The Soviet Union
at the United Nations

The Soviet Union
at the United Nations

AN INQUIRY INTO
SOVIET MOTIVES
AND OBJECTIVES

by Alexander Dallin

FREDERICK A. PRAEGER

Publisher • New York

BOOKS THAT MATTER

Published in the United States of America in 1962 by
Frederick A. Praeger, Inc., Publisher
64 University Place, New York 3, N.Y.

© 1962 by Frederick A. Praeger, Inc.

Library of Congress Catalog Card Number: 62-13751

THE SOVIET UNION AT THE UNITED NATIONS
    is published in two editions:

        A Praeger Paperback (PPS-59)
        A clothbound edition

This book is Number 106 in the series of
Praeger Publications in Russian History and World Communism

Manufactured in the United States of America

Foreword

Tʀʏɢᴠᴇ Lie, in assessing the performance of the powers at the United Nations, wrote some years ago that Soviet reasoning was always "difficult to understand. Even after seven years as Secretary-General, I cannot pretend to speak with assurance as to how the Soviet mind is made up." * Mr. Lie's uncertainty is indicative of the unique problems that confront the analyst of Soviet conduct in general and of the policies pursued at the United Nations in particular.

Friends and foes agree on the constancy of Soviet long-range objectives. Yet the motivation of the Soviet leaders and their representatives abroad has, over the course of years, remained a matter of intense speculation and dispute. How relevant are ultimate goals to current Soviet conduct? How "sincere" is Soviet participation in international organizations? To what extent can Soviet pronouncements be taken at face value? In what ways does Soviet policy differ from that of other powers? There are no simple answers.

If performance is taken as an index to motives, Soviet action in the United Nations only adds to the puzzlement. As in other

* Trygve Lie, *In the Cause of Peace* (New York, 1954), p. 18.

fields, Moscow has altered its policies in the U.N. as its analyses of political constellations and opportunities have changed. In 1945–46, it backed the efforts of the Secretary-General of the United Nations; in 1950–52, it charged him with exceeding his authority; in 1956–59, it supported him; in 1960–61, it insisted on his resignation and demanded the abolition of his office. For years, the Soviet delegation made itself the watchdog of the prerogatives of the Security Council and opposed all attempts to strengthen the General Assembly—only to wind up submitting major issues to the latter. As for the future of the U.N., Moscow has at times been bearish, at other times bullish. Do these variations reflect changes of style or of substance?

Interpreters of Soviet views are handicapped by having to rely on official Soviet sources. We have no direct knowledge of the decision-making process, and still less of the "inside" reasoning in the Kremlin. Nor have we any reliable measure of Soviet "public opinion." Thus the Soviet view of the United Nations must be inferred from a variety of evidences about Soviet intent and Soviet policy. One may think of this attempt to identify Soviet motives and objectives as moving in on the target from several directions: (1) the broad ideological assumptions and commitments of the Soviet leadership with regard to international relations and organizations; (2) the historical record, on the assumption that (everything else being equal) it is reasonable to expect a continuity of policy and outlook; and (3) the practice and promises of the Soviet Union in certain activities of the United Nations. Such a framework—broader than the specifics of the United Nations—is essential for an understanding of "what Moscow is after."

The present study does not seek to give a case-by-case description of Soviet performance at the U.N. It leaves many areas of U.N. action almost unexplored. Economic and social activities, human rights, and the International Court of Justice are among the fields that still await—and deserve—intensive analysis. In particular, the treatment of the disarmament issue does not pretend to cope adequately with the complex technical, military, and scientific problems involved. What this survey intends to do is to clarify some of the assumptions and expectations underlying Soviet policy.

While the desire to be concise rather than exhaustive prevailed throughout most of this book, the dramatic events since the first visit of Nikita Khrushchev to the United Nations in the fall of 1959 seemed to require somewhat more detailed consideration.

The paper on which this book is based was originally prepared for the United Nations Project of the Center for International Studies, Massachusetts Institute of Technology. I am very grateful to Professor Lincoln P. Bloomfield, the Director of that Project, for having provided the stimulus and encouragement to produce it. He is, of course, in no sense responsible for its contents. In writing the present, considerably expanded, text, I benefited greatly from the perceptive comments of Professor Harold Karan Jacobson, of the University of Michigan, who also kindly permitted me to read his manuscript on the Soviet role in the economic and social work of the U.N. Professor Alvin Z. Rubinstein, of the University of Pennsylvania, kindly offered competent judgments, and information not otherwise available to me. Mr. Lawrence S. Finkelstein, Vice-President of the Carnegie Endowment for International Peace, generously made available an unpublished manuscript produced for the Endowment by Dr. Irene Blumenthal that proved to be valuable on the war years and the early stages of Soviet activity in the United Nations. I had the privilege of reading several unpublished doctoral dissertations, which are indicated in the notes. I am very grateful to Professor Jan Triska, of Stanford University, for permitting me to cite his doctoral dissertation, prepared at Harvard University, and to Mr. Leopold Laufer, now of the United States Information Agency, for letting me cite his essay for the Certificate of the Russian Institute at Columbia University.

I confess to the exploitation of two of my students at Columbia

University: Mr. Norman Saul, who saved me much effort by conscientiously checking elusive evidence, and Mr. William Zimmerman IV, who toiled above and beyond the call of duty to contribute materially to the revaluation and revising of an earlier draft. I also benefited greatly from the comments of two colleagues: Professor Zbigniew K. Brzezinski and Professor Henry L. Roberts. The queries and comments of my wife, Florence C. Dallin, compelled me to seek higher standards of form and content. Mrs. Barbara Zimmerman skillfully produced a typescript under most adverse conditions. The Russian Institute of Columbia University generously provided the technical assistance needed in preparing the manuscript. For all of these I should like this to serve as a token of genuine gratitude.

Contents

Foreword   v

Part One   PAST AND PRESENT
  I.   International Law and International Organization:
         The Soviet View   3
  II. The Soviet Union and International Organization:
         The Antecedents   13
  III. The Soviet Union in the United Nations:
         The First Decade   26

Part Two   PROBLEMS AND POLICIES
  IV. Constitution and Politics: Some Key Problems   45
  V.   Specialized Agencies   61
  VI. Disarmament   70
  VII. The Domestic Image of the United Nations   88
  VIII. At the United Nations   95

Part Three   KHRUSHCHEV AND THE UNITED NATIONS
  IX. Between Success and Failure   115
  X.   The Congo: The Last Straw   135

XI. The Soviet Challenge   152

XII. The Soviet Outlook—Today and Tomorrow   182

Appendix   215

Notes   217

Bibliographical Note   245

Abbreviations   246

Part One

PAST AND PRESENT

Chapter I

International Law and International Organization: The Soviet View

THE Soviet outlook on world affairs amounts to an extension of the Communist view of society and politics. It is deeply rooted in the conception of history as progress through struggle. Both progress and struggle are essential elements of the dialectic process, expressed in our time primarily in the class conflict between "capitalists" and "proletariat" (and, by extension, other downtrodden classes and peoples).*

In the Soviet view, international relations in the age of imperialism and the rise of the "socialist world system" are marked by (1) conflicts among imperialist powers and (2) conflicts between the exploiters and the exploited, such as the struggle between the colonial powers and their colonies, and (since 1917) between the Soviet Union and the capitalist states. The former conflicts, exemplified by World War I, are considered unjust. The latter, such as the Soviet defense against Nazi aggression, are deemed just. Similarly, "national-liberation" wars are pro-

---

* These and other terms (such as "socialism" and "national bourgeoisie") continue to be used in Communist parlance with a specific meaning even where the entities involved are elusive or mythical. They are used hereinafter in their Soviet connotations.

gressive, just, and, from the Soviet vantage point, deserve full support. All "just wars" are thus identified as horizontal, geographic projections of the class struggle (between "exploiters" and "exploited") from the national to the international stage.

The classic Communist outlook—amply reiterated by Nikita Khrushchev—builds on a belief in Marxism-Leninism as the only "scientific" analysis of social and political processes, and on a vision of ultimate goals borne by an abiding faith in their inevitable attainment. The certain triumph of the exploited and alienated, whom the Soviet state purports to represent and champion, logically and explicitly entails the downfall of their exploiters and enemies—in substance, the "ruling circles" of the non-Communist world. While individual tenets of the doctrine may be amended or even discarded, the commitment to such irreducible formulas as the inevitable victory of Communism, and the identification of the Communist orbit with Good and the non-Communist world with Evil, has been so thoroughly ingrained that they are scarcely susceptible to change or eradication in the Soviet leaders' minds.

It is the permanence of this world view that permits—and commands—maximum flexibility in the choice of means in the struggle for the attainment of long-range objectives. Both Lenin and Khrushchev are explicit on this point. The zigzags in Soviet tactics, the enigmatic switches of "line," the seeming caprice and stubbornness, are to a large extent explicable in these terms; more often than not, they are a logical part of the system, not aberrations or deviations from it.

At the same time, it is important to remember that Soviet policy-makers are neither omniscient nor infallible, that they are not all of one mind at all times, and that Soviet policy does not remain static. To stress the continuity of the outlook and its ideological underpinnings is not to suggest the absence of significant variations in intensity, in method, in competence, and in short-term expectations.

Changes in strategy and adjustments in form have not, however, led to any appreciable doubt about the inevitability of the global transformation in which the Soviet Union must play a central role. Nor has it led the Soviet leaders to question the perception of tension and conflict as norms, rather than exceptions, of civil and international life. Whether or not the atmosphere becomes more clement at a given moment, the basic structure of relations between the Soviet orbit and the non-Communist world, as perceived in Moscow, remains an antagonistic one.

This is not the place to reopen the argument over the role of ideological considerations in Soviet motivation, but it may be useful to indicate that doctrinal concerns have a reality for Soviet leaders, however odd this may seem to certain political practitioners abroad.[1] This is not negated by the fact that Moscow is prone to use "ideological" arguments to justify any course it chooses to pursue, or by the fact that the translation of doctrine into policy often provokes serious doubts and disagreements within the Communist fold. Indeed, the Soviet world view is full of contradictions and ambiguities.

Communists see history as moving in stages, and specific policies are appropriate to each stage. The basic international phenomenon of the present epoch is the happenstance that during a protracted period of transition, two political types—the old and the new, the capitalist and the Communist—exist side by side; hence the problems of "coexistence" until the transition is completed and the victory of the new is achieved. Soviet policy must be planned so as to assist and speed this process.

One problem with the Soviet analysis of the world scene—and of the United Nations in particular—is rooted in a dilemma the Kremlin may be scarcely aware of: the tension between the impulses toward universality and exclusiveness. From its beginnings, Bolshevism has been impelled, on the one hand, to "go it alone," to limit the movement to an elite of devoted, professional revolutionaries, and, on the other hand, to seek a mass following, a broad base of support, and "allies" well beyond its own ranks. A sense of "leftist" uniqueness, superiority, and mission has thus clashed with a "rightist" effort to identify with the majority of mankind. The result is a split in attitudes, encompassing elements of both inferiority and superiority, and a conflict between the search for world-wide acceptance and legitimacy and a sense of proud self-sufficiency.

Another ambiguity inheres in the Soviet effort to develop the public image of a legitimate nation-state and a prime champion of "national sovereignty," while continuing to employ Communists abroad to work on behalf of the U.S.S.R. in other sovereign states. The Soviet predicament at the United Nations may thus be considered a part of the general difficulty of a regime committed to total change, one that does not feel bound by "capitalist" rules, operating in a fundamentally alien or hostile environment.[2] It is the problem of a state with a "two-camp" world view trying to operate in a "one-world" organization.

One Law or Two?

In Marxist terms, the state, its laws, and its institutions are all instruments of compulsion wielded by the ruling class. From the original, fundamentalist view that the bourgeois forms of state, law, and morals cannot be filled with socialist content but must be replaced and rebuilt *in toto,* the Soviet Union shifted, in the 1920's, to the position that for a time both state and laws must remain, "but that our laws are at all times determined by revolutionary necessity."[3] Law, it was held, expresses the will of the ruling class and strives to safeguard an order advantageous to it. The problem remained how the Soviet state and a foreign country—the two having "diametrically opposed" systems, with different codes as part of their superstructure—could share a common set of international rules of order. In theory, the problem proved refractory: If international law was socialist, it could not have antedated 1917, and could not bind capitalist states; if it was capitalist, it could not bind the Soviet Union; if it was above class, it implied renunciation of a fundamental Marxist thesis. After considerable debate, the view came to prevail in the post-Stalin years that international law was the totality of elements common to both capitalist and socialist superstructures, just as criminal law under socialism and capitalism shared certain features.[4] * This is the approach that has led Moscow at times to describe the agreed covenants and procedures of international organizations as the common denominator of two systems, and that, more recently, led Khrushchev to declare that "only such decisions should be taken in the United Nations which everyone would vote for." [5]

While the existence of a common (or overlapping) international law was thus affirmed, there remained the question of whether there did not also exist a distinct "socialist" international law to govern relations among the states of the Communist orbit. At one time, Soviet jurists had condemned such a view. But with the emergence of the "people's democracies" and the substitution of a "world system of socialist states" for the Soviet Union, heretofore the lone socialist state, Moscow affirmed in 1949 that "it is already possible to speak of the birth of elements of socialist international law." Even if the forms remain the same, it was alleged, international law under socialism obtains a new and qualitatively superior content.[6] In the following years, strenuous efforts were made to discover just what this novel content amounted to. The usual formulations included such items as "international division of labor" and "socialist internationalism" among the member-states of the Communist bloc.

During the post-Stalin "thaw," some Soviet jurists, it is true,

* This view is curiously similar to the current Soviet concept of international trade. In the words of Anastas Mikoyan, "These general world-wide economic relations continue to exist now that two world systems, the socialist and the capitalist, and consequently two world markets, two world economies have come into being. Each of these markets and each of these economies is developing according to its own laws. But at the same time the two world markets are not shut off from one another by an impenetrable wall. . . . The world market and world prices are not a fiction." (Speech of October 20, 1961, trans. in *Current Digest of the Soviet Press*, XIII, No. 51, p. 14.)

were prepared to acknowledge that the theory of distinct socialist international law was an artifice.[7] But the general tightening that followed the Polish and Hungarian crises also brought an explicit reassertion of the uniqueness and superiority of "socialist" law. It has been correctly suggested that the Soviet Union fundamentally prefers two distinct sets of law and two models of international behavior—one for the orbit it seeks to control, the other for the outside world it does not control.[8]

Soviet international-affairs specialists assert with official sanction that since capitalism "has outlived its epoch, the same is equally true of the corresponding type of international relations." Hence, "in the same way that the victory of socialism throughout the world is inevitable, so too is the complete triumph of corresponding relations between peoples. At the base of these [relations] lie the great and tested principles of Marxism-Leninism, of proletarian internationalism."[9] There are therefore no general principles of law "common to all states," the head of the legal division of the Soviet foreign office declared. Relations among socialist states, according to him, are subject to unique and superior rules. In fact, "one cannot reduce the international-legal principles of relations among the countries of the socialist camp to principles of common international law." To do so would be to "roll down onto the tracks of Partylessness, to slide into the quagmire of bourgeois normativism."[10] (Translated from esoteric jargon into non-Communist language, this assertion amounts to a reaffirmation of Communist uniqueness.) This has been the Soviet view since 1959.

The assertion that "socialist" law was superior to "capitalist" law followed logically from Soviet assumptions. The implications were considerably less obvious. At the same time, another impulse propelled Soviet international jurists in a more practical direction. In line with the Communist Party's decision of 1946 that international law could be used to Soviet advantage, a textbook by F. I. Kozhevnikov, a leading Soviet jurist, published in 1948 plainly stated that the U.S.S.R. recognizes those parts of international law "which can facilitate the execution of the stated tasks of the U.S.S.R." and rejects those "which conflict in any manner with these purposes." (Since, in the Communist view, international law is not a set of changeless rules either divine in origin or reflecting the rule of reason, the Soviet state can be selective in its use of it, frankly accepting it as an instrument of state policy.[11] "The Soviet Government's practice in international law is shaped under the influence of its foreign-policy objectives and principles, which flow from the very nature of the Soviet state." [12] * More specifically, participation does not require acceptance of all theoretical presuppositions of international organizations such as the International Labour Organisation and the United Nations itself.

"LEFT" AND "RIGHT"

In one field the Soviet Union continues to display evidence of exclusiveness, in political theory as well as in the visceral response of the Communist leadership: Moscow has consistently fought all schemes of world states and world federations (under other than Communist auspices).[13] Once an international organization threatens to become a political force impinging on the fullest sovereignty and widest freedom of choice of member states, the Soviet Union hastens to oppose such authority. These roadblocks have been constants in the Soviet response.

In addition, during periods of "leftist" intransigence, Moscow has argued that the United Nations represents governments, not peoples. Identifying governments as tools of oppression, Moscow has then arrogated to itself the role of spokesman for "all toilers of the world," for "all progressive peoples," for "the broad masses" of all nations. It has assumed that the Soviet Union and the socialist camp cannot be wrong. As one writer has put it, the subjective criteria in Soviet international law and outlook amount

---

* The manipulation of international law for political purposes has of course not been a Soviet monopoly.

to revolutionary "class justice" projected abroad.[14] In their more outspoken moments, Communists have rejected the outlook of UNESCO, based as it is on "idealistic, bourgeois conceptions concerning the causes of wars, concerning the 'nonpartisan character' of science and culture," or its hope that a philosophical synthesis of East and West can be produced.[15] On this level, a Soviet observer would concur with the view that

> if states are so fundamentally divided that international society is essentially an arena of national struggle rather than a community, there is no real possibility that an international government or international organization can be anything other than an instrument which competitive states and blocs seek to capture for use in waging the bitter struggle.[16]

Indeed, a fundamentalist (and thoroughly impractical) reading of the doctrine might lead one to think that the Soviet leaders can see no justification for participation in the United Nations or other political organizations cutting across "world systems" and not controlled by them. Yet the Soviet Union has remained a member of the U.N. (though for some years with serious misgivings)—largely out of a practical calculation that, in terms of risks and rewards, membership is preferable to nonmembership.

Throughout its history, Soviet conduct has been dotted with compromise. If, as some aver, Soviet Russia has witnessed a "great retreat," it has been a retreat not from Communist goals and attitudes, but from naïveté and purism to a mastery of politics as the art of the possible. It has been the abandonment of what Lenin called the "infantile disease" of Leftism for the sake of greater effectiveness and success. From the Treaty of Brest-Litovsk to the introduction of monetary incentives for production, from the establishment of collective (rather than state-owned) farms to the perpetuation of the army, law, and conventional diplomacy, Soviet policy has seen a "temporary" acquiescence in an imperfect present. While these adjustments—and the passage of time and men—have no doubt helped to erode some of the impatient zeal of the adolescent years of Bolshevism, they have not fundamentally changed its leaders' outlook.

Consciously divorcing the "revolutionary" Party from the state, Moscow assumed obligations in the community of nations and institutionalized the duality of its conduct by signing treaties and later joining the League of Nations, while promoting and controlling the Communist International. The problem was—and is—not one of morals but of utility. It has been shown that "the basic Soviet conception of international law is intensely practical. International law is accepted to the extent that it serves the interests of the Soviet state." [17] The same may be said of the Soviet conception of international organizations. The "two-camp" view does not preclude coexistence. To the extent that both camps accept it, international law, in its broadest sense, is thus a measure of the existing balance—the "relationship of forces," to use the Soviet jargon—among the powers of the world in the "transitional" phase. [18] In this fashion, there is no conflict between the practicality and flexibility of Soviet short-term action and the consistency of the underlying world view.

There is no doubt that Soviet policy has been shaped overwhelmingly in terms of attitudes and power relations *outside* the United Nations. Moscow has never been particularly sanguine about international organizations other than those controlled by the Soviet bloc. [19] It is precisely because of the special trucelike character of covenants between the "socialist camp" and the outside world that Moscow has insisted (as Emerson and Claude aptly put it some years ago) [20] that the United Nations amounted to a treaty relationship, to be "held within a strict construction of its contractual terms."

There will be occasion to review the consequences of this outlook, from which stemmed Soviet "conservatism" and, for a long time, commitment to a rigid and literal interpretation of the Charter. In Moscow's view, any extension of U.N. authority is bound to injure the weaker of the two contending "camps." The Soviet bloc was (at least until the recent past) the perennial minority—and some of Moscow's behavior at the U.N. has stemmed from its awareness of this inferior status. The same outlook explains Soviet hostility to compulsory arbitration. The "socialist camp" cannot be found wrong, and certainly not by a capitalist or even a mixed jury.[21]

This attitude makes it more difficult for Moscow to participate in an organization that, to be effective, requires tolerance and restraint amidst widely divergent views. Unfamiliar with, and scornful of, the tradition of loyal minority participation, Communists found a block in their own make-up when confronted with the United Nations, which by its nature cannot operate on the basis of either Soviet domination or Soviet absence.

Chapter II

The Soviet Union and International Organization: The Antecedents

THE Russian Bolsheviks, like Marxists elsewhere, foresaw the ultimate emergence of a voluntary international commonwealth.* In the meanwhile, until the state system with all its organs of compulsion "withered away," an International—a league of Communist parties, not of capitalist states—was needed.

Lenin had toyed briefly with the idea of a United States of Europe, but he came to recognize that in Marxist terms its realization under capitalism was impossible, except as a "reactionary" bloc against a socialist state. Given his conviction that as long as capitalism existed war was inevitable, Lenin was bound to reject the notion that international organizations could safeguard world peace. Peace, moreover, was not in itself the supreme objective of the Bolsheviks, adept and intensive though their use of the peace slogan has been. Surely no revolutionary state would voluntarily abandon its *élan* and mission or subordinate its decision-making to a supernational body controlled by "enemy" states.[1]

* I do not believe that the Soviet outlook has been significantly affected by the experience of Czarist Russia with international organizations. The period before 1917 is therefore omitted here as not relevant to our concerns.

The Soviet leadership was bound to view the League of Nations with suspicion and scorn. All the League could secure was a "mirage" of peace, Lenin insisted, since genuine, lasting peace could be assured only under victorious Communism. Moreover, the League was created by, and remained an instrument of, "imperialist" powers. The Bolshevik theory of capitalism, the reality of Allied intervention in Russia in 1918–20, the a-priori assumption of a "capitalist encirclement," and the belief in the unique ability of socialist states to find lasting solutions to international problems all combined to make Moscow denounce the League, which, moreover, the Soviet state had not been invited to join.

It was natural, therefore, for Moscow to describe the League either as a coalition of hostile Versailles powers [2] or as an ineffective instrument rent by feuds and "contradictions" inherent in the capitalist fold.[3] To the Soviet leaders, the League was the symbol of victorious capitalism; the Third International was the rallying point of the opposite camp.

THE LEAGUE AS AN ANTI-SOVIET BLOC, 1919–34

The view of the League as enemy headquarters remained substantially unchanged for the following decade. Occasionally, a political crisis served to confirm that Moscow had not changed its mind. In the wake of the Locarno Treaty, the Soviet leadership feared that Germany—Russia's major friend and potential ally among the "have-not" powers of Europe—might be lured into the League and might then serve, with Poland, as an approach route for enemy forces about to attack Soviet Russia. Soviet policy in cementing a Russia-centered series of alliances with Persia, Turkey, Afghanistan, and Germany amounted indeed to the formation of an "anti-League" coalition [4] predicated on the assumption that the League itself was bound to constitute an offensive bloc directed against the U.S.S.R. Foreign Commissar Chicherin was reportedly planning a "League of Peoples" to juxtapose to the capitalists assembled at Geneva.[5]

In December, 1925, Chicherin, in an interview with the German Communist paper *Rote Fahne*, explained with candor that the incompatibility of the Soviet Union and the League was due to the fact that they "are built on different principles" and that, therefore, no community of goals and methods existed between them. "Never, under any circumstances," he was quoted as saying, "will Russia join the League of Nations [which is] an instrument of capitalist machinations against the weak countries and the colonial peoples." [6] *

And yet the Soviet Union was learning to adjust to "peaceful coexistence" with the outside world, which, in its judgment, was experiencing one more "temporary stabilization" before another crisis set in. Its policy toward the League and other international organs varied with the requirements of general strategy, which now turned to the nurturing of diplomatic and commercial ties. In 1922, Moscow was proud to be invited to the Genoa Conference, to which, in Lenin's words, the Soviets went not as Communists

---

* The Chairman of the Council of People's Commissars, Alexei Rykov, declared on December 5, 1925: "The League of Nations is a little business undertaking that deals in peoples; it passes them over, as it sees fit, in the form of mandates, to the so-called states of high culture, which defend their mandate rights by force of arms and mercilessly enslave the peoples under their tutelage. For this reason, the East would naturally regard us as traitors if we were to stand behind the counter of this shop. We shall not do so. . . ." (Cited in Eudin and Fisher [eds.], *Soviet Russia and the West, 1920–1927* [Stanford, 1957], p. 321.) Commenting on the new Soviet treaty with Turkey, *Izvestiia* editorialized on December 24, 1925: "The peoples of the U.S.S.R. and of the East will . . . regulate their relations . . . without recourse to the League of Nations, outside the League and in spite of the League, which legalizes robbery and violence by the strong against the weak states."

Christian Rakovsky, among others, advanced a somewhat more practical but no doubt subsidiary consideration (in an article in *Foreign Affairs* of July, 1926): Since Soviet Russia needed peace and security to "build socialism," under the existing circumstances its foreign policy was intent on avoiding all entangling alliances and commitments such as League membership might entail.

but as businessmen. It began to cooperate with nonpolitical and technical agencies abroad, such as the League's Epidemic Commission.[7] It offered to attend an international conference on naval disarmament and in a characteristic note informed the Secretary-General of the League of Nations on March 15, 1923:

> The Soviet Government still believes that this quasi-international institution actually serves as a screen to conceal from the masses the predatory imperialist purposes of some great powers and their vassals. . . . Without in the least deviating in principle from its attitude toward the League of Nations, the Soviet Government is nevertheless prepared to consider the proposed conference as an assembly of representatives of individual states. . . . The Soviet Government believes that without the participation of Russia and her allies, this conference will prove fruitless.[8]

From 1927 on, Moscow's principled hostility toward the League weakened further. Stalin and the advocates of "socialism in one country" had triumphed in Moscow. Germany was a member of the League and would presumably help prevent an anti-Soviet move there. While the Communist International, formally divorced from the Soviet state, continued to fulminate against Geneva,* the Soviet foreign office smoothed the path for Russian participation in the World Economic Conference and the Preparatory Commission for the disarmament conference. Moscow was acting in large part out of an awareness of its own weakness, apparently fearful of a "capitalist" invasion and, during the years 1928–33, strained by the giant exertions of forced collectivization of agriculture and the First Five-Year Plan. Stalin called for a dual course of extreme radicalism by Communists abroad, but moderation and cooperation by Soviet diplomacy. Increasing

---

* The Sixth Congress of the Communist International resolved in Moscow in 1928: "The League of Nations . . . is itself more and more becoming a direct instrument for preparing and carrying out the war against the Soviet Union. The alliances and pacts concluded under the protection of the League of Nations are direct means for camouflaging preparations for war and are themselves instruments for the preparation of war, especially war against the Soviet Union." ("The Struggle Against Imperialist War and the Tasks of the Communists," Article 4.)

Soviet participation in international organizations was thus part of a pattern highlighted by Soviet endorsement of the Kellogg-Briand Pact, outlawing war as an instrument of national policy, and sponsorship of a network of nonaggression pacts between the U.S.S.R. and its neighbors.

Moscow left no doubt that such cooperation did not mean a romantic acceptance of the League system or reconciliation with its sponsors. Foreign Commissar Chicherin labeled the Kellogg-Briand Pact "an organic part of the preparation of war against the U.S.S.R." Privately, he wrote an American journalist that "I am and always have been an absolute, undiluted, unmixed, unwavering, unswerving enemy of our joining the League of Nations." His successor, Maxim Litvinov, continued to stress the impossibility of removing the causes of war so long as capitalism remained. Time and again, Moscow rejected arbitration of international disputes or, as in the Sino-Soviet conflict of 1929, outside mediation and intervention. The "two-camp" view still prevailed.[9]

THE U.S.S.R. AS A LEAGUE MEMBER, 1934–39

Until 1933, the Soviet leadership had apparently hoped that the economic depression, coupled with an intransigent radicalism of Communists abroad, would usher in a new, second round of revolutionary upheavals in the West. Such a development would also have bolstered the international position of the U.S.S.R. Instead, it found itself confronted with the double menace of a militarist Japan and a Nazi Germany—each with designs on Soviet territory. After first trying to ignore or rationalize the intentions of his two new rivals, Stalin, by the end of 1933, reversed his strategy and began to hunt for allies abroad. Before long, the Soviet Union signed treaties of mutual assistance with France and Czechoslovakia. In 1935, the Seventh (and last) Comintern Congress formally discarded its "ultraleftist" course and endorsed the "popular front," a broad political alliance with non-Communist parties: No longer were all non-Communists equally bad, and no longer was it a matter of letting the enemies fight it out. Now the strategy was to ally with the lesser foes against the greater. Soviet entry into the League was a logical part of this reversal. It was heralded by Stalin on December 25, 1933.* In reply to a question by Walter Duranty, of *The New York Times*, whether his attitude toward the League was "always wholly negative," Stalin declared:

> No, not always and not in all circumstances. Perhaps you do not quite understand. . . . The League may act in some degree like a brake, retarding or preventing the outbreak of hostilities. If that were so, if the League were to turn out an obstacle, even a small one, that made war more difficult, while it furthered, even to a small extent, the cause of peace, then we would not be against the League.[10]

It was primarily the French who, in the course of their negotiations with Moscow, pressed for Soviet entry into the League. The Soviet Government finally consented, stressing that its participation would change the League's "capitalist" character. On September 18, 1934, the U.S.S.R. became a member of the League of Nations. Maxim Litvinov, the persuasive Soviet Foreign Commissar who came to personify the "collective-security" endeavors of the following years, that very day carefully explained the Soviet reasoning to the Assembly:

> The idea in itself of an association of nations contains nothing theoretically inacceptable for the Soviet state and its ideology. The Soviet Union is itself a league of nations in the best sense of the word. . . . The Soviet state has never excluded the possibility of some form or other of association with states having a different political and social system, so long as there is no mutual hostility and if it is for the attainment of common

---

* The new Soviet history of the CPSU, eager to reduce Stalin's role, claims that a resolution adopted by the Party's Central Committee in December 1933 "foresaw the possibility" of Soviet entry into the League. (*Istoriia Kommunisticheskoi Partii Sovetskogo Soiuza* [Moscow, 1959], p. 453.)

aims. . . . The Soviet Union is entering into the League today as representative of a new social-economic system, not renouncing any of its special features and—like the other states represented here—preserving intact its personality.[11]

Here was the crux of the matter. So long as Moscow could "preserve intact its personality," it was prepared to cooperate in the search for "collective security"—and could only gain from doing so. Peace and security were the primary Soviet objectives in the League. As Litvinov declared in 1935, the Soviet Union had joined "with the sole purpose and with the sole promise to collaborate in every possible way with other nations in the maintenance of indivisible peace." [12]

Even in retrospect, Moscow makes no claim to have sought to promote international amity or cooperation. The current Soviet formula is that the Soviet Union joined the League in order to "utilize it as at least a certain *hurdle* on the aggressors' road to war and as an international *forum* for exposing the aggressors and their abettors." [13] It failed because "the principal capitalist countries . . . turned the League of Nations into a screen behind which World War II was prepared." [14] In other words, Moscow avers that even though Germany, Italy, and Japan were no longer members, "the basic cause of the failure of the League of Nations was the imperialist policy of the states dominant in it." [15]

To the extent that the League aimed at stemming aggression by Germany, Italy, and Japan, the Soviet Union loyally cooperated. Litvinov even pressed for greater authority for the League to enable it to enforce its decisions; and the Soviet Union applied the arms embargo against Paraguay and economic sanctions against Italy *—presumably because it found itself on the side of the League's majority.

However, Soviet participation in the organization did not in-

---

* It has been argued, however, that the Soviet Union adhered to the letter but not the spirit of the sanctions. See Lowell R. Tillett, "The Soviet Role in League Sanctions against Italy," *American Slavic and East European Review,* February, 1956.

volve any basic change of attitude. There is no evidence whatever that Moscow considered the League a serious obstacle to war. On a variety of issues—from the Spanish Civil War to the *Anschluss* of Austria and the Sudeten crisis of 1938—the strategy of cooperation with the "bourgeois democracies" proved barren; the popular fronts turned out to be futile, and the League itself impotent time and again.

By 1939, Moscow was again "going it alone." This solitary course led to the German-Soviet nonaggression pact of August 23, which proved to be the prelude to the German attack on Poland and the start of World War II. The secret clauses of that pact in effect ceded Finland, along with Eastern Poland and the Baltic States, to the Soviet Union, and it was in an attempt to implement this provision—and probably to bolster its defensive position before Leningrad—that the Red Army invaded Finland on November 30, 1939, after that country had refused to yield "voluntarily." On December 14, the League decided that this action constituted aggression in the terms that Maxim Litvinov himself had helped define, and it excluded the Soviet Union from membership. Seven months earlier, Stalin had jettisoned Litvinov as Foreign Commissar. The League had failed to prevent or even delay war, and once Stalin had convinced himself that he could bank neither on the Western democracies nor on "their" League, he made the outbreak of war inevitable by signing the nonaggression pact with Germany, thus untying Hitler's hands. For Moscow, the Geneva experiment had been an unmerciful boomerang.

WORLD WAR II: THE ROAD TO THE UNITED NATIONS

It is safe to say that Stalin gave little thought to the League in the years following 1939. Its demise was a part of the general failure that, in the Soviet view, characterized the "bourgeois" interwar system.[16]

The Nazi attack on the Soviet Union in June, 1941, put the

U.S.S.R. into the same camp with the West and soon led to the formation of the wartime alliance that, in 1942, came to be known as the United Nations. In the Soviet view, *the* aim of the alliance was the defeat of the Axis powers. While there was cooperation, and Soviet prestige abroad reached an unprecedented high, no great intimacy developed between the West and the U.S.S.R.

After the defeats and strains of the early war years, the allies began to plan more systematically for the postwar world. The dissolution of the Communist International in 1943 seemed to some observers to betoken the end of the "two-world" outlook in Moscow and the reintegration of the new Russia into the ranks of the peace-loving powers prepared to abide by the rule of law. Soviet propaganda surely contributed to this image. While the contours of the fundamental disagreements between Moscow and its allies were not to emerge fully for some years to come, it was soon apparent that the Soviet leadership was planning in terms far more concrete and realistic, and more attuned to its self-interest, than were the less explicit though similarly practical British and the more idealistic and at times confused Americans.[17]

Early discussions about a postwar international organization led in October, 1943, to the publication of a declaration by the Conference of Foreign Ministers in Moscow. From here to San Francisco, one and one-half years later, the road was long and perhaps thornier than any of the Big Three had envisaged. Since the story of the negotiations at Tehran, Dumbarton Oaks, and Yalta is well known, it will suffice merely to summarize the Soviet attitude.

In the Soviet view, the future United Nations Organization was to serve primarily the specific and relatively limited objective of maintaining peace. To be sure, Moscow would not bank on it for this purpose (indeed, it was still propounding the inevitability of wars), but given relative Soviet weakness and the desire to avoid war, the U.N. promised to be a useful instrument to this end. It was not conceived as a "bridge" between different systems or cultures; nor was it thought of as a first stop on the road to closer union. Soviet wartime spokesmen hinted that it was unrealistic to expect the future United Nations to establish lasting peace and universal concord so long as conflicting social, economic, and political systems existed. The common denominator of the Soviet and non-Soviet camps was the joint interest in preventing military aggression.[18]

It followed from this that Moscow would frown on the proliferation of institutions and functions under the aegis of the U.N. Indeed, it originally wanted solely a "security" organization, with no provision for economic and social activities.[19] At Dumbarton Oaks, the Soviet representative argued that one of the reasons for the League's failure had been the multiplicity of its tasks. Although it finally yielded on the inclusion of other functions, the Kremlin was not, and for ten years was not to be, interested in the many social, economic, and cultural activities of the United Nations.

This limited view of the United Nations' functions harmonized with Moscow's insistence on the broadest interpretation of national sovereignty on the part of member nations and the Great Powers in particular, and with Moscow's desire to reserve for itself the greatest possible freedom of action.

The Soviet concept of sovereignty remained to be developed in the postwar years; that of Great Power status became clear during the war. At the Moscow Conference in October, 1943, the Soviet delegates stressed the notion of a "guiding nucleus" of states—in some respects similar to the Big Three (or Big Four) "policemen" scheme that President Roosevelt had evolved. The special place to be occupied by the Great Powers stemmed from Stalin's view of the nature of power—and the fact that the Soviet Union would now be one of the Greats. By definition, the stronger states deserved special rights and were exempt from rules and restrictions binding the others. As Stalin declared at Yalta: "He would never agree to having any action of any of the Great Powers submitted to the judgment of the small powers." [20]

This position was semiofficially expounded in an article by "N. Malinin" (diplomats in Moscow considered this to be the pseudonym of a Soviet foreign-office official). The League of Nations had failed, the author insisted, for a variety of reasons, but perhaps above all because it had been conceived in sin—as one bloc of powers amassed against Soviet Russia. Harmony among the Great Powers was essential for the success of a security organization, Malinin continued, proceeding to outline the position subsequently taken by the Soviet Union at Dumbarton Oaks and San Francisco: the need for a strong Security Council with unimpaired Great Power sovereignty and veto power.[21]

It soon became clear that the Soviet Union would not delegate decisions on any sort of enforcement action to a body in which it did not possess a veto. In practice, this reflected the Soviet expectation (and deep-seated fear) of being in a minority position and thus being outvoted. When, on September 18, 1944, Andrei Gromyko told Secretary of State Stettinius that "the Russian position on voting in the Council will never be departed from," Stettinius countered that this might torpedo the United Nations. Gromyko was prepared for this: He was ready to say that no world organization would exist in which the Soviet Union (or any other major power) was denied the right to vote in any dispute, even if it was a participant therein.[22]

Moscow was playing with fire in a peculiar way. Conceivably, the Kremlin did not think enough of the United Nations to be committed to participation under all conditions. More probably, Gromyko was bluffing, expecting his opposite numbers to yield, as they had on other occasions. A few months later, at Yalta, recalling Russia's expulsion from the League, Stalin asked for "guarantees that this sort of thing will not happen again." [23] Stalin wanted both the right to withdraw and the right not to be expelled.

Altogether, he exhibited little interest in the United Nations at the various wartime conferences with his allies. When the Dumbarton Oaks Conference left open the question of whether procedural matters were subject to Great Power veto in the Security Council, the United States, on December 5, 1944, submitted a draft formula to Stalin. At Yalta, Secretary of State James F. Byrnes recalled, "I was deeply disturbed by the clear evidence that Stalin had not considered or even read our proposal. . . . If in those sixty-three days he had not familiarized himself with the subject, he could not be greatly interested in the United Nations organization." [24]

At San Francisco, three months later, Foreign Commissar Molotov's absence was generally interpreted "as a blunt confession that the Soviet Government did not attach much importance to the conference." Indeed, Stalin's shift of policy in early June served to confirm this verdict. When Molotov proved to be recalcitrant (to the point of permitting speculation on whether or not he was prepared to torpedo the whole United Nations), Harry Hopkins was dispatched to Moscow to iron out the remaining difficulties in the voting formula. After weeks of bitter debate, it turned out that Stalin was, or professed to be, simply ignorant of the problem. The United States record of the Hopkins interview with Stalin and Molotov on June 6, 1945, makes it clear "that the Marshal had not understood the issues involved and had not had them explained to him. During this conversation, Marshal Stalin remarked that he thought it was an insignificant matter"—and proceeded to yield to the Western view that parties to a dispute must abstain from voting.[25] Even at the subsequent London Preparatory Commission, the Soviet delegates played only a perfunctory part and seemed to attribute little importance to its work.

All this fitted in with Stalin's assessment of power—and the realization that the United Nations itself had none in measurable terms. He had more important things to worry about. Even before the United Nations was established, Moscow had unilaterally sponsored the Free Germany Committee, the Union of Polish Patriots, and other refugee committees destined to play a political role; it had concluded an alliance with Czechoslovakia and was

negotiating with other exile groups. Its plans for early action—
by its own forces and resources, and by local Communists—
throughout East-Central Europe were well along in 1943–44.

Stalin's hopes for the postwar world—and for his own power
position in it—lay outside the future world organization. Compared with direct Soviet action—military defeat of the Axis
powers, territorial expansion, socio-economic and political transformation of the newly "liberated" areas, and economic reconstruction and development at home—the United Nations was at
best a second-rate also-ran in the Soviet political stable.

Even at the time of the San Francisco conference, Moscow was
rather outspoken in its preference for direct commitments. The
peoples had suffered too much to pin their hopes on the United
Nations, a quasi-official Soviet publication declared; firm bilateral
treaties were far more tangible warrants of peace.[26]

And yet the Soviet Union went along, worked along, and
made a variety of concessions in the process of hammering out
the United Nations Charter. At the very least, it preferred—
then and later—joining to avoid the stigma of nonparticipation
and to prevent the body from becoming a hostile instrument.
Armed with the veto, the Soviet Union was confident that it
could prevent action against itself by the U.N. Moscow certainly
welcomed it as a forum for spreading Soviet opinion. Finally, it
apparently saw the United Nations as an institutional recognition
of the Soviet Union as one of the Big Three. So long as "Great
Power unanimity" was accepted, it had nothing to lose and perhaps something to gain.

The Soviet Union signed the Charter with a more cynical but
also more realistic assessment of the United Nations' capacities
and prospects than many of its fellow-members. Ideological and
power-political considerations—and the experience of earlier
years—combined to make the U.N. at best an ancillary instrument of Soviet foreign policy.

Chapter III

The Soviet Union in the United Nations: The First Decade

O NE may usefully distinguish several major phases in the development of Moscow's policy toward the United Nations. Never an independent variable, that policy has in its broad features followed the zigzags of declining cooperation, Cold War and Korean War, "thaw" and "peaceful coexistence."

CONFLICT

The end of the war also meant an end to Soviet moderation at home and abroad. Communist orthodoxy, militancy, and Party control were soon rekindled in Soviet life. Abroad, the early postwar years saw the extension and consolidation of Soviet dominance in Eastern Europe. By 1946–47, the revival in Soviet propaganda of the "two-camp" view of the world betrayed an expectation of new conflicts with the "capitalists." Paradoxically, the unique accretion in Communist power—from "socialism in one country" to the "world system" of ten or more Communist states—took place at a time of relative domestic weakness due to the ravages of war, and at a time of relative international weakness due to American atom-bomb monopoly. Soviet foreign policy as designed to take advantage of the opportunities—primarily the power vacuums created by the defeat of Germany and Japan —without exposing itself to undue risks at a time of reconstruction and reconsolidation.

The return to intransigence was retarded by Stalin's desire to gain all possible benefit from the pool of "Great Power amity." But he never seems to have had any doubt about the choice before him: He opted for the extension of Soviet power at the expense of "friendship" abroad. Security by territorial accretion, and the ensuing socio-economic transformations in Eastern Europe, went hand in hand with the belief in ultimate world-wide victory. For Stalin, such an orientation was both logical and historically preferable to the cultivation of good will with states that, by the nature of their economic and political interests, were bound to be unreliable friends and, in all likelihood, would sooner or later line up against the U.S.S.R. By 1947, with the Italian and French Communists out of coalition governments, the Truman Doctrine proclaimed, the Communist Information Bureau (Cominform) established, and the Cold War spreading, Communist leaders urged a more militant course on the West European and South Asian Communist parties. In 1948, the break with Tito and Moscow's refusal to accept Marshall Plan aid deepened the gulf between the Soviet bloc and the outside world.

Important for the shaping of Soviet attitudes toward the United Nations in these formative years, then, is a reflex of self-isolation and suspicion, a reliance on the Soviet Union's own strength rather than on joint international action, and a withdrawal from even the limited give-and-take that had characterized the wartime collaboration of the Big Three.

The Soviet mood after San Francisco was a mixture of hope and skepticism. At a time when both "camps" tried to maintain the appearance of amity (and many of the issues dividing them had not yet emerged), Moscow seems to have hoped to acquire for itself a more powerful position in the U.N. Perhaps the Iranian complaint about Soviet interference in its domestic affairs

—i.e., Soviet failure to evacuate northern Iran and attempts to detach it—and the overwhelmingly anti-Soviet sentiment generated in the ensuing debates helped crystallize Soviet attitudes and strategy. By March, 1946, Stalin still felt compelled to assert that (in spite of Soviet defiance of Security Council opinion and the first Soviet walk-out) the United Nations was "a serious instrument for the preservation of peace." [1] Yet, in fact, Moscow had tasted the bitter fruit of leading an apparently static bloc of five or six delegates (Soviet Union, Ukraine, Byelorussia, Poland, Yugoslavia, Czechoslovakia) that was invariably outvoted. World opinion seemed to be impervious to Soviet claims to be defending the organization against hostile onslaughts.

Moscow now strove to devise techniques to reduce the size and power of the anti-Soviet majority and, accordingly, came to insist on a strict and literal construction of the United Nations Charter. As tension mounted, it pressed for careful observance of "Great Power unanimity" and respect for the sovereign rights of all member states as conditions of effective U.N. operation. Only under "certain conditions" was "fruitful cooperation quite possible." [2] At the same time (to cite a later Soviet account), an "activization of aggressive forces" took place at the United Nations:

> As early as the work of the first session of the Assembly [a Soviet commentary explains], it became clear that two distinct courses were being pursued in the United Nations: the Soviet Union and the democratic countries supporting it in full accord with the Charter strove for the adoption of decisions aimed to strengthen peace and the authority of the United Nations; the ruling circles of the U.S.A., on the contrary, intended to subordinate the United Nations to the aims of their policy, opposing the fulfillment by the United Nations of the tasks intended for it by the Charter, and thereby weakening its authority and significance. [3]

Moscow had returned to the familiar bipolar images, and it determined to "exploit and sharpen" the contradictions it assumed xisted within the capitalist camp—conflicts between different mperialist" powers, conflicts between colonies and mother coun- ies, and conflicts within every capitalist state. In these efforts, ıe U.N. could serve Moscow's ends. Some efforts aimed at identi- ʳing the Soviet Union with the leadership of "progressive" ıuses. Thus, the Soviet and Polish delegations spearheaded the ɔndemnation of Franco Spain. Likewise, in attacking racial dis- cimination in the Union of South Africa, the Soviet Union ɔught to depict itself as the champion of humanity and decency.

More widespread and continual were Soviet efforts to identify self with anti-Western or anti-imperialist campaigns. Thus the ˊkrainian S.S.R. brought the Indonesian case before the Security ʼouncil, lodging a complaint about the British use of Japanese ʳoops and requesting a restoration of peace under U.N. auspices.[4] .ikewise, the Soviet bloc sided with Egypt and the Sudan against ʳitain, and with Syria, Lebanon, Tunisia, and Morocco against ʳance, in the various cases involving these regions.

All these issues were later described by Moscow as having een supported in defense of national sovereignty. The same ıtionale was offered for the Soviet stand on the Greek dispute. ˡather characteristically, the Soviet delegation found counter- ˡarges the most effective means of neutralizing hostile allega- ɔns. After turning down Soviet charges against Greece and ʳritain, the Security Council in December, 1946, voted to investi- ate complaints against Yugoslavia, Bulgaria, and Albania for ıterfering in the Greek civil war. While the majority of the ıvestigating commission found the three budding "people's ˥emocracies" guilty of supporting the Greek rebels, its Soviet and ɔlish members found fault with the Greek authorities only (with ıe Soviet delegate casting five vetoes and refusing to transfer ıe issue to the General Assembly). Moscow was later to charge ıat the decisions based on the reports of the Balkan Commission ˇere "illegal."

The Soviet stance was not always well thought-out or consis- ꞓnt. The priority of attention to major targets during the early

postwar years (also indicative of the Soviet perception of th
United Nations as a secondary arena of contest) implied negle
of certain regions where Soviet interests were less seriously i
volved. Such a lack of definition is apparent in Soviet foreig
policy toward Southeast Asia in 1945–48; it was evidenced
the United Nations in the Soviet abstentions (or voting with th
majority) in the Kashmir dispute.[5] Moreover, Soviet oppositic
to the terms (acceptable to the Djakarta authorities) by whic
the Indonesian dispute was settled reflected a dogmatic r
evaluation of colonial revolutions, which led to the tempora
rejection by Communists of "bourgeois nationalism" as treac
erous and of political independence as fictitious. Doctrinal rigidi
—and political consequences stemming from it, such as th
round of Communist-led revolts throughout Southeast Asia
1948—thus made it impossible for the Soviet Union to capitali
fully on potential political oportunities.

On certain issues, Moscow's stand wavered. Thus, in the Pale
tine crisis, the Soviet Union was consistent only so far as its ant
British objectives were concerned; but it joined the United Stat
in supporting the UNSCOP partition plan while striving to avo
alienating the Arab world.[6]

Everything considered, these Soviet political campaigns we
not markedly successful. On several major occasions, from th
Greek civil war to the Berlin Blockade, public opinion—in an
out of the United Nations—put the onus on the Soviet Union an
its dependencies. The Soviet position was complicated by th
fact that in some cases Moscow supported the *status quo* while
others it opposed it. Actually (as Jan Triska has pointed out), th
formula governing Soviet policy was simple: Where its ow
position tended to benefit from change—as in Iran, Greece, Be
lin, or China—Moscow favored change. It also supported chang
where the effect promised to be a setback for the "colonialis
West (Indonesia, Syria, Lebanon, Palestine, Italian colonie
Egypt, French North Africa). On the other hand, when the Sovi
Union or one of its allies was accused or attacked (Corfu, Korea

it rallied to the defense of sovereignty, domestic jurisdiction, and the *status quo*.[7]

By 1948, the situation in the United Nations mirrored the general drift toward increasing world tension and Cold War. In an epoch of rapid change, the United Nations—unlike the Holy Alliance or the League of Nations—was established before a new balance of power had been attained.[8] Indeed, the architects of the U.N. had assumed agreement among the major powers to be an essential condition of its effective functioning. That condition, it was now amply clear, would not be met.

CRISIS

The attention paid by the Soviet Union to the possibility of withdrawing from the United Nations has been markedly greater than that of other powers. Indeed, it has been the only member repeatedly to stress the legality of leaving. At San Francisco, it was Andrei Gromyko who insisted on an explicit interpretation of membership in this context. According to the Soviet delegation, it was "wrong to condemn beforehand the grounds on which any state might find it necessary" to exercise its right of withdrawing from the U.N., since this right "is an expression of state sovereignty and should not be reviled in advance."[9]

Since the Soviet Union was surely not eager to prepare a face-saving exit for one of its potential enemies, this statement strengthens the surmise that, as early as San Francisco, Moscow anticipated international crises that might require Soviet withdrawal from the U.N. Such statements were repeated, particularly during 1949–52, the period of complete deterioration of Soviet-United Nations relations, when the Soviet Union seemed to be on the verge of pulling out. What was the purpose behind such statements? They could have been intended to stress the voluntary and dissoluble nature of the United Nations, to underscore the imperfections of its operations (which might force some members to abandon it), or to warn the United Nations' majority to mend its ways. It is entirely possible that they were meant to prepare "public opinion" for a possible break. Finally, it is likely that there was disagreement within the Soviet leadership between advocates of continued Soviet participation in the U.N., frustrating though it might be, and spokesmen of the extreme "left" wing of the Party—in 1947 represented by Andrei Zhdanov and Tito [10]—who favored a "go-it-alone" policy (much like the Comintern strategy of 1928).

In early 1949, the official attitude, according to a prepared statement of the Soviet Foreign Ministry, was still one of continued participation:

> Every one sees that the United Nations Organization is being undermined, since this organization, at least to a certain extent, hampers and curbs the aggressive circles in their policy of aggression and unleashing a new war. In view of this situation, the Soviet Union has to struggle with even more firmness and persistance against the undermining and destruction of the United Nations Organization by aggressive elements and their accomplices and must see to it that the United Nations Organization does not connive with such elements as is often the case now. . . .[11]

Yet, in fact, the Soviet Union and the increasingly sovietized satellites began to disengage themselves from United Nations activities, particularly, of course, during the period of voluntary Soviet absence in 1950. Bulgaria, Hungary, and Rumania, being nonmembers, refused to discuss charges, leveled in the General Assembly, of having violated human rights guaranteed in the peace treaties signed by them (although Bulgaria and Albania had, in the preceding period, willingly testified before the United Nations). Nonparticipation was equally striking in commercial affairs.[12]

The Communist German Democratic Republic, in 1952, refused access to a U.N. *ad hoc* commission to investigate conditions precedent to all-German free elections—as North Korea had done earlier and Hungary was to do four years later. During the Korean War, Soviet participation was often more token than real. Increasingly the Soviet image was one of a doomed United Nations reduced either to futility or to an enemy tool. One analyst who examined Soviet propaganda during this period concludes:

> Probably the strongest and most persistent theme of Soviet propaganda was that the Western powers, led by the United States, wish to undermine the United Nations. This argument emerged as soon as the conflict between East and West broke into the open. It increased in sharpness and bitterness as the political situation deteriorated; since 1949, it took frequently the form of accusations that the West actually wanted to destroy the United Nations. Towards the end of our period [1951], indications were given in Soviet propaganda that the United Nations, despite all Soviet efforts to save it, was in fact already doomed and in the process of disintegration because of machinations of the "imperialists." [13]

Indeed, the legality of leaving was stressed even after the crisis had passed. Thus, the summary article on the United Nations appearing in the revised edition of the Great Soviet Encyclopedia (1955) singled out the members' right to withdraw from the Organization.[14] N. S. Khrushchev was to reassert it five years later.

In 1949, the Soviet Union began to invoke an argument that strained the ties still further. In the face of U.S. efforts to cement military alliances in the non-Soviet world, Moscow proclaimed the incompatibility of membership in the United Nations —by definition "peace-loving"—with participation in "aggressive" blocs like the European Defense Community or the North Atlantic Treaty Organization.[15] One may surmise, however, that this double-edged sword was intended to slay NATO and its analogs, not to destroy the United Nations. For, after all, the Soviet Union did remain in the United Nations even when the latter was waging war on Soviet allies, stooges, and friends.

It did so in spite of various moves by the U.N. majority that weakened the ability of the Soviet bloc to throw obstacles in the path of the dominant group.* This was true of the "Uniting for Peace" resolution, which permitted a majority in the General Assembly to by-pass the veto-bound Security Council, the continuation of Secretary-General Trygve Lie in office, and other moves to circumvent the requirements of "Great Power unanimity." [16]

The Soviet walk-out of January, 1950, over the question of Chinese representation thus came in an atmosphere already heavily laden with charges and countercharges. For over a year, the Soviet Union and its friends had been preparing substitutes for the United Nations: a narrow and rigid one in the Cominform, uniting the Communist Parties of nine countries; and a far more effective but diffuse one in the World Peace Council, which was being explicitly played up as an alternative to the U.N.† Coinciding with the ambitious "peace pact" and Soviet disarmament proposals submitted to the 1949 session of the General Assembly (and the simultaneous announcement that the Soviet Union had mastered the secrets of the atom), the many-faceted "peace" campaign was to represent a mass movement with literally "hundreds of millions" of endorsements,

---

* In November, 1947, the General Assembly established an interim committee with authority to consider issues referred to it by the General Assembly or proposed for inclusion on the latter's agenda. This move, in some ways foreshadowing the "Uniting for Peace" resolution adopted in 1950, was essentially an attempt by the Western powers to consider matters in a forum not subject to the Soviet veto. In the view of two experts, it "had the effect of radically changing the functional relationship between the Security Council and the General Assembly." (Leland M. Goodrich and Edward Hambro, *Charter of the United Nations: Commentary and Documents* [Boston, 1949], p. 69.)

† Once the United Nations declared Communist China the aggressor in Korea, Peking took refuge precisely in this device. *Jen-min Jih-pao* wrote on February 28, 1951: "The U.N. has completely disappointed the hopes placed upon it by the peoples of the world. . . . The World Peace Movement has won the confidence of the peoples throughout the world who have lost faith in the U.N."

juxtaposing the "rank and file" of the world to the majority of United Nations delegations speaking for no one but "ruling circles."

The reason why the Soviet delegates were absent from the Security Council when the Korean conflict broke out on June 25, 1950, has been amply debated. Whatever the original Soviet intent in absenting itself—a face-saving device for disengagement from U.N. activities, or a dramatic demonstration of support for Communist China, or an attempt to show that the will of the Soviet Union could not be ignored with impunity—by May, 1950, the question of representation seemed on its way toward a solution. Quite possibly, this may *not* have been the principal stimulus for the Soviet walk-out. Trygve Lie, who saw Stalin in mid-May, relates how in all their talks "Stalin had not uttered a word" on the seating of Communist China. And to Lie's efforts to impress on Stalin the value of the United Nations, Stalin "said little in answer. Recalling that the Soviet Union had been one of the founders of the United Nations, he remarked, 'We will try to do everything we can to work along a course determined by our own and the world's best interests.' " [17] In Stalin's terms, this was a statement typically cautious, leaving open the possibility of a break.

All the evidence suggests that Moscow had anticipated neither the military response of the United States and the United Nations nor the protracted warfare that resulted from the North Korean invasion. The same sedulously cultivated optimism—faith in time and history as allies of Communism—that had led Stalin into other blunders was at work again. It was compounded by Stalin's scorn for the small and the weak—as with Finland in 1939—and by his trust in the efficacy of static force—as with Tito in 1948. The same view of power on the world scene, as the corporeal product of material resources, manpower, and organization, held him firm in his conviction that the United Nations was an insignificant obstacle to expansion. Indeed, it may never have occurred to Stalin that the U.N. might act with force of arms in opposing Communist North Korea.

It is probable that this failure to take the United Nations seriously combined with a failure of coordination between the Soviet organs responsible for policy in Korea and those planning strategy in the U.N., so that the Soviet delegates were absent when the emergency session was convened on June 25, 1950.* If this is so, Soviet failure—as expressed in U.N. action in Korea—was to a large extent homemade: Stalin was once again the victim of his own political concepts. It did Moscow little good thereafter to insist that the Security Council action was "illegal" because the U.S.S.R. was not present. On July 27, Iakov Malik informed Trygve Lie that, in accordance with the monthly rotation of the Council presidency, he would assume the chair on August 1. On that date, the Soviet delegation returned.

Moscow blamed the Korean War on aggression by the United Nations; it has never retracted these charges. But, whatever its arguments, the U.N. action was a setback for the Communist bloc; the General Assembly resolution of February 1, 1951, branding the Chinese Communists as aggressors in Korea, was another defeat.[18] Stalin now charged that the U.N. had become an "instrument of aggressive war," having "ceased to be an international organization of nations enjoying equal rights. The United Nations is now not so much a world organization as an organization for the Americans, an organization acting on behalf of the requirements of the American aggressors." He concluded with another threat: "The United Nations Organization is therefore taking the inglorious road of the League of Nations. In this way it is burying its moral prestige and dooming itself to disintegration."[19] During the following weeks, the Soviet

---

* An alternative but not necessarily conflicting interpretation would be a conscious Soviet decision not to tip its hand by having the Soviet delegation return prior to the Korean operation. At any rate, Moscow clearly expected to have the latter completed before long.

press, with unprecedented bluntness, spoke in "either-or" terms
of the U.N.

And still the Soviet Union did not pull out. Everything
considered, it lost nothing from membership; certainly its presence on the East River imposed no significant inhibitions on
Soviet officialdom and policy-makers. By staying in, the Soviet
Union was not cutting itself off from the rest of the world.
Moscow kept an opportunity to discuss and negotiate, and the
Malik-Jessup talks in February, 1949, which had paved the way
to ending the Berlin Blockade, suggested the mutual utility of
such opportunities. By staying in, the Soviet Union kept access
to a well-attended, well-publicized forum in which to air its
views; and it avoided the stigma of having slammed a door that
at some future date it might wish to reopen.

Thus Stalin managed to have his cake and eat it, too—but
at a price. Above all, his moves prompted a momentary rallying
of the non-Communist world around the United Nations. By
1951, the Soviet bloc was virtually an outcast—an enemy
anomalously unnamed and continuing to sit amidst those who
voted for the military and political operations they were
jointly waging against the Soviet Union's dependents and allies.

COEXISTENCE

Just as Moscow had evidently failed to think through the
Korean attack in terms of the United Nations, so the improvement and relaxation that ensued in the mid-1950's were hardly
motivated by consideration of, or for, the United Nations. But
the new music emanating from Moscow soon found its vigorous
echoes on the East River, too.

The "turn" in Soviet conduct had various causes. There were
some harbingers prior to Stalin's death—for instance, the international economic conference in Moscow in the spring of 1952;
the appeal to national and colonial movements at the Nineteenth
Congress of the Communist Party in October, 1952; in January,

1953, Soviet agreement (after years of refusal) to join in trade consultations with the Economic Council for Europe.*

More important, Stalin's death on March 5, 1953, freed his successors to rethink the course of Soviet policy so as to extract the empire from the sterility, obsolescence, and aberrations of the Stalin era without sacrificing its power position abroad.† And finally, Nikita Khrushchev's accession to power in the spring of 1955 brought a vigorous new departure in foreign affairs. Whatever the balance of these contributing factors, they had their impact on the Soviet stance at the U.N.

The total change is indeed remarkable if one compares Soviet stature and behavior in the Sputnik era with the years of ostracism. In its new phase, Moscow strove to assert its affinity for the United Nations in various ways. The first opportunity (along with the election of Dag Hammarskjold as the new Secretary-General) was, naturally enough, the termination of the Korean War. Negotiations on the prisoner-of-war question, which had been deadlocked for many months, were concluded promptly after Stalin's death, and on June 27, 1953, hostilities ceased.

The real "thaw" was yet to come. After an outwardly quiescent 1954, Nikita Khrushchev (with Nikolai Bulganin as his temporary frontman) replaced Georgi Malenkov, retired Viacheslav Molotov, and then promptly embarked on a program designed to

* Ray L. Thurston, of the U.S. Department of State, found that "Even before Stalin's death, vitriolic criticism of American racial problems had been toned down in Soviet discussions in the United Nations. It has been noted that a change of Soviet personnel has occurred; there is more geniality." (C. Grove Haines [ed.], *The Threat of Soviet Imperialism* [Baltimore, 1954], pp. 118–19.)

† In July 1953, the U.S.S.R. made its first contribution to the Expanded Program of Technical Assistance. In September, 1953, the U.S.S.R. adhered to the U.N. Convention on privileges and immunities. Sometime in the second half of 1953, it also reversed its Stalinist policy in the international Danube Commission. (On the latter, see David T. Cattell, "The Politics of the Danube Commission," *American Slavic and East European Review,* October, 1960.)

achieve a measure of relaxation without abandoning totalitarian controls. After hesitant overtures lasting for nearly a year, serious talks on disarmament and nuclear-weapons controls were resumed in May, 1955, for the first time in seven years. The timing so closely coincided with the establishment of Soviet diplomatic relations with West Germany, the signing of the Austrian peace treaty, and the improvement of Soviet relations with Yugoslavia, Finland, and Japan, that presumably they were all part of a systematic new strategy. It appears likely that the policy decisions adopted in Moscow in the early spring of 1955 included an upgrading of the United Nations as an instrument of potential value for the U.S.S.R.

It is known from other sources that in July, 1955, Khrushchev summed up before his Party's Central Committee the new strategy he had embarked upon: a determination to wage "peaceful coexistence," avoiding war, if at all possible; substantially holding the line in Europe; and trying to take maximum advantage of opportunities in the underdeveloped areas, which were now bracketed with the Communist orbit in natural opposition to the capitalist West.[20] This is the most meaningful context of Soviet efforts, from 1955 on, to transform the United Nations into a serviceable instrument of the "socialist camp."

Suddenly the tone of Soviet commentary on the United Nations changed. As late as February, 1955, Moscow had argued that the U.N. was the child of two rival conceptions—that of the Soviet Union (peaceful) and that of the West (imperialist), and that the United States had tried to make the U.N. a tool of aggression against the Soviet Union and the people's democracies. "Full responsibility" for the "illegal" actions of the U.N. rested squarely with the United States and its allies.[21] Only a few months later, Moscow would argue (through the mouths of two of its most prominent international lawyers) that the Charter of the United Nations was based on the principles of peaceful coexistence. Without fully ignoring its "negative" features, a Soviet collection of documents on the U.N.—itself a new phenomenon—emphasized the "positive aspects" of the U.N.'s work.[22]

The General Assembly session in the fall of 1955 produced unusually favorable Soviet press comment. Moscow hailed the end of American "push-button majorities," the admission of sixteen new members, and the successful Soviet leadership of the "peace forces" in the world.[23]

It is true that the Hungarian crisis—and the setback it involved for the Soviet Union, condemned as it stood by the U.N. for violation of the Charter—temporarily muffled this increasing enthusiasm. But Hungary was balanced, after all, by Suez, and Moscow chose to comment that "time will show whether the United Nations will muster the strength to accomplish the tasks entrusted to it by mankind." [24] Within a few months, memories of the Hungarian experience receded, and the Soviet press resumed its campaign to depict Moscow as the champion defender of the United Nations.

Perhaps for the first time since its creation, Soviet policy at the highest level explicitly aimed at exploiting the new potential in the U.N. In March, 1956, a meeting in Moscow voted to establish a United Nations Association in the U.S.S.R.—an unmistakable index of the new line. In September of that year, the World Federation of United Nations Associations accepted the Soviet branch as a member and appointed a Soviet official vice-chairman of its own executive committee.[25]

In 1957, Moscow launched another new "line," since then often reiterated. The dean of Soviet specialists on international affairs, Eugene Korovin, asserted that the Soviet Union had been in the lead among the great powers in establishing the United Nations; that the U.S.S.R. had initiated both the Moscow Conference of 1943 and the Dumbarton Oaks Conference of 1944; and that the Soviet delegation had introduced a number of specific features into the Charter that had determined its spirit (though the examples cited hardly provided a convincing case). He continued:

The constant growth of Soviet economic and defensive might, of the moral authority of the U.S.S.R., the merger of the entire socialist camp on the basis of proletarian internationalism and its growing strength, the support of its international policy by the partisans of peace throughout the world vividly testify to the fact that the realization of the democratic principles of the U.N. Charter becomes increasingly the unanimous demand of all peace-loving humanity.[26]

Here was a characteristic formulation, indicative—for all its verbiage—of the new Soviet self-image, its "position of strength," and its attempts to identify itself with the proponents of peace and the "democratic principles" of the United Nations. For better or for worse, the Soviet view of new opportunities to exploit was not without some basis in fact.

Part Two

PROBLEMS AND POLICIES

Chapter IV

Constitution and Politics:
Some Key Problems

A LARGE complex of the Soviet attitude toward the United Nations may be subsumed under the sovereignty syndrome. It is a characteristic fusion of politics and principle, the protective device of a minority power, the legal basis for a keep-out attitude, and an appealing slogan in dealings with the new and small states.

NATIONAL SOVEREIGNTY

The Soviet notion of sovereignty has undergone drastic reconsideration since the Russian Revolution. Initially, national sovereignty was considered part of the bourgeois paraphernalia that had no room in a world where "the proletariat has no fatherland." But Lenin's natural espousal of "defensism" once he had seized power, and his protests against foreign intervention in Russia in 1918–20 set the stage for a new line. As the Soviet state became stronger, it insisted more firmly that it would tolerate no infringement of its sovereignty—or for that matter of the sovereignty of other "victims" of the imperialist West.

To be sure, the Soviet leadership reserved the right to

impinge through the medium of the Communist International on what other states might consider their sovereign rights. Moreover, as leading theorists asserted down to at least the 1930's, proletarian dictatorship, not sovereignty, was the slogan of the international working class. But invoking the concept of sovereign rights turned out to be extremely convenient for the Soviet Union. Like other legal formulas, its application has been politically selective. On occasion, Moscow has condemned appeals to sovereign prerogatives as attempts to shirk international obligations. In 1936, Litvinov assailed those who thus evaded enforcement of League of Nations sanctions against Italy during the Ethiopian War. Since World War II, the Soviet Union has assailed references to domestic jurisdiction when invoked by Spain, the Union of South Africa, or France.

"Sovereignty," on the other hand, has been the mantle of legality in which Moscow has cloaked its refusal to permit the United Nations entry into the Communist orbit. In 1949, it argued that the U.N. had no authority to take action in Bulgaria, Hungary, and Rumania (with respect to violations of human rights). The Soviet-controlled regimes in East Germany and North Korea refused inspection by United Nations teams. Soviet denunciation of the U.N. stand on Korea in 1950, and on Hungary in 1956, stressed that intervention into the affairs of a sovereign state constitutes a fundamental violation of international law.

The Soviet position has at times shifted in accordance with changing political desiderata. A striking example of this is its stand on the Greek elections. Apparently prepared to write off Greece, for the time being, as part of a British "sphere" (in return for a *quid pro quo* in the Balkans), Moscow in 1945 refused to participate in an international supervision of the Greek elections. In 1949, with the Greek civil war several years old and the Cold War increasing in fury, Moscow labeled the earlier election a "parody" and called for new elections under international supervision. Andrei Vyshinsky admitted the reversal, explaining that the Soviet position each time had helped Greek "self-determination"—presumably as viewed in terms of Soviet self-interest.[1]

The manipulative use of sovereignty by Moscow is likewise apparent in ratification of the U.N. Genocide Convention (March, 1954), which it considered no menace to itself but potentially a useful weapon against others; and in its hostility to the draft covenant on human rights, which moved it to voice the warning that the document was intended to give the capitalist powers "a basis in theory . . . for the policy of interference in the domestic affairs of other states." [2]

The Soviet position has had its rational and irrational components. Among the latter one might count the extreme Soviet fear of foreign infiltration—especially acute under Stalin—and suspicion of enemy conspiracies. This suspicion has extended even to humanitarian endeavors designed to relieve famine and need inside Russia, such as the ARA after World War I and UNRRA after World War II. Somewhat later, Professor Korovin implied that attempts to limit or subvert national sovereignty were merely the "legal" facet of the American drive to "liberate" Eastern Europe.[3]

More rational is the argument (never publicly articulated by Soviet spokesmen) that a totalitarian state demands the undivided loyalty of its citizens and can brook no competing focuses of authority, and that it cannot afford to give foreigners free access to Soviet installations not normally open to public scrutiny. The Soviet opposition to effective inspection schemes with regard to disarmament is, of course, intimately related to this point.*

The literalism of the Soviet position, noted earlier, has usually led to considering formal treaty provisions as the major source of international order. After World War II, it is true, a quiet

---

* So is Soviet refusal to accept the argument that individuals be recognized as subjects of international law. Once again, the effect would be to reduce the monopoly of Soviet political controls over its citizens.

debate was waged among Soviet specialists about the acceptability of certain U.N. decisions as sources of law. V. I. Lisovsky went so far as to argue, in a textbook published in 1955, that decisions of international organizations were binding on nonmembers. But Durdenevsky and other stalwarts promptly rebuked him, arguing characteristically that such a view was tantamount to a limitation of national sovereignty.[4]

In this sector, practice has customarily determined theory; and practice has required "national sovereignty" to be the cornerstone of Soviet international law. Using it as a shield of self-interest, the Soviet Union was unwilling, until 1955, to give economic and statistical information to the United Nations.[5] By posing as a defender of national sovereignty everywhere, it sought to ingratiate itself abroad.[6] Commitment to the sovereignty principle, however, has also had some self-defeating consequences, as exemplified in Soviet opposition to all ECOSOC work on crime, training in public administration, double taxation, and passport regulations as *ultra vires*.[7]

The primary purpose behind Soviet insistence on "sovereignty" has been to maintain maximum freedom of action and to eliminate outside interference. Given its bipolar view of world (and U.N.) affairs, Moscow assumed that any restriction of sovereignty was bound to benefit the stronger bloc, which would use such restrictions to meddle in the affairs of its enemies. One may speculate that a Soviet bloc in command of a working majority in the United Nations would choose to abandon the "sovereignty weapon" and seek to exploit the resulting opportunities for its own political benefit.

Logically enough, Moscow has always opposed the quest for "world law" and compulsory international jurisdiction. Neither in theory nor in practice can it see any grounds for delegating or abdicating its authority to a body or an individual over whom it has no control; hence also the practical view that the "prospects of the International Court of Justice contributing to the peaceful regulation of international relations are extremely meager." [8] While granting that the Court has served the cause of coexistence and the rule of law, Judge Sergei Krylov's assessment (1958) was that the Court's majority "pursued a discriminatory policy" toward the East European states, and in a variety of cases "assumed the position of the colonialists" or "defended the interests of the imperialist powers." [9] Indeed, says the Soviet Juridical Dictionary, "since the representatives of the imperialist state make up the majority of the International Court, the large capitalist countries can almost always count on a decision of the International Court corresponding to their interests." [10] It is symptomatic that Soviet analysts are even here unable to separate politics from law.

Equally consistent has been Soviet rejection of "world federalism" and other attempts to promote international government, or even regional federations outside the U.S.S.R. As a rule, Moscow has opposed coalitions of anti- and non-Soviet powers (other than its own "front" organizations) as tending to weaken the relative position of the Soviet Union, and it has opposed federations of Soviet with non-Communist states as naïvely impossible.[11] After all, the Soviet formula of competitive, if peaceful, coexistence rejects both fusion of the two systems and subordination of the two blocs to a common "third" authority. In all these respects, as one recent observer writes, the Soviet Union benefits from insisting on the doctrine of sovereignty, for it is "admirably suited to the tactics of a state which does not intend to constrain its policies within the fetters of international law, but sees the advantages of cultivating the law-abiding instincts of its opponents." [12]

The Soviet understanding of sovereignty—and security considerations—likewise helps explain its prolonged failure to agree to a United Nations armed force or police system, as envisaged by Article 43 of the Charter. Dismissing or ignoring the various proposals submitted since 1945, the Soviet Union argued that permanent United Nations contingents must be stationed on the territory of the states contributing them; to do otherwise would be to violate national sovereignty.[13]

During the Suez crisis in November, 1956, when the General Assembly, in special session, established a U.N. Emergency Force, the Soviet Union abstained, explaining that the Assembly must get the United Kingdom, France, and Israel to cease fighting "before occupying itself with details on the future mechanics of observation. . . ." [14] It has at all times refused to pay its assessed share of the UNEF budget on the grounds that the force was "unlawful."

President Eisenhower's proposal, in 1958, for a permanent United Nations force patterned on UNEF, evoked hostile comment from Russia. Moscow explained that this was an "old U.S. trick" to violate the Charter, which provided for an international force under the Security Council, not under the Secretary-General.[15] Needless to say, the insistence on the Security Council stemmed from the fact that its permanent members hold the veto power—that most effective of all expressions of national sovereignty within the U.N.

The extreme caution displayed by the Secretary-General and the other powers on this issue in 1958–60, in the face of known Soviet opposition, was itself a measure of the political power of the Soviet bloc. The Congo crisis was to show, in 1960–61, that Moscow's outlook had not changed.

The Veto

In an oft-cited Soviet formula, the "principle of Great Power unanimity" is the "cornerstone" of the U.N. edifice.[16] The absence of such unanimity made it even more imperative for Moscow to use the formula as a circumlocution for stubborn and unflinching insistence on the veto power. A Soviet text calls it a "most important" victory to have the principle embodied in the Charter: "It offers the possibility of not tolerating the adoption by the

Anglo-American bloc of decisions directed against peace and security, against the interests and rights of peace-loving peoples." [17]

The Soviet Union values the veto as a means to prevent action against itself or its friends. It has been available to the Soviet delegate on the Security Council as a tool to frustrate any move clashing significantly with Soviet policy, a kind of master switch turning off the energy of the collectivity. There has been nothing mysterious or malicious in its use. Moscow has availed itself of the veto not to wreck the United Nations, but to compensate for its own minority position. It has explained its need precisely in terms of the "other" powers' numerical edge—an indispensable political stilt to raise it to the level of its rivals. "The veto," Andrei Vyshinsky once declared, ". . . is a means of self-defense."

There is merit in the Soviet contention that the resolution of international disputes cannot usually be achieved by accidental "majorities" in a body in which every state, big or small, has one vote. "Arithmetic is arithmetic. But no arithmetic can solve questions [such as war and peace]," Vyshinsky explained.[18] In a speech that bears reflection in terms of future possibilities, he told the *ad hoc* Political Committee:

> The veto is a powerful political tool. There are no such simple-tons here as would let it drop. Perhaps we use it more [than others], but that is because we are in the minority and the veto balances power. If we were in the majority we could make such grandiloquent gestures as offering to waive the veto on this or that.[19]

Thus the Soviet Union has always insisted on the widest possible scope of the veto (initially, it will be recalled, seeking to include procedural questions under it, and later using a so-called "double veto" to prevent an issue it wished to oppose from being considered procedural and hence exempt from the veto). In practice, the veto (the Soviet Union has been almost the only Great Power that resorts to its use) has been applied, more often than not, to matters involving no threat to peace or security. Of the hundred-odd vetoes, more than half were cast to turn down new members—including many subsequently admitted under "package deals" with the West. One function of the veto then is to strengthen the bargaining position of its user. Moscow made this clear when it vetoed the admission of Mauritania to the U.N. in December, 1960, anticipating a *quid pro quo* in the simultaneous admission of the Mongolian People's Republic. In September, 1961, it again tried to strike a bargain with the so-called Brazzaville group of African states, offering not to veto the admission of Mauritania if the African group voted against Nationalist China in the Assembly decision on Chinese representation. Other Soviet vetoes canceled a condemnation of Albania in the Corfu Channel dispute, prevented an investigation of the Czechoslovak change of government in 1948, of the violation of Manchurian air space in 1950, and of phony bacteriological-warfare charges leveled by the Communist states against the West during the Korean War.

Moscow clearly regards the veto power as a *sine qua non* of participation in the U.N.[20] In this light, the Western debate on the ways of correcting either the abuse of its exercise or the extent of its applicability was futile. The Soviet Union strives to extend the principle of the veto, not to restrict it. The veto controversy was a consequence of Great Power disagreement— not its cause. The right was intended, at least by the Soviet Union, precisely for such a contingency.

There is an implicit conflict between Moscow's stress on the prerogatives of the Great Powers and its simultaneous insistence on the equality of nations. The problem has its roots both in the Soviet perception of power and in the ambiguity, earlier cited, between egalitarian and elitist strains in Communist thinking. On the international as on the intranational level, Moscow has often defended "equality," and it was precisely in these terms that Stalin in 1946 (in his interview with Eddie Gilmore) praised the United Nations. Since then, Soviet spokesmen have repeatedly stressed the fact that the Charter is based on the "principles of sovereign equality and self-determination of peoples." [21]

At the same time, the Soviet leaders have been full of scorn for the small, the weak, and the backward. Stalin once warned the Powers not to deal with Russia "as if it were Central Africa." At Yalta, Stalin made fun of little Albania; at Dumbarton Oaks and San Francisco, his delegates made it clear that there could be no equality of great and small states, and that some problems must remain the province of the elder and the mighty. Similar examples abounded in the following years as well.*

Here again, the Soviet view of the world scene corresponds substantially to its domestic view. In opposing "formal majorities," Russian Communists have always subscribed to the concept of "democratic centralism," which in theory recognizes the equality of all members but leaves the prerogatives of decision-making to a small central body—in this instance, the permanent members of the Security Council.[22] At the same time, Khrushchev has been only the latest Soviet spokesman to argue that form must correspond to the "realities of power" (a demand raised as selectively as other Soviet principles in international affairs).

---

* For instance, Gromyko said in January, 1945, that most of the sixteen member republics of the U.S.S.R. were "much more important than, say, Liberia or Guatemala." (U.S. Department of State, *Foreign Relations of the U. S.: The Conferences at Malta and Yalta, 1945* [Washington, D.C., 1955], p. 72.) In 1946, Molotov remarked that the cause of peace was better served in the U.N., where the Great Powers had the veto, than by the League of Nations, which had been based on the "principles of equality of large and small states." (Speech of September 14, 1946, cited in Alvin Z. Rubinstein, *The Foreign Policy of the Soviet Union* [New York, 1959], pp. 277–78.) A Soviet scholar in 1951 denounced the whole one-state, one-vote formula as absurd (*Sovetskoe gosudarstvo i pravo*, No. 7 [1951], pp. 22–23), for why should the Soviet Union and India have just one vote each, as did the Dominican Republic? In February, 1959, the Soviet envoy to Tehran complained that the Iranian authorities were dealing with the U.S.S.R. "as if it were Luxembourg." The Khrushchev proposals of 1960, discussed below, reflected this approach in a somewhat different fashion.

Moscow readily grants that sovereign states are "of course" unequal in fact and maintains that one cannot expect the U.S.S.R. to abide by the same limitations and majority decisions as does Luxembourg or any other insignificant state.[23] No sovereign state can be compelled to act against its will, and especially not a Great Power.*

The unmistakable implication, even prior to the Soviet proposals on reorganization, was the Soviet determination to adhere to United Nations decisions on a pick-and-choose basis in the absence of any effective enforcement machinery. Such an attitude is in full harmony with the eclectic Soviet approach to international law and organization.

CHARTER AND ORGANIZATION

Moscow originally looked to the Security Council, with its Great Power veto, as the key organ controlled by those who mattered in this world. Correspondingly, it tended to minimize the role of other organs—not only the specialized agencies and the Secretariat, but also the General Assembly itself. Of course, the latter could be of use as a giant propaganda forum, but the Soviet delegation found itself somewhat ill at ease in a body in which it lacked either control or veto, which was based on the politically necessary but unpalatable "one-state, one-vote" formula, and which had no power to carry out any of its recommendations. As Moscow saw it, the Assembly was a consultative body at best, and this was fine.

The experience of the early years in the United Nations

* It is interesting, in this connection, to cite the comment made by Anastas Mikoyan in July, 1960, to a group of visiting Americans (*International Affairs*, No. 8 [1960], p. 5): "If there is confidence between the Great Powers, there will be no need to employ the veto. Insofar as I remember last year, for example, no one used the veto power. If there is no confidence, will it be possible by a majority of a few votes to compel another power under conditions of international tension to do things with which it disagrees in principle? To this no one will agree. In such conditions the United Nations would simply disintegrate."

served to reinforce Soviet reliance on the Security Council. Yet it was precisely Moscow's ability to prevent majority decisions and actions by means of its veto that soon led other states to seek alternative courses of action, to explore a possible revision of the Charter, to rely on military and other alliances outside the U.N., and to endow the General Assembly, in which there was no veto, with greater authority.

The United Nations was of course not set up to act against any of the Great Powers; to this extent Soviet insistence on Great Power unanimity in the Council was in keeping with the original assumptions. Yet the need or desire to cope with issues the Security Council could not or would not handle resulted in the Western-led attempt to endow the Assembly with greater authority, which the Soviet Union vigorously opposed on legal and political grounds. Indeed, the constitutionality of the Uniting-for-Peace resolution is debatable; its net result, at any rate, was a circumvention of the body on which Moscow was prepared to rely. A shift from the Council to the Assembly—or the Secretariat—weakens the ability of the Soviet Union to obstruct or restrain a hostile majority.

In the Khrushchev era, during the years of greatest optimism, it is true, the Soviet Union tended to look on the Assembly with greater hope and favor as its membership grew and Western "control" melted away. On a number of occasions, since 1956, it has been prepared to throw questions into the Assembly— when the Security Council would not act the way Moscow wanted (e.g., because of the French and British vetoes on the Suez issue), or when "mass" sentiment among small powers or particular blocs represented in the Assembly (such as the Afro-Asian states) was likely to assure passage of resolutions in accord with Soviet desires (e.g., on Spain, Lebanon, anticolonialism, and disarmament).

However, by 1959–60, Moscow had soured on both the Council and the Assembly. Neither was performing as the Soviet Union wished. Of course, Khrushchev's two personal appearances before the General Assembly, in 1959 and 1960 respectively, gave it value in Soviet eyes—with Khrushchev singling it out in his 1960 address as the "highest, most representative and authoritative forum of the peoples." But time and again, the Assembly showed itself indecisive or impotent. Moscow, moreover, continued to oppose all efforts to give the Assembly more power, claiming that without the veto the Assembly might "well perceive a threat to international peace and security in, say, the existence of the socialist system of society." [24]

The Security Council of course continues to be "properly" organized, but so long as the United States "controls" the majority of its members, the Council—Moscow insists—"will not be able to fulfill the responsibilities" it has under the Charter.[25] Indeed:

> It is understood that, in defending the principle of unanimity of the Great Powers, the Soviet Union and the other states of the socialist camp are by no means closing their eyes to the possibility that this principle can be utilized by the aggressive forces [of the West].[26]

In 1960, having in effect split with the Soviet Union over the Congo crisis, the Security Council earned Khrushchev's comment that it was "worse than a spittoon" or at least "is a cuspidor, not a Security Council." [27] At the same time, whenever the Western powers have failed to get their way in the Council, as Khrushchev exclaimed in ire, "they have used a detour, submitting these matters directly to a General Assembly session. They have thus contravened the crucial principle of unanimity in the Security Council . . . hoping the voting machine [Khrushchev's label for the pro-American bloc of votes in the Assembly] will see them through." [28] Both key organs of the United Nations thus turned out to be, in varying degrees, operating in a fashion intolerable to the U.S.S.R.

In spite of all its strictures against the U.N.'s performance, the Soviet Union, until 1960, firmly opposed all efforts to alter or replace the United Nations Charter. It assumed that any changes aiming at greater "effectiveness" of a body dominated by forces hostile to it were bound to be detrimental to its own interests. True to its conservative strategy, Moscow therefore made itself the guardian of the Charter. From 1946 on, when several smaller states first proposed a conference to revise the Charter, the Soviet Union was uncompromising in its stand against such efforts. It insisted time and again that the Charter needed no revision, and that the advocates of change were agents promoting American plans to restrict or abolish the veto so as to "use the United Nations for their own purposes." In 1955, the Soviet Union refused to participate in discussions on organizational reform (provided for by Article 109 of the Charter). The Soviet bloc abstained from voting for a conference on Charter revision, and it was largely in deference to the Soviet position that the committee appointed to study the advisability of revision delayed submitting its recommendations.[29]

A volume published in 1957 by the Czechoslovak Academy of Sciences received warm acclaim in Moscow.[30] It stressed the fact that the veto power is not a voting device but a fundamental concept of the United Nations. The Charter could not be tampered with, for, like the U.N. itself, it is a typical product of the transitional era in which capitalist and socialist states coexist; as a common denominator of elements acceptable to both systems, the Charter is "adequate for contemporary international conditions." This was the Communist position until Nikita Khrushchev submitted his drastic reorganization proposals in September, 1960.*

Since 1957, the Soviet Union has declared itself willing to discuss "enlarging the major United Nations bodies." More specifically, it has apparently given its support to the demand of Afro-Asian states to be given a larger number of seats on the Security Council (and the Economic and Social Council), but has made the seating of Communist China a prerequisite

* See Chapter XI, pp. 153–57.

for any such amendment.[31] In addition, it is likely to insist on larger representation for the East European states as well. The support of, say, India and Indonesia for new Security Council seats (as suggested by Khrushchev in 1960) is thus used for political bargaining. This is likely to be the extent of enlargement favored by the Soviet Union, but unlike other areas of Soviet commitment, Moscow has here left itself considerable flexibility and room for negotiation.

MEMBERSHIP

Who belongs in the U.N.? The Soviet attitude toward eligibility for membership has changed significantly since 1945. At that time, it made participation in World War II against the Axis powers or Japan a precondition of admission.* Originally neutral and enemy states were thus kept out of the U.N. At one point, Moscow wanted to withhold recognition from the Red Cross as a consultative nongovernmental organization because it was also working in Franco Spain.

Once again, political utility overshadowed "principles" when it came to the admission of ex-enemy states now in the Soviet camp (Bulgaria, Hungary, Rumania). As on the seating of Communist China, Moscow's position was frankly political: It argued in favor of universality of membership on behalf of its allies and raised selective conditions when opposing the admission of nations it considered potentially inimical. The logjam on admissions was finally broken late in 1955, when a "package" of sixteen new states—some Communist, some anti-Communist— was admitted to membership. The U.S.S.R. had no hesitation in accepting the log-rolling device, which the West had initially rejected but finally came around to endorsing.

Since 1956, the Soviet Union has usually stood for universal membership. It has complained repeatedly that the U.N. "has

* On the admission of the Ukrainian and Byelorussian S.S.R.'s, see Chapter VIII, pp. 106–08.

not yet become a world-wide organization," and it has expressed its pleasure (as Khrushchev did in his Assembly speech of September, 1960) at the admission of new states. The utility of the new policy derives from the assumption that most newly admitted states will reduce the relative influence of the pro-Western bloc. Indeed—as is discussed at another point—compared with the typical 45:5 and 55:5 voting ratio of the early years, the Soviet press in 1960–62 suggested a distinct improvement in the Soviet position by listing, among the hundred or more members, some forty-three in the "Western" camp, ten 'socialist" states, and about forty-eight neutralist or uncommitted nations. A solid bloc of neutrals and Communists could thus control a majority in the General Assembly. This trend makes it "increasingly hard for the United States to maneuver," while the Soviet Union, by contrast, becomes more and more closely identified with the new nations—a crucial concern of the Khrushchev era.[32]

Soviet insistence on seating Communist China in the face of continued Nationalist Chinese representation was the occasion for the protracted Communist boycott of the U.N. in 1950. The return of the Soviet delegation, after the Korean operation began, did not end the problem, however. Branded an aggressor in 1951, Communist China had little support for recognition by the U.N. during the following years. Against an American effort to keep the issue off the agenda, the Soviet Union pressed for its consideration at every session of the Assembly. Over the years, sentiment did indeed change, and Moscow used its growing prestige to urge "realism" in acknowledging the existence of a regime that controlled more human beings than any other single state. From 1959–60 on, it also argued that without Communist China, no effective disarmament agreement was possible (although this issue was conceivably separable from that of membership); and threatened to withhold support for other measures unless Communist China were seated. The U.N.'s refusal to do so was the result of a "contemptible game played by the United

States," a course amounting to "a flagrant violation of the Charter [that] seriously undermines the international authority and role of the U.N. . . ." *

United States' consent to debating the issue at the 1961 session reflected an awareness of growing support for the Soviet position on Communist China. Most compelling perhaps was the argument voiced by Khrushchev in 1960: If Peking is barred, why not bar all other Communist states as well? Even more widespread has been support among member-states for the principle of universality of membership. (In 1950, the Soviet bloc had been alone in opposing it.) [33] But in practice, Moscow has failed to adhere to its own standards. Thus, as indicated above, its opposition to the admission of Mauritania in 1960–61 was intended in part to propitiate Morocco, in part to exact a *quid pro quo*. No less political has been the contradiction between its stand in favor of the universal right to belong and its insistence on the right of the Organization to exclude a member. Indeed, membership has become a political problem—a trend characteristic of most questions conventionally considered to be of "merely" administrative or organizational import.

* Despite speculation to the contrary and the obvious tensions between them, I have assumed that the U.S.S.R. continues to be in favor of seating Communist China, even though Soviet efforts to seat it have not been uniformly vigorous, and Communist China would not assume membership except on its own terms. For a summary of the issue before the U.N., see *International Conciliation*, September, 1961, pp. 29–36. The Mauritania "deal" in 1961 did, however, amount to Soviet support for aligning twenty African votes against the immediate seating of Communist China.

Chapter V

Specialized Agencies

THE Soviet Union traditionally has looked upon the United Nations in political terms. Correspondingly, it has had little interest in the various specialized agencies operating under the Economic and Social Council and other nonpolitical affiliates of the U.N. This selectivity of concern, stemming from the Soviet view of what an international organization can usefully accomplish, goes back to pre-United Nations days.* During the months preceding the Munich crisis of 1938, Litvinov curtly berated League members for their preoccupation with "decisions regarding the drug traffic, assistance to refugees, establishment of an international system of signaling at grade crossings, or the results of the statistical and other researches of our various commissions," at a time when peace and security were in jeopardy.[1] During the wartime negotiations over the future

* In addition to joining the League itself, the Soviet Union also joined number of specialized agencies in the medical and communications fields. But of the over one hundred humanitarian and religious international bodies active before World War II, it joined only two, and of over forty in law and administration, also only two. (Leonard Schapiro, "Soviet Participation in International Institutions," *Year Book of World Affairs 1949*, p. 214.)

world organization, Soviet representatives repeatedly strove t
minimize the U.N.'s activities in the fields of science, cultur
and economy, or failing this, to keep these apart from securit
affairs.[2]

For one thing, this policy reflected Moscow's belief that, com
pared to the Security Council, the other endeavors were trivia
at best. For another, it found little in the spirit of certai
organizations to appeal to the U.S.S.R.: the cosmopolitan an
broadly cross-cultural aspects of UNESCO were not to its liking
and the assumptions underlying the financial, commercial, an
labor agencies established under the United Nations seemed t
be tailor-made for "capitalist" conditions, with emphasis o
private property, individualism, and gradualism. In Moscow
view, these agencies simply gave organizational buttressing t
the moribund capitalist system. Finally, the Soviet Union had n
veto power in the specialized agencies and was thus often unabl
to prevent decisions and actions it did not support. It is n
surprise therefore that Soviet participation in these bodies ha
been selective and, at least during the initial stages, was littl
more than perfunctory.[3]

One may differentiate among three different groups of agencie
for purposes of Soviet response. One group has always bee
acceptable to the U.S.S.R. These are the "innocent" technica
bodies, such as the Universal Postal Union and the Worl
Meteorological Organization. Pooling weather information, a
locating radio wave lengths, exchanging technical know-ho
were desirable matters, and in these bodies there were n
ideological difficulties, no challenges to the Soviet political o
economic system, no jockeying for power.

There was a second group, which has always been unac
ceptable to the Soviet Union. This has included the "capitalist
agencies such as the International Bank and Monetary Fund
the Food and Agriculture Organization, and the Internationa
Civil Aviation Organization.

A third group comprises those agencies toward which Sovie

policy has changed markedly over the years—among others, UNESCO, the International Labour Organisation, and the World Health Organization.)

From the outset, the U.S.S.R. refused to join most of the nonpolitical bodies. In some instances, it did so ostensibly because certain nonmembers of the United Nations belonged to them (e.g., Spain, Switzerland, and Portugal were members of the ICAO). In others, it assailed the agencies as anti-Soviet tools. Thus, Andrei Vyshinsky labeled the International Refugee Organization "a recruiting and supplying bureau for cheap contract labor to plantation owners, for the recruitment of hired traitors, and for the organization of subversive and diversional activities in the U.S.S.R. and the people's democracies." [4] Finally, the Soviet Union withdrew from some organizations it had joined earlier, explaining (as Gromyko did with regard to the WHO) that they were "useless." [5]

In 1949, the U.S.S.R., the Ukraine, and Byelorussia left the WHO; Czechoslovakia withdrew from the FAO (which the U.S.S.R. had never joined). The next year, Poland and Czechoslovakia abandoned UNESCO and the International Monetary Fund, which Moscow has frequently berated as an instrument of American capitalism. In the agencies in which it kept up membership, the U.S.S.R. advocated reduced budgets and activities. It displayed no initiative in submitting realizable projects to them. It barred many of them from operating in Eastern Europe and refused to provide statistical data requested by these groups. By 1950–51, it had clearly come to view most specialized agencies as enemy tools in the Cold War.

After the nadir of 1952, however, Soviet appraisal and conduct gradually changed. In his thorough study, Harold K. Jacobson concludes that the Soviet authorities became aware of the advantages of working with the specialized agencies and henceforth assumed a more active role in them. This reorientation came as part of the shift in the broad strategy of Soviet foreign policy after Stalin's death. It was symbolized by Soviet adherence to

UNESCO and the ILO in April, 1954. Joining UNESCO, in particular—after labeling it for years an auxiliary of the U.S. Department of State—betokened at the very least a change of style.[6]

However, Soviet hostility toward the International Bank for Reconstruction and Development and the International Monetary Fund has not mellowed. These remain capitalist weapons whose ties with the U.N. "serve merely as a cover for activities actually conducted in the interests of monopolies" of certain Western countries, above all of the United States.[7] While charging that "U.S. ruling circles are using IMF credits to put pressure on other states," Moscow claims that the IMF plays only a small role in financial relations of the capitalist system and has thus failed in its stated purpose.[8] Similarly, it opposes the International Finance Corporation as an agency "of capitalist countries, whose aim is to promote the export of private capital and private enterprise on an international scale."

The Soviet Union has never joined the ICAO, for a variety of stated reasons. In addition to the general allegation that "from the moment of its creation it has been directed toward securing the interests of the largest imperialist powers," Moscow has at times voiced a more specific cause: The Soviet Union refuses to grant foreign planes "unlimited rights" to fly over its territory and land at its airports and to share with other states technical data necessary for these flights.[9]

The fundamental reason for not belonging to FAO, it would seem, is the unique system of collective and state agriculture in the U.S.S.R. and the greater sensitivity of the Soviet authorities to shortcomings in this field.

Political zigzags are well illustrated in Soviet efforts in the field of international labor organization. Traditionally hostile to the ILO (from which it withdrew before World War II), Moscow may have hoped to build up the World Federation of Trade Unions into a Soviet-controlled organization to take the place of the ILO. At San Francisco and during the following year, Soviet representatives ardently—but vainly—pushed the cause of the WFTU and backed its demand for a privileged status on the Economic and Social Council. They continued their critical harassment of the ILO until 1953, when Moscow informed its Director-General that under certain circumstances the U.S.S.R. was prepared to become a member. The Soviet reservations being rejected, the U.S.S.R. joined the ILO without insisting on them and since then, muffling its earlier strident attacks, has worked for the adoption of sweeping, "progressive" conventions with wide popular appeal. While it has not succeeded in deflecting ILO criticism from Communist countries (for instance, with regard to forced labor and freedom of association), on balance Moscow appears to have been satisfied that it has more to gain from joining the organization than from fighting it from the outside.[10]

It has continued to be critical both of the organization and the policies of the ILO. The same is true of UNESCO. While no longer berating UNESCO for endeavoring "to undermine the struggle against the warmongers . . . by abstract talk about the intellectual and moral solidarity of mankind," [11] Moscow has continued to criticize its personnel policy, its tolerance of "anti-Soviet propaganda," and its wasteful concern with trivia.[12] A recent Soviet account of the work of UNESCO speaks of the "distribution of forces" within the organization, conceiving of it as another forum for the East-West struggle. It stresses the Soviet effort to "strengthen peace and security" through UNESCO activities, and the ostensibly nefarious efforts of racist and reactionary ideologists in the agency—some of them under the "camouflage" of religious ideas. It attacks the American contention that UNESCO is apolitical as hypocritical and as denaturing the agency's work. UNESCO, Moscow concludes, can become, but is not yet, a world center in the fields of education, science, and culture.[13]

Despite these reservations, the Soviet Union has of late contributed vigorously to UNESCO publications, and participated in its conferences, and it has sponsored several seminars and congresses in the U.S.S.R. Particularly in regard to social conditions, full employment, and nondiscrimination has it sought to project an idyllic image of itself. This has been true of its part in the social-welfare work of the U.N. more generally. But even here observers have found Moscow's participation limited by the characteristic Soviet assumption that since social ills stem from the economic base of a given society, the U.N. cannot eliminate them in pragmatic fashion; by the familiar insistence that UNESCO activities must scrupulously respect the member-states' sovereignty; [14] and by periodic Soviet efforts to reduce its financial contribution to a minimum.

TRADE AND AID

During the Stalin era, the Soviet Government showed little interest in promoting international trade under the auspices of the United Nations. Pursuing a predominantly autarchic policy, it even opposed the creation of the Economic Commission for Europe and abstained from voting on the establishment of the Economic Commission for Asia and the Far East. Suspicious of multilateral trade regulations under capitalist auspices, it supported none of the various technical agreements—such as conventions on samples, advertising, and elimination of double taxation—claiming that they violated the sovereignty of the member states.

Since then, Soviet interest and participation have grown. In the post-Stalin period, Moscow has been interested in a wider exchange of technical information on fuels, plastics, and the like; on its part, it has more readily supplied statistical and technical data. It has also pressed for training and exchange of specialists under U.N. auspices in rural electrification, automation, forestry machinery, and other fields where its own economy stands to benefit.[15]

As part of its general drive for more foreign trade, the U.S.S.R. has invited an expansion of intra-European commercial arrangements, at least partly in order to block efforts at West European integration. Indeed, after initially opposing all-European recovery schemes,[16] the Soviet bloc has moved in with such zeal that it appears to have the initiative in the Economic Commission for Europe, where it can promote broad economic programs without jeopardy to its own plans—or to its assertion of sovereignty. At the same time, Moscow has continued to oppose the work carried out under GATT, labeling it "a private-enterprise club" and objecting, one may assume, to its bracketing of Western with neutral states in the successful reduction and stabilization of tariffs. As a matter of general policy, the U.S.S.R. cooperates with capitalist international economic organizations "in those instances where cooperation takes place on the basis of equality and mutual advantage and where it corresponds to the interests of the socialist economy."[17]

In the Stalin era, Soviet interest in economic and technical assistance through the United Nations was virtually nil. Soviet hostility was apparently due to a general failure to recognize the nature of opportunities in the non-Western world, and also to the relative weakness of the Soviet economy. Soviet efforts in this field were then aimed at having American aid channeled through the United Nations: Departing from its customary policy to keep U.N. authority at a minimum, Moscow preferred a neutral U.N. tag to a U.S. or U.K. label on aid to underdeveloped lands. (In similar fashion, it had favored U.N. rather than U.S. custody of atomic weapons so long as it had none to contribute.)

Here, too, a change came in 1953, when the U.S.S.R. pledged its first contribution to the Expanded Program of Technical Assistance. Since then, it has participated in various projects of economic development and technical aid. The new strategy has undoubtedly helped identify the U.S.S.R. as a mighty "giver" in the eyes of the uncommitted countries; it has offered the Soviet Union an additional opportunity to hold up its own economy and organization as a model for economic growth; and it has permitted its delegates to insist that the United Nations (rather than the United States and its allies) must sponsor vast programs to develop the resources of the new states.[18]

At the same time, the size and form of Soviet contributions remain modest * and most Soviet activity in these fields continues to be conducted outside the U.N.[19]

Soviet attitudes toward the specialized agencies have ranged from suspicion and scorn to a desire to capitalize on them for material and, especially, political ends. The latter motive has been stronger in periods of greater strength and imagination, but it has not induced any change in the basic Soviet outlook on these organs. Still, the change is dramatic—from the near-boycott of the Stalin era to the more recent awareness of "public relations," especially toward the non-Western world.† Yet even in an era of coexistence, Moscow sees no reason to moderate its opposition to international economic, social, and scientific activities it cannot control. As an authoritative Soviet account explains:

* Since the beginning of EPTA, the U.S.S.R. has contributed about 3 per cent of its total funds, the United States about 40 per cent. Percentages for the Special Fund, supported by voluntary contributions, are of comparable magnitude.

† The U.S.S.R. has joined new specialized and affiliated agencies established since this policy was launched, e.g., the International Atomic Energy Agency and the Inter-Governmental Maritime Consultative Organization. On the latter, see Alvin Z. Rubinstein, "The USSR and the IMCO," *United States Naval Institute, Proceedings*, LXXV, No. 10 (October, 1959).

The other members of the "socialist camp" in the United Nations have generally followed suit. As of 1961, the sole variations from the Soviet pattern were these: only Poland belongs to the FAO; only Czechoslovakia and Poland are members of the ICAO; only Bulgaria, Poland, and the U.S.S.R. have joined the IMCO. Czechoslavakia is the only "socialist" state to belong to GATT.

The specialized agencies play a certain role in the development of cooperation among states in the technical, scientific, and other fields. However, their role in the cause of peaceful cooperation of states should not be exaggerated. It is limited by the special (narrow) framework of its activity. More than that, the essence of certain specialized agencies is manifestly antidemocratic.[20]

Chapter VI

Disarmament

Nᴏɴᴇ of the endeavors of the United Nations has been more arduous, more important, and more fruitless than the efforts to reach agreement on reducing and controlling arms and armies. The problem goes well beyond the confines of the U.N. Indeed, the significant aspects of the disarmament complex have thus far been *outside* the United Nations.

Were one to measure Soviet intent solely by the attention paid in both domestic and foreign propaganda, the Soviet "struggle for peace" and the advocacy of disarmament would stand out among the causes championed by the U.S.S.R. The long record of disarmament talks since 1922 has shown, time and again, Moscow's uncanny ability to make sweeping and appealing proposals, while resisting the type of specific controls or inspection arrangements that other powers have deemed essential (when they have favored arms reduction or control at all). The verbal commitment of the U.S.S.R. could not be stronger than Khrushchev's emphatic and persuasive argument, in 1959 and since then, that disarmament is the "most burning issue" of our time. Nevertheless, serious doubts about his motives remain. The Soviet invitation to other heads of state to meet at the U.N. in the fall of 1960 was justified largely by reference to the importance of advancing disarmament negotiations. Yet no progress was made. Soviet domestic propaganda has continued to play up disarmament as the imperative "question of questions" in our days. But close to a thousand sessions of various commissions, committees, and subcommittees in the first sixteen years of the U.N.'s existence have produced no meeting of minds.

THE RECORD

The original Leninist position was to deny the possibility of binding and effective agreements with the bourgeois world. As a recent study well put it, in a world of capitalist powers, negotiated disarmament was impossible; in a world of Communist powers, negotiated disarmament was unnecessary.[1] But, as in other areas, political realism prevailed over purity of doctrine. Without attempting to reconcile its statements, Moscow in the 1920's came out in favor of disarmament, while candidly stating that it did not believe in the international equivalent of "class peace"; and that, therefore, in a world dominated by powers hostile to the Soviet Union, disarmament—which it was at the very same time promoting—was an invitation to suicide. The organ of the Communist Academy acknowledged that "the signing of the Kellogg Pact [outlawing war] by the Soviet Union must be considered above all as a propaganda act demonstrating once more our peaceful tendencies."[2] F. I. Kozhevnikov, in 1931, attacked a volume on disarmament (by Korovin and Egorov) because:

> After reading it, one has the impression that the U.S.S.R., in announcing its plans of total and partial disarmament, genuinely believed in the objective possibility of their realization to a

greater or lesser extent. The specificity of our policy of struggle for "disarmament" has not been shown.[3]

"The road to true disarmament," declared the official journal of the Communist Academy, "is to be seen not in diplomatic agreements but in the proletarian revolution."[4] And the Sixth Comintern Congress stated publicly with regard to the Litvinov proposals at Geneva:

> The aim of the Soviet proposals was not to spread pacifist illusions but to destroy them. . . . Disarmament and the abolition of war are possible only with the fall of capitalism. . . . It goes without saying that not a single Communist thought for a moment that the imperialist world would accept the Soviet disarmament proposals.[5]

Such remarks may have been sour grapes, the Soviet terms having been rebuffed even though negotiations continued. But they are also consistent with orthodox Communist attitudes on world affairs. Nonetheless, Litvinov continued to be the foremost advocate of a spate of disarmament schemes—immediate and gradual, total and partial—until, in 1933–34, the U.S.S.R., like other powers before it, came to place a higher priority on armed security than on the advocacy of disarmament. Whether or not, prior to that date, it would ever have concluded a binding agreement to disarm was never tested.[6]

Since World War II, Moscow has again made strenuous efforts to assume the leadership in the "fight for peace." Disarmament has been one front of this campaign. Yet there can be little reasonable doubt that in the negotiations conducted under United Nations auspices, until after Stalin's death and the Soviet acquisition of thermonuclear weapons in 1953, Moscow was purposely stalling and evading agreement.[7]

In the critical field of atomic weapons, the Soviet Union rejected the American proposals for international control and ownership of nuclear sources, materials, and production facilities (known as the Baruch Plan).* Beginning with the characteristic insistence that atomic energy problems be subject to Security Council veto, and ending with a Soviet veto of the three reports submitted by the U.N. Atomic Energy Commission in June, 1947, the Soviet delegates protested all attempted "infringements of national sovereignty" and what they claimed to be proposed intelligence operations in the guise of nuclear-weapon controls. Thus, during the time when it had no atomic weapons, the Soviet Union was interested in avoiding foreign interference with its own military, research, and industrial activities; in embarrassing the United States; and in attempting to induce it to turn over its stockpiles to international control or to destroy them. Since it was the weaker party, the U.S.S.R. stood to gain from dragging out negotiations, in the hope of speaking before long from a position of greater strength. In the meanwhile, it insisted on the application of the veto with regard to international controls and sanctions against potential violators of international agreements; and it urged the declarative prohibition of the production and use of nuclear weapons prior to negotiations about inspection or disclosure—precisely the opposite of the Western position.

While the ramifications of the disarmament debate—such as changing capabilities, weapons technology, and military doctrine —cannot be examined here, one may safely say that until 1954–55, the major stumbling block (in the eyes of those who still considered a disarmament agreement possible) appeared to be Moscow's unwillingness to deprive itself of its freedom of

---

* Philip Noël-Baker (*The Arms Race* [New York, 1958]) argues cogently that Stalin never gave serious consideration to the Baruch Plan and never acknowledged that the United States was prepared to give up its atomic monopoly for the sake of total nuclear disarmament under international control. While some have maintained that the American proposals were bound to raise Soviet suspicions and were, at any rate, unrealistic, it remains true that, whatever the Western proposals, Stalin had nothing to lose by holding out, so long as the United States was not about to embark on "atomic blackmail."

action to the extent of a binding international agreement, with inspection of its armed forces and armament industry, as well as its unwillingness to abide by the decisions of a non-Communist majority in a United Nations agency handling an issue so vital to Soviet security. So long as his enemies were "in control," Stalin deemed internationalization more harmful than the *status quo.*

Since then, the picture has changed in some essentials. A most vigorous Soviet drive in behalf of disarmament began with the note of May 10, 1955—the first Soviet approach that could form the basis of serious, realistic discussion on gradual disarmament with controls—and reached a climax with the seductive Khrushchev proposals before the General Assembly on September 18, 1959, calling for general and complete disarmament within four years; subsequent statements introduced further nuances and flexibility.

Whatever the doubts about Soviet objectives and policy zigzags, in the minds of some close observers the situation had undergone a dramatic change. Philip Noël-Baker, winner of the Nobel Peace Prize, commented, for instance:

> Until May, 1955, the Russians were overwhelmingly to blame —not only for their general foreign policy of Cold War, Communist *coups d'état* and "sponsored" aggression, but for the cynical nihilism of their approach to disarmament in commissions and subcommittees of the U.N. But a careful study of the record shows that since May, 1955, the Russians have made considerable efforts to reach agreement, including the acceptance in principle of a large measure of international inspection and control; while the Western governments have withdrawn the reasonable "comprehensive" proposal for a first stage disarmament agreement which they had previously urged.[8]

Indeed, while the Western position became more indeterminate, and at times evasive, Soviet proposals in 1955–57 showed increasing flexibility even in regard to problems previously held hopeless, such as the principle of unimpeded access for international inspection teams, the establishment of control posts at key ports and railway junctions, and aerial photography as a technique of disarmament inspection. True, there were cogent military reasons for the Soviet position—observers pointed, for instance, to the Soviet Union's edge in conventional forces even if its proposals were put into effect—and Khrushchev continued to insist on Soviet sovereignty, accusing the Western powers of seeking to violate it: "In short, set them at the table and they will put their feet on the table." Yet the mood was one of general optimism—until in August, 1957, Soviet delegate Valerian Zorin suddenly "torpedoed" the talks. Was it because the U.S.S.R. had failed to secure "parity" of representation with the West on the Sub-Committee on Disarmament; or was the change in Soviet tactics related to the successful mastery of the ICBM and the impending launching of the first sputnik, both boosting Soviet bargaining might? *

The boycott of U.N. disarmament talks precisely when some Western observers had come to believe that nuclear-weapons controls had moved into the range of negotiable issues was to be repeated three years later. The ten-nation conference on disarmament, established on the basis of equal representation of both blocs as a result of the Khrushchev-Eisenhower meetings

* A detailed consideration of the Soviet proposals since 1955 is both impossible and unnecessary here. For convenient summaries of the negotiations, see the chapter by William R. Frye, in Louis Henkin (ed.), *Arms Control: Issues for the Public* (The American Assembly, 1961); Bernard Bechhoefer, *Postwar Negotiations for Arms Control* (Washington, D.C., 1961); and Nos. 524, 526, 529, and 534 of *International Conciliation* (New York, 1959–61), which are the surveys of issues before the Fourteenth, Fifteenth, and Sixteenth General Assembly sessions; and Joseph Nogee, "The Diplomacy of Disarmament." In addition, the Khrushchev speeches before the General Assembly in 1959 and 1960 provide the essentials of the Soviet argument. See also United States Department of State, *Geneva Conference on the Discontinuance of Nuclear Weapons Tests: History and Analysis* (Washington, D.C., 1961).

The problems of controlling Outer Space have been omitted from consideration here.

in the fall of 1959, seemed to be making headway when, in the aftermath of the U-2 incident, Moscow broke off negotiations on June 27, 1960.

Finally, in the nuclear-test-ban talks, underway since 1958, the favorable prospects for agreement were dashed when, in March, 1961, the Soviet delegation began to demand a tripartite administration, which would amount to an indirect Soviet veto power over inspection, budget, and personnel. The Soviet Union now shifted its ground to insist that a nuclear-test ban be discussed only as a part of a general disarmament agreement. The resulting stalemate led, on September 8, 1961, to an indefinite suspension of the Geneva talks. A week earlier, the U.S.S.R. had resumed nuclear testing.

In all three instances, the progress toward agreement seemingly made by the specialists (most obvious with regard to requirements for policing a nuclear-test ban) was canceled by broader policy considerations. In Soviet hands (and not in its hands alone), disarmament remained a political football.

Soviet Objectives

What were the Soviet purposes in this field? That there has been a propaganda motive in Soviet disarmament policy is beyond a doubt. Indeed, in the world-wide contest of the "two camps," disarmament proposals have themselves become weapons of propaganda. Litvinov had once declared, in his oft-quoted maiden speech in Geneva, that "the peace policy of my government gives us a special right to declare that we shall not let a single opportunity slip for the most intensive propaganda for peace and disarmament." [9] And Khrushchev recognized the short-term utility of his proposals when he declared, upon returning from New York, in October, 1960, that the line-up of states on such issues was "a process that will quicken and develop, and will augment the forces that stand for peace" (i.e., are aligned with the U.S.S.R.). The idea of total and general disarmament, he remarked in the same speech, "is a potent weapon with which to rally the peoples."[10] It is no doubt effective to contrast his own simple program with allegations of Western procrastination, pettifogging, evasion, and preparations for aggression abroad. But is there more?

Soviet motives in the disarmament field are among the areas of greatest uncertainty to foreign analysts. Yet unless one considers the Soviet campaign on disarmament to be no more than one gigantic hoax—a position difficult, but not impossible, to argue—one is led to conclude that Khrushchev favors at least some forms of disarmament.

There are powerful reasons for believing this. By contrast with the Stalin era, Soviet views on the prospects of nuclear war have become far more realistic, and the attempts to avert it more rational. Having, moreover, achieved its military objectives of highest priority, and being probably more than a little bothered by the prospect of spreading nuclear capabilities to other (potentially irresponsible) powers, Moscow is eager to reduce the likelihood of war, and first of all accidental war— an issue that has cropped up with sufficient frequency and vividness in Khrushchev's pronouncements to suggest a genuine concern.

While, previously, disarmament appeared to Soviet policymakers as a device incapable of "solving" the problems of modern society or of "eliminating" the causes of war, Khrushchev sees it, by contrast, as a warrant of survival, permitting the use of largely nonmilitary means for the advancement of Soviet objectives.* To this extent, the shift in the Soviet position on disarmament corresponds to other changes in Soviet perception and strategy. The avoidance of a major military showdown is a prerequisite for the future existence of civilization as we know

---

* More precisely, as of 1961–62, the use of means short of general or nuclear war, but anticipating "just, national-liberation" conflicts.

it. This awareness of thermonuclear realities is perhaps the most compelling argument, on the Soviet side, in favor of some disarmament agreement.

Disarmament schemes usually assume that the power ratio among the participating states, after reduction or elimination of weapons, will remain substantially unchanged. They thus presuppose a willingness to accept the *status quo,* or else a belief that even a deterioration in one's power position is preferable to risking a devastating war. In the Soviet case, the predominant expectations—especially under the formula of "general and complete disarmament"—may be assumed to go substantially further. While Western efforts have, in recent years, aimed at devising a formula by which a balance of mutual deterrence can be stabilized, Moscow has not been interested in the pursuit of "perfect" stability. Underlying Soviet judgments on disarmament is the belief that, if all variables can be kept constant or canceled out on both sides of the international power equation, the historical process will move mankind "forward" toward Communism. As one recent analyst put it, "a prolonged state of mutual deterrence can be acceptable to the U.S.S.R. only if its political effects are less than perfectly symmetrical." [11]

In the Soviet view, disarmament would help tilt the international balance further toward the "socialist camp." "It should be specifically emphasized," one Soviet writer declared in 1960, "that the forces of peace [i.e., the pro-Soviet forces], already a powerful deterrent to imperialist war moves, will multiply immeasurably in a world completely disarmed. . . ."] [12] As a matter of fact, even in the absence of nuclear disarmament, a substantial cutback in weapons and troops would consolidate the natural advantages in manpower and strategic location of the Communist bloc. Furthermore, an elimination or drastic reduction of the military element in the race between the two major blocs would tend to give greater weight to techniques or forces other than overt war: revolution, guerrilla warfare, "public opinion," economic competition—fields in which the Soviet Union would be confident to excel by comparison with the West, and in which, more generally, a challenger is apt to have an advantage over the defender of the existing order.

A familiar argument in favor of substantial cuts in arms and armies is the tremendous cost of modern military establishments. Especially for a planned economy geared to the pursuit of maximum growth, the prospect of freeing 20 or more per cent of its national income, currently spent on military affairs (and millions of men), for investment in more "productive" branches is bound to be alluring. Defense spending is a greater strain on the Soviet than on the American economy, and economists have argued that the expansion of the Soviet industrial base, made possible by savings in the military field, would not only "pay off" in the short run, but even increase Soviet military-industrial capabilities in the future.

It is possible—though here the evidence is more contradictory —that the Soviet analysis of the capitalist economy adds a further argument in favor of disarmament: This is the orthodox Marxist view that the West needs arms production to forestall a giant economic crisis. Thus disarmament would tend to speed the sort of crisis that would give Communist forces new opportunities on the international scene, and perhaps on the domestic American front as well.[13]

The seriousness of recent Soviet interest is underscored by the tenor of esoteric communications inside the Soviet Union and among Communist parties. Some Soviet writers on disarmament, for instance, are authoritatively criticized for failing to stress the difference between earlier and more recent Soviet efforts, with the implication that the Soviet Union is now strong enough to mean what it says in this field: "A new stage in the struggle for disarmament has begun, and it is very important to clarify the particularities of that stage to the reader."[14]

Perhaps the most compelling evidence, in this connection, comes from the backstage controversy with the Chinese Communists since 1960. At times, Peking claimed to support the Soviet proposals, but insisted (as did Liu Chang-shang, Vice-President of the World Federation of Trade Unions) that "it is inconceivable that imperialism will accept a proposal for general and complete disarmament." Hence—in terms reminiscent of the Soviet statements of 1927–28—"the purpose of putting forth such a proposal is to arouse the people throughout the world to unite and oppose the imperialist schemes for arms drives and war preparations." [15] At other times, Peking argued that disarmament was a fine *tactical* move, but surely was not meant to be taken seriously. It "questioned" whether disarmament was at all possible while imperialism existed; the corollary question was whether disarmament was desirable if the socialist camp had the edge. Moscow, seeking to satisfy the Chinese comrades, replied that precisely the power of the bloc made it possible to "impose disarmament on the imperialists," and that "only nearsighted people who have lost contact with reality can fail to recognize the urgent necessity for full disarmament of all states, can fail to believe in the possibility of achieving this goal." [16] *

The need and ability to "impose" disarmament on the West recurs in several of Khrushchev's speeches and in the Statement of the Eighty-one Communist and Workers' Parties, hammered out in Moscow after considerable argument in November, 1960. Its somewhat vacuous formulation of disarmament as of "historic importance for the destinies of mankind" was interpreted more usefully by Khrushchev in his address to higher Party officials on January 6, 1961. After citing vivid facts and figures about the destructive power of nuclear bombs, he reiterated the warning (presumably to the intransigent "left" in Peking and elsewhere) that "a sober consideration of what a nuclear war implies is in-

* A causal connection may exist between the confrontation of Moscow's and Peking's views at the Rumanian Communist Party Congress in Bucharest on June 24–25, 1960, and the unexpected break-off in the Geneva talks on June 27. If so, it suggests a Soviet effort to satisfy militant elements within the Communist fold that Moscow was not being "soft" or "opportunist."

dispensable," that one must "warn the masses about the deadly consequences of a new world war" and that "if prevention of a new war is the question of questions, then disarmament is the best way to do it." In obvious rebuttal of the Chinese view, Khrushchev proceeded to proclaim: "Our struggle for disarmament is not a tactical move. We sincerely want disarmament." 17

Probably the clearest indication that disarmament has been an issue of bitter dispute between "left" and "right" Communist factions and powers is the indictment of Moscow voiced by the Albanians. Thus the Tirana *Zeri i Popullit,* on January 9, 1962, assailed "the dangerous views which N. Khrushchev tried to impose on the international Communist and workers movement concerning universal and total disarmament." These views amounted to a belief that disarmament was "the primary and most urgent task of the hour"—which meant subordinating the class struggle and the fight for national liberation to it, the Albanians alleged. That this is what Khrushchev wanted is shown, the paper continued, "by the practical acts of treason of N. Khrushchev and his group."

Even if all—or some—of this evidence is admitted to show Soviet interest in disarmament to be more than a propaganda stance, difficulties remain in understanding Soviet purposes. They are compounded by the fact that Soviet proposals for "general and complete disarmament" as submitted in 1959–60 are strikingly similar to those advanced in 1927 and thereafter—at a time when the Soviet leadership expected its proposals to be rejected (and thus help lay bare the hypocrisy of capitalist states). Khrushchev, too, in mid-1961 seemed to waver, stressing the expectation of Western rejection rather than of "imposing" disarmament:

Representatives of countries of monopoly capital go to disarmament talks with the sole purpose to mislead their people, to lure them with hope for an agreement, but in reality to sabotage disarmament, to continue the furious arms race.18

The ruling quarters of the Western powers, while paying lip-service to the idea of disarmament, do not really want it. Of late . . . they seek to confine the matter to control over armaments, placing under their control, above all, the up-to-date types of Soviet armaments and military equipment.[19]

Even if these statements reflect a phase of particular tension, they suggest something less than an anticipation of serious negotiations. Moreover, in contrast to the specificity and businesslike detail of which Soviet negotiators are capable, the grandstand techniques of some Soviet appeals—for instance, the Khrushchev proposals before the Assembly in 1959 and 1960—suggest a lack of seriousness of purpose.

The major consideration militating against arms reduction, in the Soviet mind, is, no doubt, the benefits Moscow feels it has derived from military strength.[20] While the policy of "smiles" helped improve the Soviet "image" in the post-Stalin years, in the last analysis it was the existence of force—and Soviet willingness and ability to use it—that were responsible for many of Moscow's successes. Why then give it up? Sometime after the U-2 flight and the seeming failure of the Soviet "soft sell," a decision was taken to return to a tougher line. In 1961, the Berlin crisis, the increase in the Soviet military budget, and the build-up of conventional land and air forces gave evidence of Moscow's continued belief in the efficacy of military power for political ends. Churchill's dictum still stood: Russia's rulers do not want war, but they want the fruits of war.

All this does not invalidate the hypothesis that Moscow wants disarmament. The difficult question is, what price is it prepared to pay for it, and how does it envisage "getting there from here?"

Some of the difficulties encountered in the negotiations may conceal the deeper causes of Soviet reluctance to conclude an acceptable agreement. Thus the earlier insistence on parity and, since 1960, the demand that the Ten Power Commission be reconstituted to represent the neutrals as well, have been patently political in inspiration: To be acceptable, disarmament agreements must be unanimous, whatever the composition of the negotiating body.

More to the point is the traditional Soviet reluctance to accept any international "interference" with its own affairs. It is here that the obsession with "sovereignty" comes back into play. Time and again, Moscow has shrunk from agreement because, it used to assert, foreign inspection amounts to espionage and, more recently, out of an apparent belief that the more complex United States proposals for "arms controls" are devious inventions to trap the unwary. As in other fields, Soviet policy-makers have sought to avoid irreversible commitments and restrictions on their freedom of movement. Indeed, the notion of submitting to the will of others—so abhorrent even in less touchy areas—is bound to be intolerable when it involves the security of the state. Even though there have been genuine advances toward agreement on inspection (increasing control "in conformity with stages" of disarmament; a specified number of "veto-free" inspections by international teams under a nuclear-test-ban treaty) and, in the fall of 1961, concurrence on "general principles" that are to govern approaches to disarmament, there remains the deeply rooted reluctance, for instance, to admit permanently a small troop of foreign observers free from Soviet control—and presumably free to interview Soviet citizens, receive their complaints, subpoena evidence, and travel throughout the land.[21]

The contrast between the Soviet and American positions has been most apparent with regard to the concept of arms control. Since the mid-1950's, the American and British views have become considerably more sophisticated and complex. Experts have argued that a fully disarmed world would be even less stable than one subject to a reasonably constant balance of terror; others have shown that inspection and control can no longer be foolproof (an assessment Moscow recognized in 1955, but not in 1959–62). As a result, considerable thought and ingenuity have gone into various devices of "arms control" by which mutual deterrence from war may be stabilized in successive stages and by which techniques of inspection may be applied that are both feasible and adequate.[22] The Soviet Union has viewed these efforts with unconcealed hostility. Its leaders would not ordinarily accept the prospect of a "stable" *status quo*. Mutual deterrence "works," as a general proposition, only so long as each side believes that it gains from the absence of war. It is precisely this objective that Moscow feels will be jeopardized by the interposition of an international inspection authority it does not control. This explains the Soviet hostility to the proposals—voiced at the 1960 Assembly session by Ireland and other states—that would extend the rule of law at the same rate as progress toward disarmament is made, so that disarmament will be achieved once all nations have accepted an explicit code enforceable by a greatly strengthened United Nations. To Moscow, such a plan was bound to be taboo.

THE ROAD AHEAD

And yet, one important measure of Soviet concern has been the general tendency—across reluctance, zigzags, and inconsistencies—to yield on questions of international control. Since 1955, Soviet negotiators have inched toward some formula more acceptable to the Western states. Khrushchev has repeatedly pledged his readiness to sign an agreement on general and complete disarmament "with any, the strictest, international control" (as he put it on June 21, 1961). What are we to make of this?

Moscow has been remarkably inconsistent in its own statements regarding the need to retain a veto under disarmed conditions. It has still not shed its deep aversion to agreements that tend to freeze the present: If the U.S.S.R. is behind, it needs a free hand to catch up; if it is ahead, it needs a free hand to clinch its victory. Yet the evidence of recent years tends to show that (a) exposure of Soviet society to foreign travelers is by no means fatal, and (b) extensive observation—for instance, by U-2 flights, SAMOS, and electronic detection—cannot be prevented under any circumstances. At the same time, the growing evidence of what thermonuclear weapons can do strengthens the view that a drastic arms cut or disarmament agreement may be worth the sacrifices and risks inherent in international inspection if it—and it alone—assures the survival of the "socialist camp" without total war. Such a basic departure would, presumably, not be justified for such "small potatoes" as a nuclear-test ban, which moreover is at times deemed undesirable for military reasons.

That such is the Soviet view is admittedly speculation. The United States has often failed to test Soviet intentions, especially at those times—like 1955 and 1960—when Moscow seemed most willing to compromise in order to reach agreement. It is manifest that the Soviet leaders have themselves reconsidered the disarmament issue several times since 1955 in the light of various military, technological, and political factors that lie beyond the scope of this survey.[23] One may surmise, moreover, that some diversity of views in Moscow helps explain certain shifts in Soviet policy, though the evidence remains highly incomplete. Khrushchev's own approach abounds in contradictions. Thus his insistence that he "will never entrust the security of the Soviet Union to a foreigner" suggests that even in a disarmed world, Moscow would demand to be the master of its own security; yet effective disarmament is hardly compatible with the maintenance of unlimited sovereignty.

The nature of international controls is therefore crucial for the Soviet view. In large measure, the key question for Moscow is: Who controls the controllers? Here disarmament merges with the broader question of Soviet confidence in international organization—and the crisis precipitated by Moscow's demand for a veto over the executive arm of the U.N.

Still another pattern has been apparent, with few exceptions, in Soviet disarmament behavior of recent years. Where the primary objective of a given move is its propaganda impact, Moscow has played it before the largest available audience—for instance, the General Assembly. Where the Soviet authorities have substantive hopes of accord, they have generally sought to pursue negotiations in smaller, or even closed, meetings. Thus the nuclear-test-ban talks, and other serious negotiations since 1957, have seen a shift from the United Nations to direct talks with the United States, or else five- and ten-nation commissions. Moscow has felt in need of a more sensitive instrument for the direction of so tricky a set of talks. Enforcement may be agreed upon more realistically among those powers that "matter"—the nuclear powers, or else the Big Two. This explains the inclusion of disarmament items on the agendas of the Geneva summit meeting 1955, the abortive Paris summit of 1960, and the Khrushchev-Kennedy meeting in Vienna in June, 1961. In April, 1961, the Soviet delegation asked for bilateral, Soviet-American exploration of "principles" of disarmament acceptable to both sides.

The failure of the "surprise attack" conference—perhaps predictable in view of the complete lack of common approach—the Soviet disruption of the Ten-Power talks in 1960, and the collapse of the nuclear-test-ban negotiations in 1961, all show that the shift of venue to a small forum does not in itself assure agreement by any means. Even the small talks have been substantially politicized, as is illustrated by the Soviet demand for reorganization on the basis, first, of parity, and then, of tripartite equality.[24] Such requests had nothing to do with the substance under discussion. (Privately, Soviet scholars have admitted that the shift in 1960–61 was due to the Soviet experience in the Congo crisis.) These have been blanket transfers of political demands, such as the *troika* principle, to areas where they were bound to prevent agreements. While there may also have been "good" military reasons for the Soviet reversals, the nuclear-test-ban negotiations are the best case in point.

In its public performance, the U.S.S.R. has wavered between crude distortion of Western intentions, and far-reaching concessions (though often coupled with a "joker") as well as seemingly sincere appeals for the imperative conclusion of agreements to prevent nuclear catastrophe. It needs no reiteration that the dis armament talks have not in the least slowed Soviet military preparedness. For the purpose of the present context, the striking disparity between verbal stress on disarmament and lack of results within the U.N. invites emphasis.

There can be reasonable doubt and disagreement about Soviet motives. But, regardless of whether or not Moscow fears or wants agreement and whether or not it will, in the interest of survival, overcome its deeply ingrained fear of foreign inspection, it is safe to say that the disarmament issue is not likely to be settled within the United Nations. At the U.N., propaganda efforts have gotten the upper hand, and Moscow is prepared to make the most of them, while apparently being committed to making real progress (if any) through direct negotiations—as the bilateral talks in 1961 confirmed. The sixteen-year record of talks under U.N. auspices invites little optimism, for under *its* roof disarmament—just as within the U.N. itself—is likely to be the object of agreement, acceptable to all concerned, only when it is no longer needed to preserve world peace.

If, on the other hand, the improbable should happen and—in spite of all the political, military, and psychological obstacles—an agreement on disarmament or arms control should be concluded, the United Nations may, in the future, play a greater role in policing it. This greater expectation reflects, on the one hand, the thinking of the United States, as shown in President Kennedy's address before the 1961 General Assembly; and, on the other, the shift in the Soviet position since 1960 regarding an international police force in a "disarmed" world—as discussed at another point below. Finally, it coincides with the thinking of the increasing number of neutral and smaller states that conceive of the United Nations as a possible policing agent. Such sanguine hopes of course presuppose that the U.N. itself survives as an effective international organism, and that a Sino-Soviet confrontation does not render early disarmament talks utterly unrealistic.

Chapter VII

The Domestic Image of the United Nations

Wнат do Soviet citizens think of the United Nations, and what do the authorities want them to know about it? To speak of public opinion in the Soviet Union is to refer either to the private and usually unuttered views of Soviet citizens, or else to the official "line" issued and reiterated from above. We have no meaningful measure of "public" opinion in the sense in which one commonly speaks of it in open societies. What we do know suggests that, whatever their grievances and doubts, the rank and file are prepared to leave policy decisions—especially in the field of foreign relations—to the government.[1] The impressions of recent visitors support the thesis that, at least until 1960, the United Nations had occupied a very minor place in the thinking of Soviet men and women not involved in the conduct or analysis of foreign affairs.

SOVIET PUBLICATIONS

The image of the United Nations that the Soviet authorities strive to convey in their domestic propaganda may be considered one of several imperfect indexes to their own thinking about the U.N.

Until recently, Soviet publications gave little attention to any international organizations other than those in the Soviet bloc. Although the Soviet press featured the speeches of Soviet delegates at the U.N., the general tenor of press comment did not suggest that the Organization was of great importance.

The relative neglect and derogation were particularly pronounced during the United Nations' first ten years. One analysis of the Soviet press for 1945–51 notes that Moscow had "little interest in publicizing the United Nations thoroughly and throughout the year to the public at large. It [did] not seek to keep the Soviet public abreast of major developments during the General Assembly sessions and in the event of important Security Council decisions." Moscow seemed "singularly uninterested in presenting systematic reports on current issues in the United Nations" to its citizens.[2]

After Stalin's death, the situation changed perceptibly. During the preceding years, almost no textbooks, monographs, or popular pamphlets on the United Nations were published in the U.S.S.R.[3] Beginning in 1955, collections of documents appeared, with some comment by the compilers—notably, a compendium by Durdenevsky and Krylov; several brochures for wider dissemination were published in 1955–58.[4] And in 1957, the first book-length account on the role of the Soviet Union in the United Nations appeared in an edition of 20,000 copies—a new departure, even though the book was limited to strictly official information.[5]

Some of these publications were no doubt a response to the encouragement given during the "thaw," when international relations began to be recognized as a distinct discipline. In 1956, several leading Soviet scholars (including Academicians Eugene Korovin and Alexander Guber) publicly urged upon their colleagues the application of this new (and presumably more tolerant and truthful) spirit to the study of international affairs. They complained, among other things, of the absence of even a single Soviet work giving a general assessment of the United Nations, or even of a collection of articles on the U.N.[6] The State Publishing House of Political Literature confirmed that, regrettably, no work on the United Nations was scheduled.[7]

Since then, textbooks on international law, surveys of international affairs, and encyclopedic yearbooks (themselves innovations in the U.S.S.R.) have customarily included a section on "international organizations," with the United Nations prominently featured. While they are formal and entirely orthodox from the Soviet point of view, these surveys do nonetheless make information on the U.N. systematically available to the Soviet reader.[8] In 1959, a Soviet yearbook provided the first detailed survey of United Nations publications. Purely bibliographical in nature, it was no doubt a useful introduction for Soviet specialists.[9] In 1960, the Academy of Sciences of the U.S.S.R. published a superb handbook on international economic organizations, both in and out of the United Nations. While the introductory comments are as one-sided as ever, the 980-page volume is rich in facts and figures.[10] In 1959–60, the Institute of International Affairs sponsored a series of booklets on international specialized agencies.[11]

By 1960, in other words, information on the United Nations was considerably more plentiful, though often superficial and dull. The number of articles on it, in such monthlies as *International Affairs*, had approximately doubled since 1956. In anticipation of the Fifteenth General Assembly session, popular accounts of the structure and operation of United Nations organs were provided,[12] and two general surveys of the U.N. appeared in book form.[13]

With regard to objectivity, the situation has remained considerably less satisfactory. Continuing to present the world in black-white contrasts, with few if any intermediate hues, the Soviet press and radio depict the U.S.S.R. as the valiant champion of all good causes, struggling against the evil forces represented by the "ruling circles" of the West—monopolists, militarists, colonialists. The first Soviet textbook on foreign policy, published in 1958, stresses the Soviet contribution to the sponsorship and operation of the U.N. It treats at length Soviet disarmament proposals and related propaganda moves as accomplishments to take credit for. Characteristic of the broad optimism of Soviet propaganda, it exclaims:

> It is not hard to imagine how tremendously significant for the strengthening of peace would be the acceptance of these constructive proposals of the U.S.S.R., which were met with warm approval by wide circles of the public in all countries of the globe.

By contrast, United States and British reactionary quarters have sought to make the U.N. an obedient tool "in the struggle against the U.S.S.R. and all democratic forces, for world hegemony." [14] The United Nations, the Soviet student is given to understand, remains an arena of struggle.

The appearances of Premier Khrushchev at the U.N. received considerable publicity. Indeed, they may have ushered in more extensive attention to the United Nations than the Soviet press had ever displayed before. And, of course, the periodic political zigzags find prompt and vigorous reflection in the domestic media —such as the vilification of Secretary-General Hammarskjold in 1960–61.

By contrast, Soviet setbacks and debates revealing seamier aspects of life in the U.S.S.R. or its allies are played down or dismissed with a few vitriolic barbs intelligible only to the initiated. Even the most substantial accounts are curiously selective.*

To the extent that one can distinguish between Soviet handling of U.N. issues for domestic and foreign audiences, certain con-

---

* Thus the Morozov volume "celebrating" the fifteenth anniversary of the U.N. (1960) ignores the Iranian case of 1946; stresses the American "provocation" of the Greek conflict; dwells at length on the Suez crisis without mentioning UNEF; presents the Korean War as a South Korean operation supported by United States forces, which were then joined by "other U.N. members"; and is crudely inaccurate in discussing the Hungarian and Tibetan crises.

trasts are apparent. One typical example may suffice. In its publications addressed primarily to foreign "targets," Moscow identifies itself with the work of UNICEF, stressing how much the Soviet Government has done along similar lines in Soviet Central Asia in recent decades.[15] At the same time, it is evidently not interested in stressing such U.N. activities for the average Soviet audience.

> A film which Danny Kaye did on his travels for the United Nations International Children's Emergency Fund was shown on Moscow TV—but a month and a half later than in twenty-five other member countries of UNICEF, and in far shorter form. The 90-minute film of Kaye's travels to hospitals, camps, and other institutions to entertain underprivileged children was cut to precisely eleven minutes.[16]

The U.N. in the U.S.S.R.

Few United Nations activities have taken place in the Soviet Union itself—except for several conferences under the aegis of UNESCO and other specialized agencies. In 1960, Khrushchev did propose—probably without serious expectation of success—that a General Assembly session be held in the U.S.S.R. While the proposal gained the support of some non-Communist officials who thought such an experience would be salutary for the Soviet Government and public alike, no such meeting appears to be in the offing.

The United Nations' own publications and documents are not easily available to Soviet citizens, though they are formally disseminated through *Mezhdunarodnaia Kniga*, the official Soviet agency purchasing and selling books abroad.

There is a United Nations Information Center in Moscow (as in other capitals) at "15 Khokhlovski Pereulok, Apartment 36." Located in an apartment house of a modest residential section of Moscow, the three-room "center"—maintained at U.N. expense —consists of an office nicely furnished with bookcases full of

United Nations volumes, a reading room with a few tables and chairs, and a storeroom of U.N. documents. A recent visitor reports that there is no card catalog or filing system, and that during his stay of an hour or more not one other visitor was in sight. "My impression," he remarks, "was one of fundamental inactivity and almost minuscule value." [17]

The Soviet Association for Cooperation with the United Nations is a somewhat more "visible" organization. While it has contributed little toward informing the general public, it has sponsored some lectures and publications. With some prominent names featured on its board, its purpose, however, appears to be primarily ornamental, designed for foreign consumption. [18]

A survey of Soviet publications produces the impression that a real difference exists between the fairly extensive and "technical" discussions of U.N. affairs among the professionals in world affairs and the virtual silence in media representing those who hold the levers of power. Mention of the U.N. in schools is often perfunctory.* The official syllabus on Soviet foreign policy and international affairs makes no reference to the United Nations as a separate topic. Likewise, the Party's model outline of the lecture on recent Soviet foreign policy and world affairs does not list the U.N. [19] Some of the most authoritative documents produced, studied, and circulated in the U.S.S.R. ignore the Organization entirely. [20]

No doubt, with the multiplication of contacts abroad, the United Nations, too, comes into sharper focus in Soviet communications media and in the Soviet citizen's mind. Yet the Soviet people have felt no direct benefits from the U.N.'s existence and

---

* An official Soviet report claims, a bit lamely, that all graduates of secondary schools know about the United Nations through courses on the history of the U.S.S.R. and on the recent history of foreign countries. It asserts that U.N. Day is observed in schools and that discussion groups for students fourteen to eighteen years old deal, among other things, with the General Assembly and specialized agencies of the United Nations. ("Teaching of the Purposes and Principles, the Structure and Activities of the United Nations . . ." [UNESCO, Doc. E/3322, February 4, 1960], pp. 68–69.)

hence have no reason to consider it deserving of special devotion or loyalty, whatever the current Soviet propaganda line.[21] There is no basis for expecting international activities through the United Nations to stimulate a sense of community and transnational objectives. Indeed, the Soviet authorities continue to be jealous to maintain their monopoly over the loyalties of their citizens, and they will not tolerate conditions under which the U.N. could become a challenger or rival.

At the United Nations

SOVIET PERSONNEL

Emerging on the international arena in 1945, after years of semi-isolation and purges, the Soviet Union found itself faced with a shortage of men trained in world affairs. While it wished to make effective use of its newly won opportunities, Moscow was unwilling to denude its foreign office and foreign service of qualified personnel. As a result, the Soviet mission at the United Nations during the first years included men not noticeably qualified for their positions and others who were serving their diplomatic apprenticeship at the U.N.

While much in early Soviet behavior—the walkouts and vituperation—was calculated, something in the heavy style of Soviet performance suggested a lack of familiarity not only with the give-and-take of parliamentary procedure, but also with the general atmosphere of diplomatic intercourse. If it is generally true that in an age of "instant diplomacy" (as Dana Adams

Schmidt has called it) the envoy becomes a glorified messenger, the Soviet diplomat in particular has been deprived to a remarkable degree of freedom to maneuver and negotiate. Full of suspicions and inhibitions, he has often not been prepared to listen and learn in the "hostile environment" into which he has been thrust. For a good many years, it was harder to meet Soviet delegates and their families—and for that matter, Soviet secretarial personnel—in relaxed and informal surroundings than virtually anyone else at the U.N.

Here, too, the passage of time and of Stalin has wrought some change. More specialists have been trained and are now available for service at the United Nations; more diplomats have been stationed abroad long enough to gain a "feel" for foreign lands and customs. According to some observers, Soviet representatives are now at times allowed some latitude for negotiation without prior reference to Moscow—although such room must be narrow indeed.

While there are wide variations, one gains the impression that Soviet personnel stationed at the U.N.—be it with the U.S.S.R. mission or on the United Nations staff—tend to be more practical and pragmatic in outlook than those in the "home office"; at times, they seem less concerned with doctrine than with success. And while it is easy to exaggerate such nuances, there are occasional suggestions of different perceptions of reality. Thus there is nothing to suggest that in 1960 any member of the veteran Soviet staff at the U.N. believed the Khrushchev proposal for tripartite reorganization of the Secretariat to be a practicable scheme. But if disagreements have developed between Moscow and its U.N. mission, these remain carefully concealed from the outsider's eye.

Some Soviet representatives have remained morose and sullen, mouthing stereotypes and feeling ill at ease; but others have gained enough of an understanding of how the outside world operates to dispense with some of the wild misconceptions so prevalent a decade ago. This, to be sure, has not led them to deviate one inch from the most irresponsible tactics whenever Moscow has demanded them.

A few senior Soviet delegates may be taken to represent a certain "U.N. type," as it has emerged since 1945. Semion Tsarapkin, for instance, had attended the Dumbarton Oaks and other wartime conferences, then worked at the Soviet Embassy in Washington, in Korea, and on disarmament affairs. After several years at the U.N., he became, in 1954, head of the Division for International Organizations in the Soviet Foreign Ministry—the link between the policy-makers in Moscow and their staff in New York. Neither very subtle nor very deep, he was accepted by many colleagues as a sincere, fairly predictable fellow.*

Valerian Zorin is a man of greater polish and sophistication, perhaps, but he, too, is able to rise out of his customary non-violence to heights of righteous wrath. After an ambassadorship to West Germany and extensive experience with disarmament negotiations, Zorin, a Deputy Foreign Minister, became Permanent Soviet Representative at the United Nations in September, 1960.

His predecessor, Arkadi Sobolev, was widely regarded as a "reasonable" man who knew his business well. Characteristic in his career was his dual exposure to the U.N. Secretariat and the Soviet Delegation—first, as Under-Secretary on Hammarskjold's staff, then as Permanent Representative of the U.S.S.R. Indeed, the dividing line between the two is not so sharply drawn by the U.S.S.R. as by other nations, personnel being at times shifted from one to the other. At least some Soviet citizens serving as U.N. officers keep closer contact with the U.S.S.R. Mission than would appear proper. At times, Trygve Lie relates, a high Soviet member of his Secretariat (Konstantin Zinchenko) would openly

---

* "I am not the gentleman from the Soviet Union," he shouted one day in the Security Council when so addressed, "I am the representative of the Soviet Union."

tip him off that an important Soviet note was about to arrive.* It is not being unfair to the U.S.S.R. to suggest that the entire principle of divestment of national commitments in the Secretariat is alien to its personnel. As one comment at the United Nations put it, "Sobolev was an absolutely first-class administrator, but not working for this Organization." [1]

A minor incident was touched off on January 30, 1962, when, during a Security Council debate on the Congo question, Under-Secretary Georgi Arkadiev passed five penciled notes to Soviet representative Valerian Zorin. Non-Communist delegates suggested that such communications—presumably about fine points of parliamentary procedure—were highly improper. In March, 1962, Arkadiev resigned and was replaced by another senior Soviet diplomat, Eugene Kiselev.

The close relationship of senior Soviet nationals on the U.N. payroll to the U.S.S.R. Delegation has had its useful aspects, too. Particularly during the incumbency of the "moderate" Sobolev and of Anatoli Dobrynin, Secretary-General Hammarskjold was apparently able to explore the likely Soviet response informally by trying out projected moves on the Soviet Under-Secretary first.

Over the years, the competence of Soviet personnel at the U.N. has grown. Even before the Korean War, one probing analyst finds, Soviet representatives on U.N. commissions showed a detailed knowledge of U.N. decisions and reports as well as of the debates underlying them.[2] More recently, a harsh critic of Soviet policy in the United Nations acknowledged that the Soviet diplomats were of depressing industry, considerable technical skill, and impressive versatility.[3] And a leading American official who for years made the United Nations his central concern, commented about the extent to which, by 1960, the Soviet bloc had developed its knowledge of parliamentary tactics and procedures.[4]

---

* Trygve Lie, p. 341. Thus on July 26, 1950, Zinchenko intimated that Iakov Malik would return to his chair in the Security Council on August 1.

By now, enough Soviet diplomats have served at the United Nations to provide the Foreign Office in Moscow with a corps of veterans who know how the organization works.* Khrushchev's own experience at the U.N., on the other hand, may hardly be considered typical of, or conducive to, such an understanding.

TECHNIQUES AND BEHAVIOR

Soviet negotiatory behavior has been amply commented on.[5] On the whole, such observations hold for the United Nations, too. One striking facet of Soviet conduct has been the refusal to "play" when miffed, outraged, or uninstructed. The long list of walkouts, from the Iranian case in early 1946 to recent boycotts of the Disarmament Commission and the Committee on the Peaceful Uses of Outer Space, is not, however, a measure of Soviet impulsiveness. Walkouts and boycotts have been calculated tactics, used at will and terminated whenever practical reasons of sufficient magnitude have appeared. The Soviet absence from the Security Council in 1950 was terminated when Moscow decided to interfere with the U.N. effort in Korea; Soviet refusal to take a seat on the Trusteeship Council was forgotten when the Palestine issue came up before it in 1948.

In addition to its dexterity in the use of the absence-and-presence game (perhaps destined to be used less frequently in the future), the Soviet Delegation has over the years made a mark for itself by its virtuosity in the use of legal and verbal technicalities to defend its point of view, often against heavy odds of logic and fact.[6] It has tried to wear down the opposition by reiteration. It has been quick to level countercharges whenever accused of wrongdoing. When Iran complained of Soviet interference in its internal affairs, Vyshinsky within two days filed

* Andrei Gromyko, of course, became Foreign Minister; V. A. Zorin, Ia. A. Malik, V. V. Kuznetsov, and Sobolev are among the deputy foreign ministers; Anatoli Dobrynin, who, until 1960, was Under-Secretary at the U.N., became head of the Soviet Foreign Ministry's American Division and, in 1962, Soviet Ambassador to the United States.

charges against British interference in Greece, and Dmitri Manuilsky (for the Ukrainian Delegation) accused the British of intervention in Indonesia. The formula remained substantially the same, down to the Soviet response to the Hungarian case in 1956–57. Finally, Russia has seen fit to ignore the United Nations whenever convenient—for instance, in relations among "socialist" states. In sum, the range of Soviet behavior has amounted to an adaptation of earlier Bolshevik experience at home.

Soviet tactics have of course not always been a success. Not only were they unable to propel the U.S.S.R. out of its position of habitual loser, but, especially in the Stalin era, the Soviet Union often antagonized the small powers by treating them cavalierly as appendages of the "imperialists" or as "obedient lackeys" of the United States. There was good reason to wonder why the Soviet Delegation wrote them off, as it were, in advance. In a very real sense, "the Soviet Union [was] itself responsible for the consistently large majorities which the United States [was] able to muster on political questions." [7]

Those days are past. The Soviet Delegation's tactics have, by and large, become more subtle. Its representatives have taken to systematic "lobbying," long an American specialty, in order to round up votes on their side, with their approach "tailor-made for each delegate, according to a geographical and ideological situation." [8] Soviet diplomats, writes an astute observer, "are now encouraged to make full use of small but important diplomatic techniques that mean a great deal—personal contact, the press conference, the conference room show of affability, the corridor appeal for understanding." [9] Khrushchev's own performance in New York in 1960, which, of course went dramatically against this trend, was an exception to this, as to so many other rules.

Yet even the most optimistic observer of the learning process among Soviet delegates will not claim that they have emancipated themselves sufficiently to report home in meaningful terms, regardless of whether or not Moscow approves. No one expects them to pass the acid test of public service with integrity—to tell their superiors the truth when it hurts.

PERSONNEL POLICY

Until about 1955, the Soviet Government apparently preferred not to fill all the positions that its citizens were entitled to under the rules governing apportionment of U.N. jobs among member states. Of the more than one thousand professional employees at U.N. Headquarters in 1951, only fourteen were Soviet citizens. In 1955, with a potential quota of from 131 to 175, there were only 19 Soviet nationals on the Secretariat staff.[10]

Since then, the number of available Soviet specialists and administrators has increased; and the number of positions held by its nationals has come to assume the significance of crude representation or equity.° Moscow, therefore, has made more serious efforts to fill the existing vacancies and has complained of discrimination against its candidates. Only 1.6 per cent of technical assistance experts used by the U.N. in 1958 were Soviet citizens, Moscow claimed. Of the 3,700 members of U.N. missions sent to underdeveloped countries in 1955–59, only 40 came from the U.S.S.R., while more than half came from the United States or its military allies.

As time went on, Moscow provided further figures. The U.S.S.R. claimed to have supplied only 2.2 per cent of the UNESCO staff, while contributing 13 per cent of the budget. When the Congo operation took shape, Deputy Foreign Minister Kuznetsov complained that twenty-one experts out of sixty-five employed by the United Nations were citizens of Western powers, while there was not a single expert from the socialist states. And of the top twenty-eight positions in the U.N. Secretariat, the U.S.S.R. held only one, whereas seventeen were held

---

° Moreover, U.N. commissions have provided good vehicles to bring Soviet personnel in contact with underdeveloped areas.

by citizens of NATO countries. On the next lower level (of directorial rank), the Western powers had twenty-eight men, the "neutralist" states five, and the Communists one.[11]

Soon this became a major theme in the mounting campaign against the Secretariat. Former Under-Secretary Chernyshev publicly assailed the "flagrantly unfair selection of personnel" and went on to proclaim that "it seems high time for the Secretary-General to lend an ear to this criticism" and redistribute positions on his staff.[12] Khrushchev reiterated these charges as part of his broadside against the Secretary-General at the 15th Assembly session the following year. In line with its increasing emphasis on equal weights and numbers for the major blocs of states, Moscow chose to stress the Charter's requirement for the widest possible geographical spread in hiring U.N. personnel. United Nations officials, on the other hand, insisted that according to the Charter (Article 101), the geographical requirement was subsidiary to the "paramount" criteria of "efficiency, competence, and integrity" of employees.

In regard to sheer numbers, the Soviet Union had a case.[*] The administration readily recognized that the quota for Soviet citizens was some three times larger than the number actually employed; officials advanced a variety of explanations for the discrepancy. Perhaps the most important was the impossibility of recruiting Soviet citizens directly: Soviet authorities nominated candidates for the vacancies, and in a number of instances the men so proposed proved later not to be qualified for the positions. In some cases, Soviet personnel considered or hired by the U.N.

---

[*] In 1960, for instance, only one of Hammarskjold's Under-Secretaries (Georgi Arkadiev) was a Soviet citizen, while three (Ralph Bunche, Andrew Cordier, and David Vaughan) were Americans.

However, some Soviet charges were completely wild. Thus *Izvestiia* alleged (October 8, 1960) that U.N. officials (i.e., largely Americans) "take in a rich harvest of salaries, roam around the world with fat traveling allowances in their pockets, and are engaged, to put it bluntly, not in political business alone." It went on to accuse a number of U.N. officers of illegal financial transactions, sometimes at U.N. expense.

failed to appear. Moscow has usually insisted on rotating its citizens working for the United Nations, returning them to the U.S.S.R. after one, two, or at most three years—an unsatisfactory arrangement for the U.N.*

And still Moscow bitterly complained about discrimination.[13] In January, 1961, it followed up its blasts in the Assembly with specific demands for fifty additional positions. The U.N. administration seemed eager to show, in the course of the following year, that it was impartial in hiring, and gave more positions to citizens of Communist states.[14] One year later, the Soviet Union again asked for eighty key positions. In June, 1961, the eight-man advisory committee on the reorganization of the U.N. Secretariat proposed a new formula under which professional positions would be allocated with regard not only to the several states' financial contribution (as heretofore), but also to their population and geographical distribution. The result would not have significantly changed either Soviet or American entitlement, but would have increased the quotas of African and Asian states at the expense of Western Europe. The committee did recommend, however, the addition, without Charter revision, of three under-secretaries for Special Political Affairs, presumably representing the three major power blocs in the U.N. All this, the Soviet member of the committee declared in a vigorous last-minute dissent, would fail to remedy the "intolerable" state of affairs in the Secretariat. Returning to the Khrushchev demand for tripartite reorganization, the Soviet spokesman insisted that "the entire staff of the United Nations Secretariat should be reorganized on the same basis." [15] Once again, the specifics of administrative arrangement had been politicized and inflated so as to become an integral part of the crisis of confidence that confronted the U.N.

* As Dag Hammarskjold put it in his Oxford speech, a national official released by his government for a year or two with the U.N. is psychologically and politically in a different position from the permanent international civil servant who does not contemplate a subsequent career with his national government. (U.N. Press Release, SG/1035, May 29, 1961.)

FISCAL FIAT

There is some irony in the fact that, to the extent that entitle-ment to staff positions is measured by the magnitude of contribu-tions to the United Nations budget, for some years Moscow's own efforts tended to reduce the Soviet Union's quota. The Soviet delegation's pressure for reductions in United Nations budgets and expenditures is revealing as an index of the low priority Moscow assigns the United Nations.* Communist delegates have repeatedly asked for a cut in United Nations programs; they have argued for eliminating what they consider lavish and wasteful activities, unessential trips and benefits; they have refused to pay for what they declare to be Cold War maneuvers carried on by the U.N.; and they have advocated a reduction in the U.N.'s public-information and field-service activities.

The political intent of the major Soviet effort, in 1960–61, to cut the budget was indicated by the fact that it coincided with the blast against the Secretary-General. A budget of $50 million for the central U.N. system instead of the proposed $70 million or more was quite adequate, Soviet delegate Alexei Roshchin alleged.[16]

The Soviet Union and its allies have been notoriously selective in their contributions to United Nations activities financed by separate budgets. While the United States has borne over 60 per cent of their cost and the British Commonwealth about 20 per cent, the Soviet Union—even prior to the Congo operation—had contributed only 1.67 per cent.[17] It has not contributed to the U.N. Refugee Fund, the U.N. Relief for (Arab) Palestine Refu-gees, or the U.N. Korean Reconstruction Agency. Its contribution

* The U.S. contributes 32.5 per cent, the U.S.S.R. 13.62 per cent of the regular United Nations budget (raised to 14.97 for 1962–64). The nine Communist members (without the MPR) jointly accounted for 19.09 per cent of the regular budget until 1961, and 21.14 from 1962 on.

to the Technical Assistance Program has remained meager.*

In recent years, the U.S.S.R. has, above all else, refused to contribute financially to activities it chooses to consider illegal. The U.N. Emergency Force in the Middle East and the U.N. Force in the Congo are the two primary examples of continuing and expensive operations financially boycotted by the Soviet bloc. Indeed, the U.S.S.R. has challenged the right of the General Assembly to approve funds for the Congo operation and has served notice that it would not heed such decisions.[18] It has argued that the Security Council alone is empowered to establish such forces and that, moreover, the costs should be borne by the states responsible for the outbreak of the crisis.

Unless the U.N. embarks on the suspension of members in arrears on their payments (a most unlikely contingency, despite the fact that the Charter permits depriving a member state that is in arrears for two years or more of its vote in the Assembly), there is no way by which the collective can constrain any state to pay. The result is, of course, a severe financial crisis. As of mid-1961, less than half of the authorized budget for the Congo operation ($100 million for the first ten months of 1961) and less than one quarter of the current UNEF budget had been paid in. By the end of the year, the U.S.S.R. alone owed the United Nations over $40 million. The whole concept of assessment geared to ability to pay seemed to invite reconsideration.[19] Neither the $200 million bond issue authorized by the General Assembly on December 20, 1961 (over Soviet and French opposition), nor the advisory opinion asked of the International Court of Justice about the obligatory nature of assessments for the UNEF and the Congo operations is likely to solve the problem.

---

* However, a recent survey indicates, "it is worth noting that while the number of Soviet experts is still low (only 47 out of 2,208 in 1960), that country [the U.S.S.R.] is host to the largest number of fellows of any country in the world." In part, this is due to the fact that Soviet contributions are paid in nonconvertible currencies. (*International Conciliation*, No. 535 [September, 1961], p. 163.)

What is involved for the Soviet Union is, after all, not a particular device of apportioning costs or a ratio of contributions. Under the Soviet interpretation of sovereignty, it is free to pick and choose which of the offerings of the United Nations "cafeteria" it wishes to select. In this fashion, Moscow had not only preserved its own freedom of choice, but also secured for itself the equivalent of a "financial veto" over the U.N.'s special—and more expensive—activities.* The implications for U.N. finances and, beyond it, for U.N. action and survival, are self-evident.

Three Cheers

As early as December 19, 1943, Moscow asked the Allies that in the future world organization all sixteen constituent republics of the U.S.S.R. be given separate representation. This was presumably one of the reasons behind the constitutional amendments adopted on February 1, 1944, which granted the Union republics the right to enter into direct diplomatic and treaty relations with foreign states instead of having such contacts handled for all the sixteen federal units by the Foreign Ministry in Moscow.[20] At Dumbarton Oaks, the Soviet Delegation accordingly asked for sixteen seats in the United Nations—a request that promptly ran into Western opposition. At Yalta, as part of a larger settlement,

---

* In 1961, the Soviet bloc demanded a division of the budget into three budgets—a regular administrative account, a separate one for "extraordinary" action for the maintenance of peace and security, and an operational budget for technical, social, scientific and other voluntary activities. Interested members, Moscow suggested, would sign such agreements for each of the three budgets as seemed proper. (Doc. A/4776, June 14, 1961.) "Adoption of this proposal," a commentary declared soundly, "would be tantamount to dissolving the United Nations into a series of bilateral arrangements, with each state deciding in the light of its own interests what it would or would not contribute to." (*International Conciliation*, No. 535, pp. 200–201.) Radio Moscow voiced a new theme (January 2, 1962) when it began to assail the "revolting" position of the U.S. and U.K. as based on "the money principle." In the "cynical" Western view, Moscow asserted, "money is the criterion of power," and therefore the West wants the U.N. to follow the "principle of 'he who pays the piper calls the tune.'" The Soviet Union has declared that it will disregard the "illegal" Assembly resolution authorizing a bond issue.

this demand was whittled down to three votes (adding delegations from the Ukrainian and Byelorussian S.S.R.'s to that from
the Soviet Union); and President Roosevelt, who had left Washington determined to prevent such a deal, found himself accepting it (as did British Foreign Secretary Anthony Eden) in return
for a Soviet promise to support the grant of three votes to the
United States. Within less than two months, the three-vote bargain "leaked out" in the American press, producing "one of the
worst all-around botches of the war" and prompting an official
statement by which the United States renounced its extra two
votes. The Soviet Union, however, stood firm on its demand and,
at San Francisco, obtained the three seats.[21]

Here was a crude political maneuver, presumably intended to
compensate the Soviet Union at least partially for the numerical
strength of the Western "bloc." Moscow has apparently not been
bothered by the illogical situation that led to the separate membership and dual representation of two republics (by their own
missions and by the U.S.S.R.), while the remaining "sister republics"—legally on an equal footing with the Ukraine and
Byelorussia—have only the Soviet Union as their spokesman.

The U.S.S.R. has made use of the quasi-independent status
formally accorded these republics to have them conclude treaties
and agreements. At the U.N., both the Ukrainian and the Byelorussian S.S.R.'s have served on various boards and councils. The
situation has remained anomalous, nonetheless, for these republics have repeatedly refused to establish direct diplomatic relations, e.g., with the United Kingdom. On the other hand, Moscow
has made it a custom to have premiers and "foreign ministers"
of other Union republics (such as the Uzbek, Kazakh, but also
the Russian Republic), which are not separately recognized by
the U.N., attend sessions of the General Assembly and other U.N.
bodies as part of the Soviet delegation.*

* On several occasions in recent years, Americans heard high officials of
the Uzbek S.S.R. express regret over the failure of the U.N. to admit such
"sovereign" republics as Uzbekistan to membership, implying that it is
as much entitled to it as are the Ukraine and Byelorussia.

With the passage of time, the Ukrainian and Byelorussian delegations (elevated to permanent missions at the United Nations in April, 1958) have come to be accepted as appendages of the Soviet representation. They have never acted independently of Moscow. They have served their original purpose, for they have been useful as additional votes and speakers, and sometimes as "frontmen," when the Soviet ventriloquists have preferred to have others utter their words.[22]

THE SOVIET BLOC

More difficult and, in many ways, more important to the Soviet Union has been the cementing of its "bloc" at the United Nations —a mirror image, though perhaps distorted, of the Soviet bloc created in Eastern Europe. While the behavior of its allies at the U.N. requires separate investigation, it may safely be said that the Soviet Union to date has been eminently successful in forging and using its bloc of votes; indeed, the record of successes may be deceptive.

During the early postwar years, Moscow's command over the votes of East European states was not always automatic.[*] But by 1948, the consolidation of Communist rule in Poland and Czechoslovakia was completed. One of its many expressions was the consistency of votes at the U.N. The three Soviet votes, augmented by the Polish and Yugoslav on most occasions, still constituted a solid bloc of five—counting Czechoslovakia, but not Yugoslavia after the Stalin-Tito break. With the admission of new states in December, 1955, the Soviet contingent rose to nine,

[*] In 1945, Jan Masaryk, Czechoslovak Foreign Minister, is reported to have objected strenuously to Soviet Foreign Minister Molotov's demand that Czechoslovakia propose inviting the so-called Lublin (pro-Soviet) "government" to represent Poland. Masaryk complied only after Molotov threatened to denounce the Soviet-Czechoslovak treaty. (Josef Korbel, *The Communist Subversion of Czechoslovakia* [Princeton, N. J., 1959], p. 118.)

thanks to the addition of Albania, Bulgaria, Hungary, and Rumania. The admission of the Mongolian People's Republic in 1961 made it ten.

As Thomas Hovet has demonstrated, (the Soviet bloc has operated with more cohesion and unanimity than any other combination of states in the U.N.[23] The Soviet and East European delegations hold regular joint meetings; their "common" decisions are binding; and their voting has been virtually unanimous. If, on occasion, because of the alphabetical voting order, a minor member of the bloc proves to have voted differently from the U.S.S.R., he usually requests amendment of his vote after the Soviet ballot has been cast.

Whatever the strains among the Communist delegations, Soviet control over them has been outwardly effective. As a matter of principle, prestige, and practical benefit, Moscow will probably continue to insist on the "unanimity of the socialist camp." How long it will be able to maintain this cohesion is a matter of speculation. For various reasons, the accretion in Soviet power has, in recent years, not seen a concomitant consolidation of authority within the "socialist commonwealth." On the other hand, even during the Polish and Hungarian crises of 1956, and the Chinese and Albanian heresies of 1960–62, Moscow insisted on a façade of unanimity toward the outside world. It may well be that, even as substantial disagreements on strategy and tactics —and personality—develop within, the bloc will for some time continue to vote as a unit.

There is little doubt that, left to themselves, some of the East European delegations would have acted and voted differently on occasion. H. G. Nicholas is correct in saying that the Communist states form "a monolith, chipped only where Poland may register an individual voice, though hardly ever an individual vote." [24] Yet the Polish abstention on the Hungarian question, in 1957, was of course full of political innuendos. Closer scrutiny would no doubt reveal other instances of Polish efforts to convey unique nuances.* In all likelihood, the significant differences have not come to light. A close reading of speeches by East European delegates suggests that—even on the central issue of reorganizing the United Nations—differences in emphasis and selectivity of arguments may reflect more fundamental divergences from the Soviet view.

The closest the Communist missions have come to showing a rift at the United Nations was the ostracism to which their colleagues subjected the Albanian delegates at the 15th and 16th Assembly sessions. For months before the 15th session, Albania's dictator, Enver Hoxha, had feuded with Khrushchev, rejecting departures from Stalinism, such as the attempted reconciliation with Tito and, more generally, Khrushchev's approach to "peaceful coexistence." Having, in effect, aligned himself on the side of Communist China, Hoxha was the only East European Communist leader not to heed Khrushchev's invitation to attend the 1960 Assembly session in New York.

At the U.N., Albania openly fractured "socialist unity" by attacking the proposals of the Polish, Rumanian, and Bulgarian delegates on disarmament and the creation of an atom-free zone in the Balkans. While disagreements on these issues related to specific proposals before the United Nations, the causes of dissension—foreshadowing the Soviet break with Albania a year later—were, of course, to be found in the broader fissures within the Communist camp.[25]

Exceptional though it is, this experience suggests that it would

* For instance, the Polish assertion that a future nuclear war would destroy both capitalism and Communism (General Assembly, First Committee, January 21, 1957) came at a time when Moscow decried this thesis as revisionist defeatism. At other times, the Polish delegate is likely to have had mental reservations; to cite a minor instance, Poland with the rest of the bloc abstained from voting on a General Assembly resolution on November 29, 1959, that would have put it on record as opposing the spread of nuclear weapons to additional countries. Privately, it is understood, Poles were eager to oppose such a development. The Warsaw press stressed the "restraint" of Premier Wladyslaw Gomulka's address of September 27, 1960, coming on the heels of Premier Khrushchev's blood-and-thunder performance.

be risky to assume that, in the face of an unstable equilibrium within the Communist camp, the "monolithic" operation of the Soviet bloc at the U.N. must continue indefinitely. As George Modelski has pointed out, this assumption is particularly dubious because at present only the "homogeneous" bloc nations (other than the Albanian anomaly) are represented in the United Nations. The absence of Communist China and the three divided Communist states (North Korea, North Vietnam, and East Germany) in itself makes it easier for Moscow to control its bloc and, obversely, contributes to a greater sense of isolation, resentment, and virulence on the part of the nonmembers. Whichever the cause and effect, these states include those most violently hostile to the *status quo;* and if they are ever admitted to the United Nations, they might well provide an element of intransigence and intractability rarely found today. By the same token, their membership would increase, however slightly, the prospect of terminating the unanimous bloc voting of the Communist states.[26]

If Moscow is concerned over the effect of seating Communist China in the U.N., this has not been reflected in overt Soviet advocacy of Peking's representation.[27] Indeed, a bonus Moscow would expect to derive from the adoption of its *troika* plan would be that, China or no China, the U.S.S.R. would be the senior spokesman for its "camp," which would then be organizationally constrained—from the outside—to speak with one Soviet voice.

Part Three

KHRUSHCHEV AND THE
UNITED NATIONS

Chapter IX

Between Success and Failure

U NTIL 1955, Moscow, along with the rest of the world, saw the Communist bloc as a permanent minority, both in the real world and in the U.N. It followed that, as a matter of Soviet self-interest, the United Nations must be kept weak so long as it was considered to be an overwhelmingly hostile body. Since then, a significant change in the Soviet assessment of world affairs has taken place. In and out of the U.N. the Communist powers made significant gains in power, prestige, and opportunity. Moscow perceived the new trend with undisguised elation: For the first time since 1919, there was serious expectation of having the socialist camp emerge as the leader of mankind in the near future. A new stage in the world-wide struggle seemed to have begun. In moments of euphoria, Moscow now looked upon the United Nations as a tool it might eventually come to control.

The experience of recent years has, no doubt, confirmed Moscow in the reality of Soviet emancipation from its protracted status of an insecure survivor in a "capitalist encirclement"—and from that of an embattled, consistently outvoted minority at the U.N. In Soviet eyes, the decisive shift in the international balance of power has been due to the growth of Soviet might and the inherent crises and antagonisms of the non-Communist world, as well as to a change of policies that has benefited the Communist cause. Of these shifts in policy, two are of particular importance: the explicit and elaborate option in favor of "coexistence," with the concomitant assertion that both international and civil wars may (though not necessarily will) be avoided in the future; and a keener understanding of what nuclear warfare would mean— making the avoidance of total conflict so much more imperative than ever before. Khrushchev is plainly convinced that the continuing shift in the balance of power assures ultimate Communist victory on a world scale without major war. In his view, this shift has been marked not only by the strengthening of the Communist camp—proof ranges from the ICBM and space satellites to the rising standard of living in the U.S.S.R.—but also by the emergence of the new nations. They have been the target of Moscow's second major change of strategy.

Moscow and the Emerging Nations

The underdeveloped countries were an object of special Bolshevik attention from the start. But, while welcoming, and at times fostering, their "anti-imperialist" aspirations as akin to its own, Moscow's attitude toward the independence movements in the non-Western world has vacillated between hope and suspicion. Early Soviet attempts to strike at the "imperialists" through their colonial back doors (e.g., in China in 1926–27) invariably failed. After World War II, Stalin, slow to utilize the potential friendship of the newly independent nations, labeled the leaders of India, Burma and Indonesia as lackeys of imperialism. But in Khrushchev's world, with military conflict hopefully put on ice, the conflict between the two "world systems" shifted to other areas, among which the uncommitted countries were the major prize.

Only in the mid-fifties did Moscow determine to launch a vigorous and often imaginative campaign, extending moral and material aid to some of the new nations, pointing to its own experience of rapid economic development as a model, and depicting itself as their foremost friend and champion. The time-honored dictum of "He who is not with us is against us" was jettisoned at last to make common cause—temporarily and up to a point—with anyone who shared the same enemy. Another doctrine now found obsolete was the unarticulated but significant concept of contiguity, which had led the U.S.S.R., especially during the Stalin era, to concentrate on territorial expansion along its borders while being prepared to sacrifice Communist regimes far away. In the nuclear age, more territory did not spell more security; and with the "downfall of the colonial system," there beckoned, far from Soviet borders, opportunities that good Communists dared not miss.

Soviet policy was based on the assumption that the interests of the formerly colonial areas—in fact, of the entire non-Western world—tended toward the Communist rather than the capitalist camp. This assumption has been fundamental to Khrushchev's foreign policy, in and out of the U.N. In the Soviet view,

> the Afro-Asian countries are developing in a world which is split into two systems. Because they desire to preserve and strengthen their independence, the nonsocialist countries of Asia and Africa, despite the fact that their social systems have affinities with those of the Western powers, are nearer to the peace-loving position of the socialist states than to the aggressive position of the U.S.A. and its allies on a number of international-affairs questions.[1]

Whatever the changes in other regards, this thesis has continued to be held—with Latin America added to the brace of "progressive" forces which are the "main allies of world socialism." [2] In the official reformulations of 1960–61, the collapse of the colonial system is defined as one of the most important historical events of the century, second only to the emergence of the "socialist camp." [3]

Somewhat less explicitly—for good political reasons—Soviet optimism also extended to changes *within* the emerging nations, which were to take place either by peaceful means (such as a national revolution developing, step by step, into a people's democracy) or by "national-liberation war" (which by definition commanded the support of the Communist states). In the Soviet view, "the revolutionary energy of the popular masses of the countries of Asia, Africa, and Latin America, having awakened to political life, acts as an accelerator of the historical process and progress of all mankind." [4] While both the violent and the non-violent paths toward Communist accession to power remained open, Khrushchev was banking on an increasing number of "peaceful" transformations. Here his expectations were to lead him astray; yet the initial success of this strategy must have seemed gratifying indeed.

At the U.N., Soviet attacks on racial discrimination and colonialism, and the general inclination to support the Afro-Asian states—especially pronounced since the Suez crisis of 1956—naturally evoked favorable comment among the "uncommitted."

In Soviet eyes, the Suez crisis marked a Soviet victory. Not only did Moscow take credit for stopping the Franco-British-Israeli campaign by its own threats to come to Egypt's aid, but it was intensely gratified by the sight of the "imperialist whales" falling out—the United States voting with the U.S.S.R. against Britain and France. Would the capitalist universe no longer stand together against an outward challenge? While the General Assembly resolution on Hungary of course spelled a verbal setback for the U.S.S.R., in terms of actual control even the Hungarian crisis demonstrated the unwillingness or inability of the capitalist world—and of the U.N.—to intervene overtly in the Communist camp. During the following two years, Moscow was comforted by further evidence of Western weakness and retreat from the Middle East—for instance, American failure to underwrite the Aswan Dam; Anglo-American failure to "hold" Iraq; and, with the assistance of the United Nations, the U.K. and U.S. evacuation of Jordan and Lebanon. The West was on its way out!

Another significant bit of evidence for the quickening pulse of history was the change in the very composition of the United Nations. With good reason, the Soviet bloc welcomes the growing membership of the U.N., which has been giving the sum of Soviet-oriented and uncommitted states an increasing edge.* This is precisely the combination of "blocs" that Moscow, since 1956, has sought to juxtapose to the "imperialists" as the "zone of peace." Stressing the Communists' "united front with those from the Afro-Asian countries," a Soviet commentary in 1957 concluded with marked satisfaction that the Western countries "cannot rule the U.N. roost as they used to." [5] And in 1958, it found that

> to an important extent, the increasing role of the United Nations is due to the recent entry into it of a number of countries of Asia and Africa, which, together with the Soviet Union and other socialist states, come out for a strengthening of international peace and security.[6]

By 1960, it could note that "the *composition* of the U.N. had substantially changed; accordingly, the *significance* of that international organization must also change." [7]

COLONIALISM AND TRUSTEESHIP

Moscow's policy has been tailor-made to appeal to underdeveloped and "neutralist" countries. Its support of independence and sovereignty went hand in hand with the anticolonialist campaign at the U.N., climaxed by its resolution in 1960, calling for the immediate end of all colonies. Its appeals for peace were coupled with the persuasive argument that the emerging nations needed economic development rather than a prohibitive share in the arms race. However transparent to "old Soviet hands," and however much contradicted by other Soviet words and actions,

---

* Soviet journals have compared the situation as of 1945 (51 members, including 15 from Asia and Africa, and 5 from what became the Soviet bloc) with an expected membership of about 110 in 1962, including about 57 from non-Communist Asia and Africa and 10 from the Communist bloc.

the effect of the antiwar and anticolonialist campaigns was by no means nil.

The Soviet drive against colonialism was of long standing and of legitimate origin in the Marxist creed. One of its by-products between the wars had been Soviet condemnation of the League's mandate system. When the drafters of the United Nations Charter came to the proposed trusteeship system, however, the Soviet negotiators evinced surprising interest. This appears to have been due, first, to a hope of gaining a direct voice in colonial affairs—since in the Soviet view it behooved a Great Power to be consulted on all matters; [8] and second, to an attempt to obtain a trust territory for the U.S.S.R. to administer—specifically, Italian Tripolitania.[9] The effort, never pushed with vigor, failed, as did a Soviet attempt to secure supervision jointly with Italy—contrary to the customary Soviet aversion to joint authority.[10]

After this failure, Moscow's interest cooled. The Soviet representative refused to participate in the election of the Trusteeship Council in December, 1946, claiming that the first eight agreements that had been completed were in conflict with the Charter. The U.S.S.R. absented itself from the Council until April, 1948; then, when the Palestine issue was under discussion, political considerations induced it to appear.

Since then, the Soviet Union has used the Trusteeship Council as a forum for propaganda aimed at the colonial and "trust" peoples themselves. Advancing recommendations substantially identical for all the areas involved, Moscow has accused the administering powers of resorting either to veiled annexation or to purposive stagnation of the entrusted territories. As late as 1959, a major Soviet work on the U.N. identified the U.S.S.R. as a "principled opponent of the trusteeship system," while charging that the United States looked upon it as a tool for the penetration of monopoly capital into new areas.[11]

In 1956, the U.S.S.R. proposed independence for all trust territories within three to five years. In 1960, its draft "Declaration on the Granting of Independence to the Colonial Countries and Peoples" was to proclaim:

> The powers exercising "trusteeship" flout the principles of the United Nations and virtually preserve the colonial regime; they ruthlessly exploit the population and plunder the natural resources, taking repressive measures against those who have addressed petitions to the United Nations; they block the economic and political development of the trust territories. The trusteeship system has not proved its value anywhere and must be buried together with the entire obsolete system of colonialism.[12]

Even earlier, it was clear that the Soviet Union could not fundamentally consider trusteeship as an acceptable "solution." Why then Soviet support for the institution, to start with? A Soviet monograph explained with unusual candor and cogency:

> The international system of trusteeship represents an attempt to solve the national-colonial question by means of reforms, through a partial improvement in the conditions of the colonial peoples, without threatening the foundations of imperialism. This system, as it were, legalizes the colonial system. . . .
>
> How then can one explain that the Soviet Union signed the Charter of the U.N. and consequently has recognized the trusteeship system? Is not such an attitude toward trusteeship equivalent to a renunciation by the U.S.S.R. of the revolutionary solution of the national-colonial question? . . .
>
> So long as the trusteeship system contributes to the struggle of the colonial peoples for freedom, the Soviet Union will continue to support it, since trusteeship not only legalizes the colonial system, but also provides a vehicle for attaining independence. . . . The Soviet Union does not idealize the trusteeship system, considering it merely an insignificant concession on the part of the colonial powers, thanks to the struggle of the colonies' population. The Soviet Union has stood, and unalterably stands, for the revolutionary method of solving the national-colonial question.[13]

While some of the forms and the speed of the independence movements in former colonies and trust territories are certain to have surprised the Soviet Union as much as they did other foreign offices, the events confirmed Soviet expectations that the Trusteeship Council and its problems were of a transient nature. By the 1960's, most of the trust territories were well along toward political statehood,* and the Council itself was contemplating self-dissolution; the struggle in the U.N. had shifted to other fields.

THE FAT YEARS AND THE LEAN

One dominant impression of the following years is the rapid alternation of Soviet foreign-policy moods between unreasonable euphoria and a sense of intemperate frustration. In oversimplified terms, the period from the second half of 1957 to the beginning of 1959 stands out as one of exuberant optimism.†

The greater Soviet confidence in the U.N. was reflected in the unprecedented initiative of Communist states to submit issues to the General Assembly, a course of action they had previously scorned. Adlai Stevenson related his conversation with Khrushchev in August, 1958, at the time of the Middle Eastern crisis, when the Soviet Premier turned down the Security Council as the forum for a high-level conference.

> He proposed a special meeting of the General Assembly, "with all countries participating, to condemn the aggressors and

---

* Togo, Cameroon, and Somalia became independent in 1960. The British Cameroons were divided between Nigeria and Cameroon. Tanganyika and Western Samoa became independent at the end of 1961. Belgian-administered Ruanda and Urundi may gain independence in 1962. What remains are the Australian trusts of New Guinea and Nauru and the network of United States-administered "strategic" islands.

† The same period is suggested in a Soviet review of a Czech volume on the United Nations: "The enormous economic, scientific, and technological successes of the Soviet Union, the launching of the first Soviet Sputnik, tipped the world balance of power in 1957–59 in favor of the Socialist camp." This new situation, the article continues, demanded a new approach in the United Nations, too. (A. Lukanin, reviewing Miroslav Potočný's *OSN 1945–1960* [Prague, 1960], in *International Affairs*, No. 9 [1961], p. 106.)

demand the withdrawal of their troops" from Lebanon and Jordan. . . . It was apparent that the General Assembly looked to him like a better forum for a Soviet effort to mobilize opinion against Britain and America.[14]

Moscow was appealing to the majority of states: Here was a new phase indeed!

The growing hopes for the U.N. were also reflected in the Soviet backing of Hammarskjold for a second term as Secretary-General and in Khrushchev's unprecedented invitation to the Secretary-General to join in an impromptu summit meeting on the Near East.

A similarly jubilant attitude underlay Soviet articles over the growing difficulty of the Western powers to contain or control a majority of U.N. votes. Moscow saw defeat for the "imperialists" in the inclusion on the Assembly's agenda of such questions as West Irian, Algeria, racial discrimination in South Africa, and the definition of aggression. Soviet officials, in 1957–58, rather openly talked of a future situation in which the Soviet Union and Communist China—once it was seated—would be joined by another permanent member and perhaps a majority of nonpermanent members on the Security Council. "And then," a Soviet delegate to the U.N. is reported to have remarked, "the United States will be glad to have the veto."* Less directly but more openly, Soviet publications asserted that "the time is not far off" when (with the ex-colonial states voting with the Soviet Union) the "architects of the Cold War" can be "isolated" in the United Nations.[15]

If Soviet statements reflecting this optimism are projected into the future, they inescapably lead one to conclude that,

* The persistence of such expectations is suggested by a variety of similar statements in later years, including Khrushchev's remark to Walter Lippmann in the spring of 1961 that "You'll be glad you have the veto" (cited by Lippmann on CBS-TV, June 15, 1961). However, the forecast no longer seemed to carry the conviction and convey the sense of reality and immediacy it possessed for the Soviet leader in 1957–58.

in however vague a fashion, the long-range prospect Khrushchev saw for the U.N. was Soviet control of a working majority of its members. While such an expectation cannot be demonstrated, the spirit of his own and his deputies' comments suggests strongly that during these years, the ultimate vision of the U.N. was a vast "front organization" manipulated by the Soviet Union and its allies.

Yet before long, Khrushchev's strategy encountered challenges and disappointments. In brief, the successive failures to achieve its maximum objectives in any of the three "blocs"— the underdeveloped areas, the West, and the Communist "commonwealth" itself—led to some consternation, perhaps argument, and, above all, a sobering in Moscow, in regard to the *speed* with which the anticipated changes could be expected. The essential assumptions and the basic strategy remained unaffected hereby. Yet the reassessment, and the ensuing adjustment of the Soviet time-table to a longer time perspective, had an important bearing on Moscow's expectations and conduct in the U.N.

Among the various experiences that contributed to this reconsideration, relations with the underdeveloped countries were first in time and probably first in importance. By the time the Twenty-first Congress of the Soviet Communist Party met, early in 1959, after three or more years of Soviet economic aid to a dozen countries, the political pay-off was still in doubt. While the U.S.S.R. had no doubt gained some prestige, not a single country had moved from the uncommitted into the Communist column. Nor had the political support that Moscow gave the emerging nations always been reciprocated in kind. What, economic isolationists in Moscow were bound to ask, was the sense of strengthening the economy and military establishment of non-Communist states at the expense of the socialist camp? [16]

Moscow met its most telling disillusionment in the Near East. Here Gamal Abdel Nasser had been identified as a likely "bourgeois" ally of Communism in the struggle against Western "imperialism" and against "feudalism" and "big business" at home. Military and commercial agreements, a Soviet loan, and a pledge to finance the building of the Aswan Dam were followed by promises of direct support during the Suez crisis. Even more than in Egypt, Soviet hopes were high for Syria, where, in 1957, Communist leaders moved to gain key positions in preparation for what looked like control of the government. Given the Soviet theory that the national "bourgeois" revolution constitutes only the first of a two-part transformation, it was axiomatic that a second, Communist, revolution was to follow—either by force or else by "peaceful" take-over.[17]

Nasser's actions, from 1958 on, rendered both techniques unworkable. Indeed, the very formation of the United Arab Republic was in large measure intended to neutralize Communist influence.[18] To Nasser's charges that Communist activity in the Arab lands was "being waged not without the influence of the Kremlin," Khrushchev replied in January, 1959, by dismissing the Egyptian leader as a "young hothead" who would know better in time. Communism, Khrushchev declared, was not an enemy of nationalism, and the Soviet Union would continue to support the U.A.R. on the international stage.[19]

While the estrangement was by no means total, Nasser shunned any closer ties with Moscow. By 1959, indigenous Communists in Egypt and Syria were outlawed or suppressed and their leaders jailed or exiled. Moscow had exaggerated the ease, or at the very least the speed, with which it could hope to take advantage of Arab nationalism for its own ends.

Soviet hopes shifted to Iraq, where in July, 1958, the "imperialists" were also ousted by a "national-liberation" movement that initially had accepted Communist help. Moscow began backing Iraq against its Arab rival, the U.A.R. But the Iraqi experience proved equally disheartening to Moscow. Once he had come to feel strong enough and to suspect the motives of the local Communists, General Abdul Karim Kassim outlawed the pro-Moscow Communist Party.*

By mid-1959, it was thus apparent that Khrushchev had failed in the three areas of the Arab world in which he had expected to move the revolutionary process to a "higher" stage. To be sure, it was good politics to continue offering economic and diplomatic aid to Nasser and Kassim (and for them to accept it). But this was still merely sowing, with no reaping in sight. Some old-timers in Moscow—and others, no doubt, in Peking—were bound to mumble that the leader's hopes had been naïve and the failures predictable.

One of the first victims of the less extravagant outlook that came to prevail in 1959 was the expectation of a reasonably early take-over of the United Nations by the Soviet bloc and its friends.

Such a summary statement does, however, some violence to the complexity of Soviet attitudes. Pronouncements of leaders and publicists suggest that there was, throughout these years, a certain duality in Soviet arguments about the U.N.—on the one hand, the insistence that American "dictation" was on the wane; on the other, the assertion that the forces of evil were still in control.

The evolution of Khrushchev's own views is reflected in some of his public statements. Until mid-1957, he was skeptical in his appraisal of the U.N. In an interview with Turner Catledge, of *The New York Times,* Khrushchev stated:

* There is evidence of disagreement in Communist circles, in 1958–59, on whether conditions were ripe for an early seizure of power or whether a further "consolidation" of forces in alliance with "bourgeois nationalists" was in order. From September, 1958, on, a number of statements suggested that at least some Soviet spokesmen argued for a "new stage" in the approach to revolutions in non-Western areas. The more militant policy, perhaps stimulated by an effort to reassert Soviet leadership in the face of tacit Chinese and Yugoslav challenges, was apparently discarded before it was applied. By the summer of 1959, Moscow reprimanded those Iraqi Communists who had supported an abortive attempt to seize power— and by implication other extremists "prematurely" advocating "direct action."

The United Nations can, of course, be regarded as a useful instrument. But I would be going against my conscience if I called it an important instrument for the settlement of international problems today. So long as a situation exists in the U.N. where everything is bossed by the United States, where the United States commands countries receiving sops from it, that organization will in effect be not an international organization but a branch of the U.S.A. Of course, even today it happens that the U.N. expresses the aspirations and desires of the peoples. But, regretfully, such cases are rare.[20]

Such reserved comments were virtually absent during the next two years—the phase of greatest optimism.* Now Khrushchev found it convenient or desirable to introduce an element of welcome apology for American "victories" in the U.N. by asserting that anti-Soviet votes were not really anti-Soviet, but merely reflections of economic indebtedness to the United States—a situation apt to end, Moscow trusted, as Soviet economic might and contacts abroad expanded in the years ahead. Khrushchev explained, in an interview with United Press correspondent Henry Shapiro:

Some of the U.N. delegations often vote with the United States, but after the voting they come up to our delegation and apologize for not having voted for the Soviet proposals even though they believe them to be correct. (What can we do, we depend on American credits?) How can the many member

---

* There were two exceptions. One was part of Khrushchev's plan to use the General Assembly for a debate on the Middle Eastern crisis: In a letter to President Eisenhower, he exclaimed that "under United States pressure," the Security Council had become a committee composed "in the main" of NATO, SEATO, and Baghdad Pact powers, who "are not free to undertake anything that is contrary to the position of the United States." (*The New York Times*, August 6, 1958.) The other exception was Anastas Mikoyan's explanation—one may assume the best he could think of—why the U.N. had condemned the U.S.S.R. over Hungary: "It [the resolution] was adopted through the voting machine, the majority which is at the disposal of the United States." (*Ibid.*, January 19, 1959.)

nations of the United Nations which are in debt to the
United States act independently?

The United Nations of course does something useful, and
that is why we belong to it. But it is a mechanism that stalls
in its work. This must be taken into account.[21]

In 1958, even this type of dialectical explication disappeared.
Now Moscow claimed that, thanks to Afro-Asian support, it
had been possible to stem the tide by which the West had
striven to "impose an American *diktat* on other countries."[22]
The United States was "steadily losing support" in the U.N.,
where, in 1958, it suffered "serious moral and political defeat."[23]

By late spring of 1959, the sweet smell of victory had faded.
Once again, *Izvestiia* returned to the old motif: "The drill-
sergeant system that American representatives have imposed on
the United Nations for fourteen years is the main reason why
that organization has not lived up to the hopes resting upon it."[24]
In his debate with U.S. labor leaders a few months later, Khrushchev rejected Walter Reuther's suggestion that the U.S.S.R. and
the United States jointly channel their aid to underdeveloped
countries through the U.N., adding that "In the United Nations
we are always outvoted. . . ." When Reuther mentioned parity
of representation for both major power blocs in the U.N.,
Khrushchev replied pessimistically; "That would already be
progress, but it won't be accepted."[25] In the returning spirit of
gloom, it was natural for Dmitri Poliansky, Premier of the
Russian Republic of the U.S.S.R., to say that "it's common
knowledge that the United Nations is controlled by the United
States."[26]

On at least three occasions in the latter part of 1959 did
Moscow find bitter evidence to support this view. The 14th
Session of the General Assembly again condemned Soviet "disregard" of its earlier resolutions on Hungary—and did so by an
overwhelming margin (53:10, with 17 abstentions). Over the
protest of Soviet Deputy Foreign Minister Vasili Kuznetsov that
it was "a dead question which has already begun to stink," the

General Assembly voted to debate charges of Chinese Communist terror in Tibet and called for "respect" of Tibetan human rights, religion, and culture.[27]

The third problem, that of Laos, presented even greater difficulties for the U.S.S.R. The establishment of a fact-finding subcommittee on Laos entailed a Soviet defeat over the question of the so-called "double veto"; * the Soviet Government labeled the creation of the subcommittee a "violation of the United Nations Charter" and declared that it would not recognize the resolution establishing it. When the Secretary-General personally proceeded to Laos, Arkadi Sobolev admonished him in writing that he had no business to go and no authority to station a representative there: "All such steps cannot be considered otherwise than attempts to use the United Nations for covering the actions of certain powers."[28] As for the fact-finding subcommittee itself, its members could not possibly make an objective report: "Look who they are: representatives of Japan, Argentina, Italy, all of them countries economically and politically dependent on the United States."[29] Such comments were dangerously reminiscent of Soviet "go-it-alone" tactics of earlier days. The U.N., so recently expected to become a Communist front, turned out to be an enemy tool!

U.N., U.S., AND U-2

After the Middle Eastern developments of 1959, Soviet diplomacy concentrated its efforts on the United States. It was to take another year before Soviet strategy was to suffer shipwreck here, too. The central argument pressed on the West

---

* The Soviet representative on the Security Council argued that the question whether the establishment of a fact-finding subcommittee on Laos was procedural or substantive, was itself subject to Soviet veto. But this time, unlike several earlier instances dating back to 1946, in which the Powers had agreed on the legality of the "double veto," the chair held the motion procedural and went on to let the subcommittee be established by majority vote.

since 1956–57 was that it had failed to recognize the passing of its "position of strength." What the United States must do, Moscow preached time and again, was to adopt a "position of reason," i.e., a willingness to acknowledge soberly that the relationship of forces has changed, recognize its own impending demise, and hence seek a "reasonable compromise."[30]

In 1959, the Soviet Premier's dramatic trip to the United States provided the occasion for his first visit to the United Nations and his speech before the General Assembly on September 18. The U.N. itself, he exclaimed optimistically, was the "embodiment of the idea of peaceful coexistence"; Great Power relations were on the mend; and there were many facts to "exemplify the new favorable trend in world affairs." In fine, "everything goes to show that the time has come to usher in a period of international negotiations, conferences, and meetings." The United Nations must merely "cleanse itself of the elements of the Cold War, which often hamper and handicap its activities." What he meant was that it was impermissible for a "group of countries" in the U.N. to "pursue a policy of imposing the will of some states upon others."

The over-all impression of Khrushchev's performance was one of positive support for the U.N. "The important conclusion" from the Assembly session of 1959, Moscow itself commented soon after, was that "increasing possibilities are opening up for the struggle to maintain and reinforce peace"—the customary circumlocution for the Soviet Union's getting its way.[31] No less positive were Moscow's comments about the "spirit of Camp David" and the prospects of improved relations with the United States.*

But it was precisely this period of new hopes that flushed out an unusually sharp attack on the United Nations by a senior

---

* For the official version of the trip, see, for instance, the Soviet volume *Face to Face with America: The Story of N. S. Khrushchev's Visit to the U.S.A.* (Moscow, 1960). On his return from the United States, Khrushchev declared (September 28, 1959) that he was certain President Eisenhower would do his level best to "bring about agreement" and "create friendly relations" between the Soviet Union and the U.S.A.

Soviet official. Ilia S. Chernyshev, who had spent four years as Under-Secretary at the U.N. (in 1953–57), summed up his views on United Nations Day, 1959. Building on several themes introduced by Khrushchev in his Assembly speech, Chernyshev went well beyond them. Where Khrushchev had been optimistic, Chernyshev was pessimistic. The U.N. had "become coated with quite a crust of Cold War ice." For the first time in years, he seriously raised the possibility of a Communist withdrawal: "One could understand the indignation of men who for years had watched Anglo-American diplomacy use its obedient mechanical majority to cloak pretty questionable doings with the United Nations flag." But he went on to argue that, even if some people with an "ultrapessimistic view" had questioned this, the United Nations was after all "worth keeping up."

It is of some interest that the three priority issues mentioned by Chernyshev were precisely the problems identified by Khrushchev one year later in his major attack on the United Nations:

> The United Nations' efforts should be focused, first of all [Chernyshev wrote], on solving the problem of *disarmament*, the importance of which is self-evident. Further, past injustices in the *Organization's functioning* must be remedied. A prominent feature in its activities should be assistance to *colonial* and dependent countries in their striving for independence and progress.[32]

And the organizational questions specifically listed included the inadequate representation of Communist states on the Security Council, the "flagrantly unfair selection of personnel for the U.N. Secretariat," and the unsatisfactory work of the Secretariat itself.*

* The tenor of the Chernyshev article is so much out of keeping with the then predominant Soviet "line" that one is tempted to speculate that Chernyshev was a spokesman for what more recently has been called the "Molotov position"—fearful of illusions fostered in Moscow as a result of the "coexistence" policy. It is curious that Chernyshev, who had been on diplomatic assignments abroad since before World War II, was brought back to the Soviet Union in 1957 and remained there in relatively obscure

The charge that the United States was "running" the U.N. and that the Secretary-General was in effect a stooge of the U.S. foreshadowed the Soviet offensive at the 1960 session. But during the six months following the Khrushchev visit to the U.S. and U.N., Moscow was primarily concerned with—and apparently committed to—the general strategy of implementing its "coexistence" policy and, for its own benefit, propitiating the United States. In the view of the Soviet leadership, world prospects were good; the socialist camp, Asia, and Africa were on the move; and a "phase of negotiations" among the Great Powers had begun.[33] As one Communist spokesman summed up the general atmosphere: "Why should the Soviet Union plunge headlong into a devastating war when the socialist system . . . is winning the peoples without war?" While the "ruling circles" of the West were clearly split between war-thirsty monopolists and "reasonable" men, the trend was in favor of those "opposed to 'brinkmanship.'"[34] The summit conference due to take place in Paris in May, 1960, was to strengthen the links.

By April, it is true, distinct elements of caution had crept into the Soviet analysis of American policy, perhaps suggesting uncertainty or differences of interpretation. No agreement on Berlin or disarmament was in sight. In at least some Soviet quarters, a variety of basically unrelated moves in the United States °

---

positions (such as Deputy Chairman of the State Committee for Radio and Television) until appointed Soviet Ambassador to Brazil in December, 1961.

° These included "anti-Soviet" speeches by Vice-President Richard M. Nixon, Secretary of State Christian Herter, and Under-Secretary Douglas Dillon (Khrushchev refers to these three in his letter to Prime Minister Macmillan of August 3, 1960); an intensification of attacks on the U.S.S.R. in Voice of America broadcasts (or so Moscow claimed); the release of a State Department "White Paper," which Moscow interpreted as minimizing the value of summit conferences; and on April 9, the unpublicized overflight of Soviet territory by a U-2 reconnaissance plane (which Khrushchev may have alluded to in his April 25 speech). It is likely that the virtually unpublicized visit to the United States, in mid-April, of Georgi Zhukov, a top foreign-policy and Party official, was intended to explore the reality of the suspected shifts in American policy.

appears to have prompted the view that the "Cold War" contingent in Washington had "again" gained the upper hand. In his Baku speech on April 25, Khrushchev, too, referred to these trends; he was forewarned, skeptical, and perhaps defensive—for Western failure to play his game amounted to a setback for his general plan. Yet there are no indications that, prior to May 1, he was preparing to wreck the conference.

Then came Francis Gary Powers' flight. The deep penetration of Soviet air space, the successful downing of the U-2 plane and apprehension of the pilot, the propaganda potential inherent in the American violation of Soviet sovereignty, the challenge that the flight constituted to Soviet security and to the coexistence policy, as Khrushchev saw it—all these revealed a sensitivity and violence of reaction Washington had not foreseen but probably compounded by its handling of the "story." It was clear that the American President, whom Khrushchev had hailed as an earnest partner in the search for world peace, had treacherously engaged in warlike provocation and thereby exposed Khrushchev's own policy: In reply, the Soviet Premier torpedoed the entire summit meeting and canceled the impending Eisenhower visit to the U.S.S.R.

Before long, Moscow caught its breath. The policy of peaceful coexistence was not jettisoned, only reinterpreted: It had not failed, but had merely met a momentary setback. In spite of everything, Khrushchev declared himself an "optimist." What was the basis of his "inexhaustible historical optimism"? The Communist Party editorially explained: "The postwar years are filled with the struggle of these two trends [coexistence and Cold War, i.e., East and West]. And while the prevalence of the former trend is evident, from time to time the enemies of peace succeed in passing to the counteroffensive. This is what happened this spring. . . ." [35] United States policy "has not killed—nor could it kill—the idea of normalizing international relations." [36] In short, Moscow was telling its critics, it was all a natural and trifling zigzag, soon to be reversed.

Khrushchev's "inexhaustible optimism" was to be taxed further. In June and July, 1960, the Soviet Union suffered defeat on three more issues at the U.N. First came its demand that the Security Council condemn the United States as an aggressor and the U-2 flight as a threat to peace. Gromyko's warning that failure to act would make the Security Council "a willing or unwilling acolyte in the aggression" was to no avail. In July, after shooting down an American RB-47 plane in the Barents Sea, the Soviet Union again called for Security Council action against American "aggressive actions." Given the mood of the Council (and, one may take it, the fact that, in this instance, the Soviet case was far more dubious than its case with respect to the U-2), Khrushchev granted in advance that he did not expect the Security Council to take any satisfactory steps but insisted that the question must be raised—if only to "discredit the dishonest judges once more." [37] Yet the Security Council refused to sit in judgment, and the Soviet case was further impaired by the Soviet refusal to accept an American offer of an impartial investigation.

In a third case, the Soviet delegate gave strenuous support to the Cuban complaint against United States "economic aggression" and interference in the internal affairs of Cuba. But in an unusual side-stepping of the United Nations, this case was referred to the Organization of American States, a decision that, by implication, denied the legitimacy of Soviet interest in the area covered by the Monroe Doctrine.[38]

Just then the Congo crisis confronted the Soviet Union with one more challenge, both in the Security Council and outside. Its course was bound to reinforce Moscow's view of the United Nations as a weapon wielded against it. The days when Soviet control had appeared to be around the corner seemed strangely remote.

Chapter X

The Congo: The Last Straw

INTERNATIONAL POLICE FORCE: AN OVERTURE

THE founders of the United Nations had soberly assumed that the maintenance of peace and security required an instrument for enforcement. In accordance with the modest commitment agreed upon by the member states, under Article 43 of the Charter, "armed forces, assistance, and facilities" were to be made available to an international police force under Security Council jurisdiction. Such a force never came into being. By 1947, the Military Staff Committee reported that its members were unable to agree upon a formula governing the size, strength, location, and command of the international force.

As earlier indicated,[1] the position adopted by the Soviet Union was consistent with its general tendency to limit United Nations authority and safeguard its own freedom of action. It was always suspicious of "supernational" armies; privately, a Soviet delegate pointed to the Hungarian crisis of 1956 as an instance in which the U.N. might have been tempted to establish an armed "presence" had such a force been in readiness. Indeed, the U.S.S.R. argued, so long as its bloc was in the minority, such a force was more likely to be used against, rather than in support of, the U.S.S.R. Placing military forces under the control of the Secretary-General, beyond the veto of the Great Powers, was unthinkable to the Soviet Union, as indeed it was to some other powers, too.

As usual, the Soviet Union could find support for its restrictive interpretation in the letter of the Charter; and the American tendency to push beyond it was bound to intensify Soviet suspicions.* 2

At any rate, the cleavage of the postwar world frustrated all efforts to create an international army under the Security Council. Of course, the Korean experience provided a somewhat anomalous precedent for joint action; and the Emergency Force dispatched to Egypt, however limited its purpose, gave encouragement to those who were looking for some device by which —without altering the Charter—an instrument for international enforcement could be forged.

The question gained new poignancy in connection with Khrushchev's disarmament proposals of September, 1959. What, American and British spokesmen were quick to ask, would fill the power vacuum if the world were really to disarm? British Foreign Secretary Selwyn Lloyd had included the creation of just such an international force in the disarmament proposal he submitted to the U.N. the day before Premier Khrushchev's address. Secretary of State Christian A. Herter several times referred to the need for such a contingent during the following months; and Ambassador Henry Cabot Lodge more formally inquired of the Soviet Delegation what type of international

---

* Bound as it was by the rule of "Great Power unanimity," the Security Council and, therefore, its military arm could never act against a Great Power. Hence, Moscow argued, the military contingents needed by the international police force could be relatively small. The United States, on the other hand, favored more powerful forces, with mobile air and naval units to be supplied largely by the West.

police force a disarmed world would need, what principles of international law would govern it, and what security forces could be left to each nation.[3]

Surprisingly enough, the Soviet Union found itself on the defensive over an issue it had expected to exploit. The vigorous and cogent discussions in non-Communist circles of the problem of a police force invited systematic Soviet rebuff. Moscow had labeled a proposal for an international force made by Eisenhower in 1958 an attempt to create "punitive units operating against national-liberation movements," a "gendarme" force of a "colonialist" character. Likewise, the proposals drafted by the U.N. Secretariat drew sharp Soviet comment. After all, Moscow had ridiculed an earlier Secretary-General as the self-styled commander of United Nations troops "on a white horse"; it had vetoed the creation of a U.N. force for Lebanon, and it never acknowledged the legitimacy of the UNEF in Gaza. Under the Hammarskjold plan, it claimed, the international army would be placed "in effect into the hands of the United States and its partners in NATO and would be used for causes having nothing in common with the objectives of the United Nations."[4]

During his American tour, to be sure, Khrushchev had told Adlai Stevenson that Moscow would be prepared to "discuss" an international police force to keep the peace after disarmament. But was this more than a gesture calculated to propitiate an influential American? On October 2, 1959, *Pravda*, over the signature of Georgi Zhukov, an authoritative spokesman for the Kremlin, ruled out the establishment of such a force: The West would use it to impose capitalism and to suppress those who were "determined to change the social system in their countries."[5]

Soviet dissent was sharpest precisely in the half year after Khrushchev's visit to the United States. Moscow assailed Western statesmen who implied that effective coexistence presupposed permanence of the "capitalist" order, including armed resistance to Communism.

It is with this purpose [wrote *International Affairs* in March, 1960] that the absolutely artificial question of a special "international police force" to maintain "order" (read, to suppress the democratic struggle of the masses) has been raised. The question of organizing this force has been raised in the United Nations and is being artificially hitched to the disarmament problem. . . .[6]

In April, a detailed article rebuffed the proposal as similar to Western efforts to subvert the veto. What the West sought, it asserted, was an

international military instrument which, officially an organ of the United Nations, would in practice be at the beck and call of a certain group of powers . . . to use the U.N. flag to secure privileges, to promote their selfish interests . . . to fight the national-liberation movement in the colonies and dependencies . . . to crush any action by the democratic forces within the capitalist countries . . . [and] to exert military and political pressure on the disarmed Socialist countries.[7]

The May issue of the same journal (put together before the U-2 incident) carried a letter by Professor Eugene Korovin vigorously attacking the U.N. police-force scheme.[8]

And yet, somewhat unexpectedly, it became clear that Moscow had reconsidered. In commenting on the disarmament terms the Soviet Union had submitted for discussion on June 2, 1960 (originally, it seems, intended to be released at the ill-fated "summit" in May), Khrushchev explained:

After our proposals were submitted in September last year, the question was raised of how to ensure the maintenance of international law and order under conditions of general and complete disarmament. . . . We carefully studied these considerations and drew the conclusion that the only realistic possibility in present conditions would be, in accordance with the United Nations Charter, to place, when necessary, police (militia) detachments at the disposal of the Security Council to ensure keeping the peace.

He went out of his way to stress that these units would be intended exclusively to maintain international peace, not to intervene in domestic affairs or to "suppress" any forces struggling for colonial emancipation or social progress. In response to a question, he made it clear that the use of such contingents was to be subject to Great Power veto in the Security Council.[9]

The change was significant if one contemplates that it required overcoming a deeply ingrained hostility and ceasing the intense campaign just waged in opposition to such a plan. Once reached, the decision became part of the Soviet disarmament scheme. In his address to the General Assembly on September 23, 1960, Khrushchev confirmed the need to set up "armed forces under international control." But by then, he could point to the involvement in the Congo, where "the U.N. forces are being used precisely in the direction against which we have warned and that we resolutely oppose." What was needed were "safeguards" against a repetition of such an experience; and these the Soviet reorganization proposals were to provide. As a leading Soviet military analyst spelled out soon thereafter, the command structure of the contemplated international police force—after disarmament—"should naturally be on an international basis reflecting the world correlation of forces: the socialist countries, the countries of the West bloc, and the neutral countries." [10]

A few months later, Korovin restated in franker terms his opposition to a police force without disarmament, tying it directly to the Congo experience.

> The formation of an international army before general and complete disarmament would lead in practice either to the rise of unprecedented "supermilitarism," if the international armed force were stronger than the armies of the Soviet Union and the United States, or to the perpetuation of extreme inequality in international relations, if the international force were employed only against small and weak countries. The experience offered by the use of the United Nations force in the Congo makes us approach this issue with extreme caution.[11]

The benefits of hindsight had of course not been available to Soviet policy-makers in mid-1960, when the Congo crisis erupted.

MOSCOW AND THE CONGO

Khrushchev had made the Soviet bloc the self-appointed champion of the emerging nations. Blaming all their ills on the colonial and "neocolonial" powers, Moscow strove to work with the nationalist leadership of these countries, realizing the weakness of Communism in most of them. Africa in particular raised a host of problems, ranging from the near-absence of Communist parties to the inapplicability of many concepts of Soviet "class analysis." Moreover, Moscow had not foreseen the rapid and wholesale achievement of independence in 1960, which brought the Black Continent into the United Nations in considerable numerical force.

But Soviet promises were on record. Mikoyan had told a Baghdad audience on April 15, 1960, that "all the peoples of Asia, Africa, and Latin America can be fully confident that the Soviet Union will protect their interests everywhere and at all times," and Khrushchev emphasized that "the Soviet Union will be their most loyal and unselfish friend and ally." [12] In mid-July, Moscow pledged 2.5 million rubles for economic aid to Africa through the U.N. and embarked on one of its most intensive propaganda campaigns under the banner of anticolonialism.

Moscow had nothing to lose and everything to gain from these efforts, which embarrassed and tended to divide the West. Khrushchev's assertion that "the Soviet Government is prepared to do everything for the collapse of colonial slavery" no doubt endeared it to some of the new nations during "Africa year." Yet for many of them, the Soviet image changed perceptibly as the Congo crisis unfolded.

Within a fortnight after the proclamation of independence on June 30, 1960, the Republic of the Congo was in the throes of chaos and terror. Fighting among warring tribes, and between

Africans and Europeans, and the nearly total absence of governmental authority set the stage for the reintervention of Belgium, which in turn led the young republic's President, Joseph Kasavubu, and Premier Patrice Lumumba to appeal for help to the United Nations. Within a day, the Secretary-General had convened the Security Council, which on his recommendation unanimously called on Belgium to withdraw its troops from the Congo and authorized the Secretary-General to provide military assistance. As Dag Hammarskjold formulated its ground rules (later endorsed by the Security Council) the U.N. force (known by its French initials, ONUC) was to be recruited primarily from other African states and was to exclude nationals of the Great Powers; it was not to intervene in the internal strife of the Congo Republic.

Here was an international armed force precisely of the sort that the U.S.S.R. had heretofore opposed. The Soviet vote in favor of its establishment was above all an extension of its policy to befriend the African states, for the Congo crisis looked like an ideal case in which the Communist states could "protect" the new nations against the West. It could not very well fail to support this first showdown on colonialism in Black Africa. Indeed, the initial Soviet statement on the Congolese request for aid accused the United States, Britain, and France of violating international law and the U.N. Charter by "unleashing armed aggression" and warned NATO against being the "international gendarme in the colonial subjugation of the peoples of Africa." [13]

In this, the first and "hopeful" stage of the Congo operation, Moscow claimed that "the firm stand of the U.S.S.R. in defense of the Congolese people's lawful rights undoubtedly had an exceptionally important role in the adoption of the [Security Council] decision." [14] Later, Moscow looked back wistfully on the initial prospects: The U.N. "could have emerged from the Congo tangle with flying colors. . . . At first it seemed that that would be the outcome." [15]

The Soviet Union even suppressed its customary concern

with national sovereignty once it became apparent that the United Nations Force could not restrict itself to token operations. When in early August, 1960, the ONUC command had to choose between failure (because of its commitment not to "interfere" in internal Congolese strife and because of its inability to do its job without the use of force) and shooting its way into Katanga, whose independence had been declared by the pro-Belgian Moise Tshombe, Soviet representative Vasili Kuznetsov urged the U.N. to enter the area by force, arrest the Tshombe regime, and use arms to suppress all resistance. The awkwardness of the Soviet position was apparent when Kuznetsov, isolated among his colleagues, wound up voting for the milder resolution (introduced by Tunisia and Ceylon), which called for an immediate Belgian withdrawal from Katanga and instructed the Secretary-General to help carry out the move. The Soviet Union, Kuznetsov explained, was still pursuing the primary goal of getting the "imperialists" out; nor was it prepared, he might have added, to publicize a split with the unaligned states, which were advocating a more moderate policy.

By early September, the U.N. operation looked like a near-total success. The Belgians had completed the withdrawal of their combat troops (though assuredly not of various military and civilian "advisers"), and the U.N. contingents had taken up positions in Katanga. But all this Moscow chose to ignore. Instead, it charged that Secretary-General Hammarskjold had not even tried to get the Belgians out.

The special position adopted by the U.S.S.R. had its roots in the first days of the Congo crisis. Unable to regard ONUC as a "neutral" force, Moscow was bound to look for evidence of an "imperialist" (and above all an American) plot. As early as July 13, it charged that United Nations Under-Secretary Ralph J. Bunche—an American citizen—was being used in Léopoldville to promote plans for the intervention of the Western powers. When, on request from the U.N., the United States Army provided communications personnel and aviation technicians to help ONUC in Léopoldville, Arkadi Sobolev on July 19 demanded the "immediate withdrawal" of American troops, whatever the "pretext" for their aggressive presence in the Congo.

Hand in hand with its efforts to keep the United States out, Moscow began to develop a conspiracy theory whose full fruition was not to come for another six months. In essence, Belgian "aggression" was blamed on its stronger partners in NATO. How indeed would little Belgium dare act on its own? Too weak to satiate their colonialist appetites singly, the imperialists in the era of their decline had embarked on "collective colonialism"; "the bayonet was Belgian, but the bosses were the United States, Belgian, British, and West German big monopolies." [16]

The logical corollary of these allegations was the Soviet offer to support the Congo Republic outside the framework of the United Nations. In an increasingly vituperative campaign, Khrushchev promised the Congo "the necessary help that may be required for the victory of your just cause"—if need be, by unilateral action defying the West. The political support pledged by Moscow was supplemented by Soviet promises of economic and technical aid and, beginning in late July, the dispatch of transport planes, trucks, and other equipment from the U.S.S.R., without any reference to the United Nations. In the following weeks, a variety of (partly unverified) reports spoke of other, unpublicized forms of Soviet and Czechoslovak aid to the Stanleyville regime, including food and medical supplies and, apparently, also small arms.

This was the occasion of the first serious clash between the Secretary-General and the Soviet Union over the Congo. According to the Secretariat's rules (approved by the Security Council, including the Soviet Union) the Great Powers were not to intervene with troops or matériel, directly or indirectly. When reminded of these terms, Moscow remained silent. On September

5, Hammarskjold reiterated his demand that Soviet shipments to the Congo cease. By then, Lumumba (backed by the U.S.S.R.) and Kasavubu (backed by the United States) had "dismissed each other" from office. Moscow saw the Congo situation finally polarized into friends and foes, and Hammarskjold had lined up with the foes.

As a matter of principle, Moscow asserted, the Soviet Union was free to enter into such agreements as it desired. The United Nations resolution, it argued,

> does not restrict and, of course, cannot restrict the right of the government of the sovereign Republic of the Congo to request assistance from the governments of other countries besides the United Nations and to receive such assistance.

The Secretary-General's note was therefore labeled

> an attempt at taking control over the relations between the Congo Republic and other states, especially the Soviet Union . . . [whereas] not a single United Nations administrative official has the right to intervene in the relations between sovereign states if these states do not request it.[17]

But there was more involved than principle. Hammarskjold had been the one to challenge Moscow's right to act unilaterally after voting not to do so. Even earlier, Hammarskjold had been publicly identified by Moscow as "scandalously" partisan and as "playing a very unseemly part in this NATO plot against Africa." [18] Now the Soviet Union charged the senior representatives in the Congo (above all, Ralph Bunche, who was replaced by Rajeshwar Dayal of India in September) with "outrageous colonialist behavior" and protested the Secretariat's "functioning most unashamedly on the side of the colonialists."

Moscow was witnessing the failure of its hopes that the Congo operation would open new opportunities for Soviet influence, via ONUC. The U.N. administration was unwilling to leave an ambiguous and hazardous vacuum in the Congo. Whether or not it could in fact fill it remained to be seen, but it would not tolerate Soviet efforts to short-circuit the attempt. This was the essence of the Secretary-General's response to Soviet charges that he had violated the Security Council's instructions. Moscow was once again stymied by the Secretary-General, who was beyond the reach of its veto. But so also was the General Assembly: Gathered in special session when a Soviet veto forestalled Security Council action, the Assembly, on September 20, passed an Afro-Asian resolution (by a vote of 70:0, with the Communist bloc abstaining) explicitly calling upon all states to refrain from direct or indirect military assistance in the Congo "except upon the request of the United Nations through the Secretary-General."

What could Moscow do? Behind the scenes, Soviet advisers were active with Lumumba's staff, and help appears to have come to his forces from other Communist states. Moscow supported him against his domestic rivals—Kasavubu and Colonel Mobutu in Léopoldville, Tshombe in Elisabethville—and against the United Nations force. But Khrushchev had clearly decided to avoid a total break with the U.N. Confronted with the choice between risking conflict—with the West as well as with many Afro-Asian states—by giving Lumumba outright support, including arms, and having its policy exposed as a bluff, Moscow in obvious frustration opted for the safer though more distasteful course. (Moreover, while it might have produced a mobile force to serve abroad, Moscow and its allies had no overseas bases—and ONUC had taken control of airports in the Congo Republic.) The broad needs of "peaceful coexistence" had to come before victory in the Congo.

This was a bitter pill. How had the runaway Congo operation resulted in such a failure for the U.S.S.R.? How could Moscow make sure that such a sequence of events would never recur? What moves could it take to restore its position? The Congo experience prompted top-level Soviet rethinking in the first half of September, 1960. By the time Khrushchev addressed the General Assembly on September 23, the new strategy had been set.

Blood and Boycott

From that time onward, the Congo operation ceased to be a precipitating factor in Soviet decisions relating to over-all policy toward the United Nations; the crucial decisions had already been made. What remained for Soviet diplomacy, as Khrushchev's speech at the U.N. made clear, was (1) to associate itself with the Lumumba regime as the only "lawful" government "enjoying the confidence of the Congolese people"; (2) to avoid any commitments that might involve the Soviet Union in a conflict in the Congo; (3) to assail—as part of a broad Soviet attack on the U.N. administration—the Secretary-General as the man directly responsible for the "disgraceful" events in the Congo; and (4) to repair some of the damage to Soviet ties with the Afro-Asian states caused by previous policy.

Moscow knew that these bonds needed mending. In the Security Council, the U.S.S.R. had used its veto to kill a resolution introduced by the unaligned members; in the General Assembly, the Soviet bloc had abstained from the Afro-Asian resolution upholding the United Nations Secretariat. The differences between the Soviet Union and India, the most influential of the unaligned powers, over the general attitude toward the United Nations and the role of the Secretary-General had become painfully apparent. Moscow now stepped up those appeals that tended to identify the "socialist" bloc with the "uncommitted" nations. At the same time, Khrushchev in his United Nations speech of September 23 developed a thesis first voiced in the Soviet proposals of July 13 and elaborated at a later date: Only African (and perhaps Asian) troops were to remain in the Congo, for service "only at the discretion of [the Lumumba] government." What, if any, functions the U.N. was to have in this operation remained unspecified.[19] *

Largely for reasons unrelated to Soviet conduct, the balance did indeed begin to swing back before the year was out. With the Congo Republic balkanized, the seating of the Kasavubu delegation in the United Nations antagonized the more ardent proponents of African nationalism. Several neutralist states withdrew their contingents from ONUC and recognized the Lumumba regime in Stanleyville. The United Nations effort—attacked by Lumumba, Tshombe, Kasavubu, and the Belgians—was seemingly stymied. In the Security Council, the Soviet Union again used its veto to prevent an endorsement of Hammarskjold's actions; in the General Assembly, on December 20, neither a Western-sponsored nor a neutralist (Soviet-backed) resolution was able to secure the necessary two-thirds support: *no* bloc was in clear control, and the Secretary-General could no longer count on a solid majority of Western plus unaligned states to support his Congo policy.[20]

It was both convenient (to explain past setbacks) and politically astute (to "expose" the amalgam of its enemies) for the

---

* The appeal to let the African nations themselves supervise the Congo operation "without U.N. or other outside interference" (a proposal pressed especially after Lumumba's death) was diametrically opposed to the Soviet efforts to involve the United Nations in Latin American affairs, denying that these were the exclusive preserve of the region's member states. The principal reason for the difference, one may take it, is the presence of the United States as an American but not African power. In connection with the Cuban problem, Khrushchev declared on July 12, 1960, that the Monroe Doctrine "has died a natural death." Soon after, the Soviet Union asked the U.N. to endorse the call of the Organization of American States for sanctions against the Dominican Republic (August 20). However, the United States and other American countries prevented such an endorsement, fearing that it would give the Soviet Union a precedent to claim a veto over decisions of quasi-regional organizations like the OAS or even NATO. (See, e.g., *The New York Times*, September 9, 1960.) On the general problem, see Klaus Törnudd, *Soviet Attitudes Towards Non-Military Regional Cooperation* (Helsinki, 1961).

Soviet propaganda machine to revert to the conspiracy theory of imperialist "aggression" in the Congo.* When Lumumba was jailed, Moscow charged that his captors were linked to the assassins of Ceylonese Premier Bandaranaike and of pro-Communist African politician Felix Moumié, as well as those who had made attempts on the lives of Sukarno and Sékou Touré. It claimed to have evidence of French and American complicity in the build-up of Tshombe's mercenary army. Hammarskjold's reports and messages, containing "scurrilous fabrications of the imperialist propaganda machine," were part of "psychological preparation for aggression." [21]

The news of Lumumba's murder, on February 13, 1961, provided Moscow with the occasion to bring this campaign to a climax. The Soviet Government officially declared that "the crime was prepared methodically, step by step, and it was sanctioned in fact in no other place but the capitals of the states that bear the responsibility for the criminal aggression unleashed against the Republic of the Congo." It was clear, Khrushchev wrote Prime Minister Nehru on February 22, that the murder "was, to all practical purposes, predetermined when the colonialists saw that [Lumumba] was an obstacle to the realization of their plans." [22]

At the United Nations, the Lumumba murder led Moscow to break with Dag Hammarskjold. A Soviet Government declaration on February 14 opened the campaign to label the Secretary-

---

* There were various attempts to link the "colonial conspirators" with financial, "militarist," and "racist" groupings in the West. On his return to Moscow, Khrushchev declared on October 20, "It is no accident that U.S. Secretary of State Herter handed Mr. Hammarskjold a $5 million check to be used at his discretion in the Congo for the purpose of consummating this sordid business." On December 5, 1960, the Soviet Union asked for an investigation into the sources of Colonel Mobutu's financial backing. The mutual-assistance pact concluded between the central Congo and Katanga regimes (and Kalonji's "Mining State") was in Soviet eyes a "pact to divide up the money Tshombe gets from the Union Minière." Both his and Mobutu's forces were being "openly financed by West European and American monopolies." (Y. Bochkaryov, "The U.N. Congo Operation," *New Times*, No. 11 [1961], p. 7.)

General a "murderer" and a "Judas." The U.S.S.R. officially declared that Hammarskjold's policy "from beginning to end was a policy of foul betrayal of the interests of the Congolese people, of the principles of the United Nations, of elementary standards of decency and honor." As "a miserable lackey of the colonialists," he could expect nothing but "the scorn of all honest people." Hence his continued tenure in office was intolerable to the Soviet Union, which would no longer recognize him as an official of the United Nations.[23]

Despite the general indignation at the murder, Moscow was overplaying its hand. When it finally came to a vote in the Security Council, a week later, the Soviet resolution, based on the declaration of February 14, was defeated (8:1, with two abstentions). Instead, a neutralist resolution reaffirmed the earlier United Nations decisions under which the Secretary-General had acted and demanded an immediate withdrawal of all Belgian personnel from the Congo. Apparently afraid of being isolated, the Soviet delegate abstained rather than vote against this move.

How much of his own charges Khrushchev believed would be interesting to know, but is not decisive for an assessment of Soviet strategy. In Moscow's estimation, the murder of Patrice Lumumba provided a perfect occasion to dramatize the gap it claimed to see—and strove to widen—between the Soviet-neutralist coalition and the "imperialist" West. Yet in his immediate purposes, Khrushchev failed: The bulk of African states stayed "unaligned," the Secretary-General remained in office, and the Congo operation went on.[24]

A CLASH OF CONCEPTS

Within little more than six months, Soviet policy had completely reversed its course. From its position of vigorous proponent of United Nations action, Moscow had shifted to press for prompt cessation. Instead of seeking to guide ONUC, Moscow was now opposing it as inimical to its own and its friends' interests. Hopes of alighting in the Congo on the back of the United Nations had been frustrated. Once again, Khrushchev had miscalculated.

The difficulty was compounded by Soviet unwillingness to break out of the circle it had drawn around itself. Even when it attacked the United Nations action, it reluctantly complied with U.N. decisions and refrained from massive unilateral support for its friends. It refrained from vetoing several resolutions sponsored by neutralist states it was seeking to befriend. Yet it was precisely the small and unaligned powers on whose support the Secretary-General hinged *his* policy, and successfully so. Logic would have invited the Soviet Union once again to "go it alone." But in the age of "coexistence," Moscow deemed it essential to fight for the sympathy and support of the underdeveloped world. The circle could be neither squared nor broken.*

The Congo operation—Moscow acknowledged this much—was decisive in triggering the Khrushchev attack on the Secretary-General and the structure of the U.N. Behind it lay the fact that Moscow once again saw the United Nations as an obstacle to progress. The culprits, Khrushchev wrote Prime Minister Nehru after Lumumba's death, were "those who would like to hold back the march of history"—the theme of inevitability abundantly familiar to readers of the Premier's remarks.

Perhaps an international force operating in the setting of civil war cannot remain neutral and must choose between competing personalities and programs.[25] But even if the United Nations had remained fully "neutral" in Congo politics, its commitment to preserve the *status quo* would have been intolerable for

---

* Soviet discomfort may have been compounded by comparisons with the Spanish Civil War of 1936–39. The sequence, on the Soviet side, had not been so dissimilar then: involvement, surprise, conflict with the League of Nations' policy; failure to defy the League completely, but also failure to follow through with troops of its own; and unwillingness to risk involving itself in war. Both conflicts took place in remote areas during periods of general "coexistence."

Moscow in the long run. In all comparable crises, the U.N. would henceforth see its task, at least at the outset, as upholding the existing governments—and then, if need be, working through them for gradual change. The United Nations was therefore bound to be suspect in Soviet eyes as a "holy alliance" committed to opposing the process of change with which the U.S.S.R. is identified.

Although Hammarskjold's own philosophy clarified the problem, it also exacerbated it, for in his view it was proper for the United Nations to act "in cases where the original conflict may be said either to be the result of, or to imply risks for, the creation of a power vacuum between the main blocs [of states]. Preventive action in such cases must in the first place aim at filling the vacuum." This doctrine of interposition sprang from his view of the U.N. "as a universal organization neutral in the Big Power struggle over ideology and influence in the world." United Nations action must take place explicitly "on the basis of its noncommitment to any power bloc, so as to provide to the extent possible a guarantee in relation to all parties against initiatives from others." [26]

In Soviet terms, the U.N. would thus amount to a barrier athwart the course of history. While inevitably appealing to neutralist advocates of political prophylaxis, the concept was intolerable for the Communist world: Instead of providing a welcome vehicle on the road to the "underdeveloped" countries, the U.N. would loom as a barricade. So much the more reason then for Moscow to insist on a free hand to act outside the organization, as the dictates of political prudence, the pursuit of advantage, and the principles of sovereignty (as expounded by the Kremlin) would seem to demand.

Chapter XI

The Soviet Challenge

On July 19, 1960, Prime Minister Macmillan wrote Premier Khrushchev: "I simply do not understand what your purpose is today." Soviet policy in 1960 was indeed marked by contradictions that baffled observers in Moscow and abroad. On the one hand, the strategy of coexistence had become more belligerent; the Paris summit had been disrupted before it had even begun; in June, the Soviet and East European delegations abandoned the disarmament negotiations in Geneva; in the summer, the Congo crisis embroiled the Soviet Union in new arguments with the West; soon a new military build-up was begun in the U.S.S.R. On the other hand, in spite of all the "tough" talk in each successive crisis—the U-2 incident, the shooting down of an RB-47, the Congo war, and the promise of rocket support for Fidel Castro—Soviet conduct still sought to avoid major showdowns. The Soviet call to all heads of state to attend the 15th session of the General Assembly likewise seemed to foreshadow Soviet support of the U.N. Indeed, the Moscow press labeled it the "most significant Assembly meeting in the whole history of the United Nations." For the Soviet Union this was true: For the first time perhaps, the U.N. was a focus of Soviet policy in its own right, not the by-product of other political decisions.

The two issues most publicized by Moscow in connection with the Assembly session were disarmament and anticolonialism. But they involved little that was new or significant. The surprises came with regard to organization, administration, and personnel.[1]

THE TROIKA

The essential feature of the new Soviet proposals was revealed at the end of the lengthy Khrushchev address of September 23, 1960, before the General Assembly. Referring to the Congo experience, where, Khrushchev charged, the Secretary-General had been able to ignore the will of the Security Council, the Soviet Premier demanded "safeguards" that would "preclude a similar state of affairs in the future":

> It is necessary that the executive agency of the United Nations reflect the actual situation now obtaining in the world. . . . We deem it wise and fair that the United Nations executive agency consist not of one person, the Secretary-General, but of three persons enjoying the confidence of the United Nations.

The proposal thus amounted, in part, to establishing

> a collective U.N. executive agency consisting of three persons, each representing a definite group of states. This would provide a definite guarantee that the activity of the U.N. executive agency would not prove detrimental to [any] one of these groups of states.

The three "groups of states" were, of course, the Communist, the Western, and the unaligned blocs.

Until 1960, the U.S.S.R. had refused even to serve on the General Assembly's committee to consider amendments to the Charter: It had ardently and consistently opposed all such change.[2] Now Moscow put forth its proposals "in view of the obsolescence of the United Nations' structure." To formalize the suggested terms, Khrushchev urged adoption by the General Assembly of a single amendment to the Charter—a relatively simple procedure. Still, he knew well that such an amendment would have binding force only if ratified by two-thirds of the U.N.'s members, including all the Big Five.[3]

Since the proposals were first voiced, Soviet negotiators have raised similar demands for the reorganization of other international agencies. In 1961, the notion of a tripartite organization —or *troika,* as the Russians called the threesome—came to prevail in Soviet proposals for the international control commission on Laos, on nuclear-test-ban inspection, on disarmament, and in Soviet demands for the administration of UNESCO, ILO, IAEA, and ECOSOC. In almost mechanical fashion, the device was now applied to diverse groups and circumstances. Moscow was prepared to argue that "this principle of tripartite representation should be applied in all international organizations and agencies since it reflects the real situation in the world." [4]

However novel and striking at first sight, the *troika* may be considered the logical extension of several principles and arguments that Moscow had adduced for a long time.

(1) *The Soviet demand for "parity."* Since 1957, the demand for parity had been raised by Soviet negotiators, without any significant theoretical foundation, as a reflection of a growing Soviet sense of strength. In 1959, the U.S.S.R. refused to participate in the work of such U.N. bodies as the Disarmament Commission and the Committee on the Peaceful Uses of Outer Space unless the total number of Communist (in some cases, Soviet and neutralist) members represented at least equaled that of the Western nations.[5] The Soviet Union was in effect demanding that the U.S. acknowledge its status as a coequal on the world scene. While it felt that it could not yet ask for more, Moscow in the sputnik age was determined not to settle for less—while in the meanwhile safeguarding its freedom of action and immunity from foreign inspection or interference.[6]

To be effective, operational recommendations must have the

unanimous support of all participants, regardless of the formula of representation. This is especially true of security matters. To a large extent, the "parity" problem was then a matter of prestige. It also revived the unresolved contradiction between Moscow's insistence that power "realities," rather than "arithmetic," must rule and Soviet propaganda in favor of equality of member states in the U.N. Likewise, the concentration, in 1959–60, on Soviet-American parity was difficult to reconcile with the simultaneous Soviet effort to align the uncommitted nations against the United States.

In 1959, Khrushchev—hopeful of an improvement in Soviet-American relations and probably ignoring latent implications for Soviet relations with the neutralist states—plugged for parity *à deux.* In 1960, with the abortive Paris summit behind him, he extended the concept to parity *à trois:* Now the under-developed countries were to be brought in as a third coequal member.*

Since the Soviet leadership professes to take for granted an inherent gravitation of the neutralists toward the Communist camp, the eventual prospect under the *troika* is the alignment of two "progressive" elements against one "reactionary" one, each with a veto.[7]

(2) *Soviet stress on "realism."* Form must correspond to content, and institutions must correspond to political facts if they are to be viable; and international realities had changed—in Moscow's favor—since 1945. The Soviet bloc had grown, and the "third" grouping had emerged, each "speaking for" approximately one billion people. Such was the Soviet argument, politically opportune, even if novel in terms of the traditional Soviet

---

* As a matter of fact, Korovin linked both types as precedents for the Khrushchev reorganization proposals: "I have in view the composition of the committee on the peaceful uses of outer space, of the disarmament and some other commissions, set up either on a parity basis (capitalist and socialist states) or on the principle of tripartite representation (countries of Western blocs, socialist states, and neutralist states)." (*International Affairs,* No. 12 [1960], p. 8.)

hostility to the legal argument of *rebus sic stantibus*.* Taking account of the increased "economic and military potential of the socialist camp" would give the Soviet Union more weight in the international organization than the nine votes its bloc commanded in an assembly of ninety-nine or more states.[8] Khrushchev proudly contrasted the "stagnation" of the American economy with the rapid growth of Soviet steel production— 65 million tons in 1960, 75 million tons in 1961: "That is what is more important than voting in the United Nations." [9]

In another context, Khrushchev was to revert to the primary yardstick of international relations, the "correlation of forces," contrasting it with the "parliamentary stereotypes":

> It is not the number of states on the respective sides—the side of socialism or that of capitalism—that in the final count determines the correlation of forces. . . . One must be ever mindful of Lenin's advice that politics is not arithmetic.[10]

This, too, was by no means novel. It was precisely in these terms that Vyshinsky had earlier justified Soviet use of the veto. But in 1960, the gap between "real" Soviet influence in the world and the strength it commanded in the U.N.—despite its veto— seemed to represent a more legitimate grievance than ever before.†

* In the summer of 1961, a Soviet specialist on the U.N. extended this approach into an entire "theory" that organizations must constantly change to bring form in line with changing "reality." (G. Morozov, "Usovershen-stvovanie sistemy struktury OON—nazrevshaia zadacha," *Mirovaia eko-nomika i mezhdunarodnye otnosheniia*, No. 8 [1961], pp. 31–44.) For a recent Soviet affirmation of the traditional view, see V. M. Shurshalov, "Juridical Content of the Principle *pacta sunt servanda* and Its Realization," *Sovetskii ezhegodnik mezhdunarodnogo prava* (Moscow, 1959), pp. 166–68.

† A related point is the Soviet prediction that before long the majority in the U.N. would be against the West and that therefore the West as a matter of self-interest should support the shift in the basis of international decision-making and administration from "arithmetic" to "realities." (See, for instance, Khrushchev's speech of September 18, 1959, and his remarks to the United Nations Correspondents Association in New York on October 7, 1960.) The same point was reiterated at the 1961 Assembly session.

(3) *The Soviet concept of sovereignty.* The rigid insistence on the principle of sovereignty runs across all the zigzags of Soviet policy like a red thread. The United Nations itself is viewed as the product of a collective treaty among sovereign states and cannot be placed on the same level as these states. "The rights of the U.N. are not primary, but derivative from the rights of the member states."

As earlier discussed, the sovereignty syndrome informs Soviet demands for self-determination, its anticolonialist campaign, its attack on the U-2 flight, and the Congo operation as well. Defining the authority of the United Nations as minimal, such an outlook lends itself to a reinterpretation by which action is possible or permissible only in those instances where all the powers concerned (or all major powers, or all three power blocs) concur—when, in other words, no violence is being done to their sovereign will.

The inflexible position that the "unanimity rule" in the Security Council is a cornerstone or prerequisite for the United Nations' existence is part of this outlook. The 1960 proposals extend the notion of a veto from the Security Council to the Secretariat (and, it has been argued, indirectly to the General Assembly as well, since its decisions would be subject to administrative control in the course of their implementation). In the *troika,* the failure of any one member to pull his load would inevitably stall the other two, thus preventing effective action. That indeed is the purpose of this "safeguard."

A CHAIN OF EVENTS

While the tripartite plan can thus be considered to fit onto the continuum of Soviet attitudes and operating principles, it nonetheless required a specific series of irritants and stimulants to lead Moscow to offer these terms as an imperative proposal. The decisive element was the succession of failures to achieve the maximum objectives Khrushchev had set for his own policy toward each of the three blocs. His disillusionment with the neutral camp came in 1959. With regard to the West, the "spirit of Camp David" had evanesced by the spring of the following year. Within the Communist family—as will be shown—the spirit of reasonable unity achieved by the end of 1957 was exorcised by bitter backstage recrimination with Peking. At the United Nations itself, themes of major Soviet concern, such as disarmament, had been sidetracked; sensitive Soviet nerves had been trodden upon in a most unkind fashion: the political initiative of the Secretary-General and imperialist "packing" of the Security Council were only two of Moscow's many objections. After all this came the Congo: We need not doubt Soviet statements that it was this experience that triggered Khrushchev's decision to take a firm stand.

There is some evidence that the reorganization plan, as presented by Khrushchev, was decided upon at a very late date. Until early September, 1960, there was no hint of the coming proposal.* On September 5, the Secretary-General dispatched a vigorous protest to Moscow over unilateral Soviet intervention in the Congo. On September 9, Khrushchev, accompanied by the leaders of the other Communist states, left for New York aboard the liner *Baltika*. On September 10, it is reported, Peking

---

* In his press conference of June 3, 1960, Khrushchev declared: "Our proposals raise the question of disarmament and nothing is said there of a revision of the United Nations Charter. We do not even think of submitting such proposals for a revision of the Charter, but on the contrary intend to uphold this Charter." In July, a Soviet article assailed the Western campaign for Charter revision, ridiculing the contention that some of the initial assumptions on which it was based no longer held true. (V. Gantman, "The United Nations," *New Times*, No. 29 [1960], p. 30.) In an article in the September issue of *International Affairs*, which went to press on August 20, Korovin declared that the Charter "has become the foundation of contemporary international law" (p. 7). Both the editorial board of that journal and Korovin himself may be considered sensitive to the latest political impulses. Finally, a survey of "What the U.N. General Assembly Will Discuss," sent to the printer on September 7, makes no reference to any reorganization proposals, while listing six other major issues that came up in New York. (*New Times*, No. 37 [1960], pp. 27–28.)

sent Moscow its reply to an earlier Soviet Central Committee letter regarding the areas of disagreement between them: Without a doubt, this message was promptly communicated to the conclave aboard the *Baltika*. Four days after his arrival in New York, Khrushchev voiced the *troika* demand from the rostrum of the General Assembly.

The scheme had not enjoyed any prior publicity. Yet even though its contents betrayed haste and improvisation, it was not an impulsive or petulant response. Its substance had probably been discussed and drafted, as one of several alternatives, in the Soviet foreign ministry months, if not years, before. Yet only a few elements in its genealogy can be traced.

Participants in the nuclear-test-ban talks in Geneva recall that Soviet delegate Tsarapkin had momentarily opposed the appointment of a single administrator for the inspection program as far back as 1958. In the fall of 1959, the Chernyshev article, cited above, had contained the gist of Khrushchev's later critique. Perhaps most important, the Soviet disarmament proposals published on June 3, 1960,[11] called for representation of all three blocs—Western, Communist, and neutral—in equal numbers on the suggested Control Commission, which would normally require a two-thirds vote for "questions of essence." The notion of a tripartite plan was clearly in the air—and on paper. The notion of a veto for each of the three blocs and its application to the Secretariat emerged as a consequence of the events of the summer of 1960.

SAINTS AND SECRETARIES

The Soviet Premier's outbursts against the Secretary-General in the fall of 1960 may have come as a surprise to the public. Actually they represented but the latest in a long series of opportunistic, but by no means erratic, shifts in the Soviet position regarding the authority of the chief executive officer of the United Nations.

When the major powers agreed in 1945 that the appointment of a Secretary-General was to be subject to the veto, the Soviet Union went furthest in stressing the prerogatives of the Great Powers over him. It sought, in vain, also to have deputy secretaries-general appointed with the concurring vote of all the permanent members, one deputy being in effect allocated to each Great Power. It likewise strove to make the top appointees in the Secretariat political officeholders rather than experts hired on the basis of their competence.[12]

Though it had originally approved his appointment, the Soviet Union came to consider the first Secretary-General, Trygve Lie, hostile to its interests. During the U.N. action in Korea, Moscow identified him as an "accessory of the American aggressors" and opposed the extension of his term of office; throughout his "extended term" it refused to deal with him, corresponding with his office, but not with him personally.[13]

One of the first tokens of the post-Stalin "thaw" at the U.N. was Soviet consent to the election of Dag Hammarskjold. On several occasions between 1955 and 1959, the U.S.S.R. even departed from its stand in favor of minimal authority for the Secretariat and supported his initiative, as for instance in the Suez and Palestine questions.°

Yet even then, Moscow had doubts about his allegiance and therefore about the prerogatives it was prepared to accord him. On several occasions, the Soviet press accused him of acting as an agent of the "imperialist" camp. When the U.S. proposal on air inspection of the Arctic zone was under discussion in the Security Council, *Pravda* rebuked Hammarskjold for "hurrying to the rescue of the American diplomats." He had evidently forgotten, *Pravda* cited an observer as saying, that he was Secretary-General of the United Nations, not of NATO.[14] Moscow's unhap-

---

° In September, 1957, the Soviet Delegate expressed Soviet "appreciation" for the Secretary-General's "devotion to our Organization" and the "scope of his activities and endeavors." (Cited in *International Conciliation*, No. 543, p. 209.)

piness over the involvement of the U.N. in the Laotian crisis in 1958 included the "most regrettable" discovery that "U.N. Secretary-General Hammarskjold gave his countenance to the State Department version" of events.[15]

The Soviet Union was putting him on notice. "It is not clear," an authoritative Soviet journal remarked, "whether he has made the necessary efforts to overcome the resistance of those who . . . have no intention of carrying out" the General Assembly's resolutions.[16] The test of his desirability to the Soviet bloc, in other words, was the extent to which Hammarskjold was able to emancipate or dissociate himself from the West. In these terms, Khrushchev's dramatic attack in 1960 seems logical, if extreme. Once the Congo crisis precipitated the showdown,* the U.S.S.R. demanded not only his resignation, but the abolition of his office. Since "the executive organs of the U.N. have been transformed into something like a chancery of the Western powers," [17] the problem was not that of the individual incumbent, for, Khrushchev maintained on October 2, "any other Secretary-General will also fail objectively to represent the three different groups of states."

Here the Soviet Premier returned to a fundamental Bolshevik conception. As far back as the Hague Conference of 1922, Maxim Litvinov had rejected international arbitration because "it would be impossible to find a single impartial judge in the whole world. It was necessary to face the fact there was not one world but two." This was the recurrent leitmotiv. "Only an angel could be unbiased" in a conflict between Communist and non-Communist regimes.[18] In 1948, *Pravda,* arguing against the U.N. plan for international control of atomic energy, reiterated that it would be impossible to find "independent" administrators immune to political considerations.[19]

---

* "The Congo events," Moscow wrote, "are a striking illustration of how peace can be jeopardized by concentrating in one official—and moreover one that can lay no claim to objectivity—all executive power and the right to interpret General Assembly and Security Council decisions." (Observer, "The Record of Fifteen Years," *New Times,* No. 43 [1960], p. 7.)

Now Khrushchev elaborated the same theme by declaring that no person could fairly represent the interests of the three blocs of states: "It is said that God alone was able to combine three persons in one. But then, no one has ever seen him, and so let him remain in the imagination of the people who invented him. But we can see the Secretary-General." [20] A week later, he told the Assembly that "there neither are nor ever have been saints on earth. . . . Mr. Hammarskjold—whose saint is he?" [21] The answer was obvious. Foreign Minister Gromyko soon suggested that if the Soviet plan were adopted, Hammarskjold might be acceptable as the Western representative among the three members of the *troika*.*

As Walter Lippmann reported in April, 1961, Khrushchev had made unmistakably clear to him that he "would never accept a single neutral administrator. Why? Because, he said, while there are neutral countries, there are no neutral men. You would not accept a Communist administrator, and I cannot accept a non-Communist administrator." [22] The whole philosophy of the United Nations was in jeopardy.

THE REST OF THE PACKAGE

Another part of the Soviet proposals was the suggestion that the United Nations should "consider choosing another site" for its headquarters. In support, Moscow cited the various restrictions to which United Nations personnel and members of missions have been subjected in the United States—in the early 1950's, the so-called security investigations of the McCarthy

---

* In Khrushchev's words: "Whose candidate is Mr. Hammarskjold, the present U.N. Secretary-General? It is clear to everyone that he is the candidate of the United States. The Swedes say he is a representative of Sweden. Yes, by birth he is a Swede, but in terms of his political views he is a representative of the monopoly capital of the United States and serves that country. I hope the Swedes do not take this amiss. We, too, have our Hammarskjold in the United States—Kerensky. He is Russian by birth, but whom does he serve? He serves American imperialist capital, and see how many years it is now that the Russian people have been managing quite well without him." (Speech of October 20, 1960.)

era; in 1960, the restrictions on the freedom of movement of Communist delegates; and at all times, the scandalous instances in which non-white personnel (especially Africans) have been subjected to discrimination around New York. That Moscow wished to embarrass the United States while making itself the champion of decency and dignity requires no elaboration.

The Soviet Union, Khrushchev volunteered, would gladly "guarantee the best conditions for [the United Nations'] work, full freedom, and security for the representatives of all states, irrespective of their political or religious convictions or the color of their skin." But, suspecting that the U.S.S.R. was not likely to be accepted as a venue, Khrushchev proposed moving the U.N. to Switzerland or Austria instead. During his meeting with President Kennedy in June, 1961, it became known that the Soviet Union had indeed explored with the Austrian authorities the whole question of transferring the United Nations to Vienna.[23] While the likelihood of such a move was slim, the issue promised to provide Soviet representatives with continuous ammunition. In the interim, Moscow might press for sessions of U.N. bodies in other lands, including the U.S.S.R.[24]*

A third issue concerns U.N. personnel. Soviet complaints once again hinge on charges of collusion between the organization and the Western powers, on the one hand, and discrimination against Soviet (and neutralist) personnel, on the other.† As discussed earlier, the demand for greater representation of non-

---

* While Vienna remained Moscow's first choice (to judge, e.g., from A. A. Roshchin's statement of October 9, 1961), the Berlin crisis became involved in the reorganization proposals when the Soviet Union urged moving U.N. headquarters to West Berlin (Khrushchev orally to Konnie Zilliacus and Paul Reynaud, and *Izvestiia* editorial, September 20, 1961). This was a more sweeping proposal than the plans considered in the West, which ranged from a minimal U.N. "presence" in Berlin to the establishment there of one or several U.N. organs or agencies, but not presumably the Council, Assembly, or Secretariat.

† In addition, Moscow has complained for many years that the Western powers ignore the "gentlemen's agreement" of January, 1946, by which one of the nonpermanent Security Council seats would normally go to an East European country. Similarly, the Soviet Union has protested failure ever to elect Communists to other offices, such as the presidency of the General Assembly.

Western personnel at the U.N. was not unfounded, even though the criterion of geographical distribution was decidedly subordinate to that of competence. The U.N. Secretariat was well aware of the problem.* In June, 1961, Andrew W. Cordier, an American citizen and a close aide of Secretary-General Hammarskjold, announced his intention to resign as Executive Assistant; he was to be replaced by Chakravarthi Narasimhan, of India.† Such gestures did not suffice to mollify the U.S.S.R. Once the Soviet Union had committed itself to the tripartite formula, its representative demanded the reorganization of the "entire staff of the United Nations Secretariat" on the basis of tripartite equality.[25] In spite of its patently nonsensical implications, he reaffirmed this demand on October 9, 1961, adding that "all the practical work in the reorganization of various links of the Secretariat must be aimed at the achievement of this task." Moscow has refused to distinguish in its demands between policy positions and clerical personnel.

THE SHADOW OF CHINA

The concatenation of pressures under which Nikita Khrushchev labored in the weeks prior to the Assembly session of 1960 and during his stay in New York would not be adequately conveyed were one to omit from consideration the Sino-Soviet relationship. Tensions within the Communist universe, especially between Moscow and Peking, happened to assume crisis proportions just at that time. They had a direct bearing on Khrushchev's conduct at the U.N.

Stalin's death spelled the end of Moscow's unquestioned

---

* The recommendations of an eight-man committee of experts to the Secretary-General, in the summer of 1961, included a new, and perhaps more equitable, formula for geographical distribution of staff members. (Document A/4776, June 14, 1961.)

† Cordier left the U.N. as of March, 1962, once U Thant had taken effective charge of the administration. The interim Secretary-General designated eight of the under-secretaries as his principal advisers, including two Soviet bloc citizens and two nationals of NATO states, along with four nationals of neutralist states (India, U.A.R., Nigeria, and Brazil).

authority over all Communist parties. The challenge to Moscow's ability to impose its will—manifest in the Polish and Hungarian crises of 1956 and in the questioning of Soviet omniscience by Communist notables, such as Palmiro Togliatti—gained poignancy as the very success of Communist expansion created an autonomous power base for some of those who disagreed—not over ideals and long-range perspectives, but over some of the strategic concepts and perceptions current in Moscow during the "era of peaceful coexistence."

After 1956, Khrushchev did, by and large, succeed in placing relations with the East European members of what was now called the socialist commonwealth on a more stable and more rational foundation, with somewhat greater latitude for the component members to pursue divergent policies and techniques within a common framework of ideology, economic system, and political controls. He was markedly less successful in adjusting relations with Communist China and, as a consequence, with the international movement as a whole.

While the record of friction and recrimination between Moscow and Peking is complex and old, the issues that precipitated a confrontation were of more recent vintage.[26] Whatever the admixture of national, economic, military, and personal elements, the dispute (to the extent that we know it) was couched largely in terms of divergent perceptions of world affairs and, consequently, differing prescriptions for action. Communist China had embarked on a program of rapid and violent change, and its leadership looked with suspicion on Khrushchev's efforts to stabilize conditions and build bridges abroad.

Until 1960, Khrushchev had perhaps been inclined to dismiss the Chinese Communists' position as a mild variant of the "infantile disease of Left-Wing Communism" that Lenin had so mercilessly torn apart. But sometime after the Soviet Premier's return from his first trip to the United States, it became apparent that Peking's insistent questions could no longer be ignored. Moscow found itself obliged to demonstrate to China's satisfaction that it had in no sense "betrayed" Communism, that Khrushchev remained a good and orthodox Marxist-Leninist, and that the policy of *détente*—which, Peking feared, meant an abandonment of revolutionary steadfastness behind the façade of coexistence—was not only proper and sound, but essential.

The Chinese were willing to accept many Soviet moves—on disarmament or more generally, on coexistence—as propaganda tactics but not as policy. They insisted on the immutability of imperialism, the improbability that capitalists would adhere to peaceful settlements, and the necessity to expect war (even if they, too, granted that theoretically it was no longer inevitable). Behind the scenes, Peking viewed with amazement and some scorn Moscow's efforts to "whitewash and embellish imperialism," i.e., Soviet-American relations in the "spirit of Camp David." After the U-2 incident in May, 1960, Mao Tse-tung was reported to have commented victoriously: "We hope that some people will learn a lesson from this, that they will realize that the nature of imperialism is immutable." Agreements with the secular foe were bound to be illusory if not suicidal. "Lenin and Stalin never held," *Red Flag* proclaimed, "that the inner contradictions of imperialism would enable it to change its nature. . . . Facts have amply demonstrated that it is nothing but wishful thinking to regard Eisenhower, Herter, and their ilk as constituting the reasonable group of the American ruling clique . . . and to place hopes on diplomatic negotiations with them."[27]

In June, Moscow counterattacked. D. P. Shevliagin, Deputy Chief of the Foreign Section of the Party's Central Committee, wrote disparagingly:

> Modern "leftists" feel that the present course for achieving peaceful coexistence, the end of the armament race, and the establishment of peace and friendship among peoples is a "departure" from Marxism-Leninism. The slightest deterioration of the international situation is taken by them as proof of their sectarian convictions. Their views may look "terribly revolutionary," but they do harm to the cause. . . .[28]

At the congress of Rumanian Communists in Bucharest and in a letter to the Chinese Party, in late June, the Soviet leadership took a firm stand, blaming the "sectarians" for naiveté, dogmatic reference to irrelevant quotations from Lenin, and failure to understand the nature of thermonuclear war. Publicly, *Izvestiia* again denied that the U-2 incident strengthened the argument of the extremists: "Such reasoning can come only from dogmatists who draw their conclusions without considering or analyzing the true relationship of forces on the world scene—an obligatory demand of Leninism." [29]

Yet there was no denying that Moscow was on the defensive. Khrushchev and his allies henceforth leaned over backward to demonstrate that they were not selling out or watering down the faith. Peaceful coexistence, as it was now reinterpreted, did not mean a lessening of the class struggle. On the contrary, it represented the pursuit of struggle by other means; it was its "highest form." [30] Coexistence did not entail a neglect of revolutionary solidarity and obligations. On the contrary, the growing might of the "socialist camp" permitted the U.S.S.R. and its allies to "impose" agreements—regarding disarmament, a nuclear-test ban, and "atom-free zones"—on the unwilling enemy. Peking skeptically demanded to be shown. Certainly the Congo crisis did not strengthen Moscow's hand: If this was the new policy Khrushchev wanted his fellow-Communists to adopt, it proved to have little to recommend it.

By the time Khrushchev left for the United Nations, in early September, Sino-Soviet relations had reached a new low. The issues involved in the argumentative exchanges had multiplied, and their outward repercussions had become impossible to conceal. The formal reply sent by the Chinese Communist Party to Moscow on September 10 ushered in some of the most violent polemics—precisely during the twenty-five days of Khrushchev's stay in New York.

It took several weeks of heated arguments and lengthy expositions before the meeting of eighty-one Communist parties agreed on an important manifesto that, for the moment, healed the breach. But when Khrushchev was in New York, that hard-won agreement still lay ahead. He knew that Peking was skeptically watching his moves—and so were others, including one of his own colleagues at the U.N., Albania's foreign minister, Mehmet Shehu, whose regime had taken substantially the same line as had the Chinese.[31]

Underlying Khrushchev's position was a time perspective strikingly different from that of Peking. The seasoned Soviet leaders repeatedly reminded their Chinese comrades of what Peking itself had known and taught a few short years before: Not everything is possible, even for Communists; history moves in stages that cannot be bypassed or skipped; each stage demands specific policies proper to the circumstances of that stage. A wise policy refrains from "adventurist" efforts to push too far. Assailing those who still believed in forcibly "pushing revolution," if need be by war, another Soviet voice reminded the Chinese that "at the present juncture, the revival of views like those of the 'left Communists' would be right up the imperialists' alley: it would help them spread tales about the 'aggressiveness of Communism.'"[32]

Similarly, Moscow sought to teach the Chinese, sophisticated policy-makers anticipate setbacks and zigzags and take them in stride. The U-2 incident had been a futile attempt of the imperialists to stage a counteroffensive; the Congo was another. But, Moscow indicated, "failures are inevitable, and so are errors, misjudgments, and disappointments. The art of attacking has to be supplemented by the art of defense and sometimes also the art of temporary retreat."[33] Such arguments did not make the Chinese leadership more confident about Soviet diplomacy. This was particularly true with regard to the U.N.

Communist China had, after all, been branded an aggressor in Korea—a label that has not been torn up. For ten years, China had been an enemy of the United Nations, and conceivably, it might even welcome the collapse of the U.N.—an imperialist agency apt to engender dangerous illusions among Peking's "softer" allies. In public, it had little to say about the United Nations, confining its references in the press almost entirely to "illegal" U.N. efforts to intervene in Laos or to raise the issue of

Tibet.[34] During the Congo operation, Peking found "U.S. imperialism" once again hiding "behind the fig leaf of the U.N." It asked unidentified but unmistakable quarters: "Countless historical facts of the past fifteen years have repeatedly proved that United States imperialism has all along used the United Nations as an instrument of aggression. In the face of these cold, hard facts, how can anybody believe that the U.N., which still remains under United States control, will stand for justice and will help the struggle against colonialism?" [35] There was obviously not the slightest enthusiasm in Peking about Premier Khrushchev's mission to New York, which received slight coverage in the Chinese Communist press.* As for taking its seat in the United Nations, Communist China professed to be in no rush. "It is not China but the United States which has become more and more isolated. . . . As for the restoration of China's seat in the United Nations, this is primarily an urgent need not of China but of the United Nations as a world organization." [36] Premier Chou En-lai made it clear, in his interview with Edgar Snow in October, 1960, that his government would "definitely refuse to take part in the United Nations" so long as any "Taiwan clique" was seated there.[37]

The day before Khrushchev delivered *his* major report to the Soviet people on his stay at the U.N., the *People's Daily* in Peking took its own measure of the United Nations: "The people of the world should in no way place their hopes for liberation and world peace on the United Nations. . . . We should in no way cherish any unrealistic illusions regarding American imperialism and the United Nations under its control." [38] †

If such were some of the public pronouncements, it is likely

---

* It has been asserted that the Communist *New Evening Post* in Hongkong stated editorially on September 3, 1960, that Khrushchev's trip to the United Nations would be a waste of time. (Marvin L. Kalb, *Dragon in the Kremlin* [New York, 1961], p. 239.) I have not been able to verify this item.

† Contrast this statement with the remarks made by Deputy Premier Frol Kozlov at the Chinese Embassy reception in Moscow on September 30, 1960: "Look, comrades, at the progress of the 15th session of the United Nations General Assembly. With what consistency the head of the Soviet Government, N. S. Khrushchev . . . [and others] defend the cause of peace and expose the intrigues of the imperialist-colonizers!"

that there were other communications which passed behind the scenes. There have been suggestions that Peking may have objected to the Soviet endorsement of ONUC from the start. More broadly, as a competitor in Africa, Communist China was free from the inhibitions and restrictions under which Moscow labored. Khrushchev no doubt resented this, but what could he do? Communist China was not in a position to compel the U.S.S.R. to change its policy. Moscow still held the trump cards. And yet his awareness of the "dogmatists" on the sidelines was bound to affect Khrushchev's conduct at the U.N. Thus he was torn between attempts to identify himself—and be identified—with at least two different audiences. In the Communist camp, he strove to be recognized as a full-blooded, successful, imaginative, bold leader of revolution. In the company of the world's mighty statesmen, he wished to be esteemed as the master of a Great Power, to be dealt with on the basis of respect and parity, to be a success at the U.N.

To suggest that he sought membership in both leagues is not to imply that to him Moscow was equidistant from Washington and Peking: It was not. Khrushchev has sought no *rapprochement* with the West—only his particular brand of coexistence. Yet both his friends and his enemies made it hard for him to make a success of his strategy. Perhaps he found relief in thumping the desk with his shoe. Perhaps his vicious blasts against Dag Hammarskjold would also prove to the boys in Peking that he could be as tough as any of them.

IF NOT TODAY, THEN TOMORROW

Most of the Soviet demands and proposals of September, 1960, were subject to postponement or negotiation. The problem of membership was likely to be solved before long; the personnel issue was being considered; the expansion of the Security Council was actively being explored; even the location of U.N. headquarters was not of primary concern. What was central, in Khrushchev's mind, was the tripartite reorganization of the Secretariat.

Yet this was the one proposal that was unacceptable to the majority of members; moreover, the United States and others whose support would be required for passage of an amendment to the Charter were bound to oppose it, if need be by use of the veto.*

Khrushchev was no doubt aware of the legal, logical, and administrative imperfections of his proposal. They mattered little (indeed, some of them helped) if they served the immediate goal: to shatter "United States control" and neutralize the United Nations; to prevent having the U.N. used in any way inimical to the interests of the Soviet bloc. Until such time as Soviet control of the organization could increase, the dialectical effort required a weakening of the United Nations.

What weapons could the Soviet Union use to bring about acceptance of its terms? None, in the short run, that would suffice. But given the frequent Soviet reference to withdrawal from the United Nations, it was natural that the possibility of a Soviet departure was raised. "It is clear that no international organization can survive in our days if it caters to the tastes and interests of one group of states." [39] The threat, reiterated on at least three occasions, was most pronounced in Khrushchev's comments on the U.N.'s refusal to seat Communist China:

> And if we were to go away from the United Nations? We, the Socialist countries. And if we were to organize our own United Nations with an appeal to those countries which would wish to take part and become members of our United Nations? That is what will be the burying ground of the United Nations. . . . We do not wish to see that.[40]

Still, he was careful not to express any threat of wrecking the U.N. His major address before the Assembly contained no menacing statements. Asked privately about any plans of withdrawal, he told a correspondent that the Soviet delegation would not

* For the opinions of twenty delegations opposing the proposal, see United States Department of State, *A United Nations or a Disunited Nations?* (Washington, D.C., 1960).

walk out if his proposals were rejected.[41] The reorganization proposals were not even formally put on the agenda. By November, 1960, the Soviet Union had decided to put off any action until at least the next year; and the following spring, Andrei Gromyko privately gave American officials to understand that Moscow recognized it had no choice but to live with the existing organization until the expiration of the Secretary-General's term of office in April, 1963.

Even while failing to achieve his objectives, Khrushchev seemed full of hope. Once again, what was needed was *time*. Here was his reply to all setbacks: Time would convert the draw into Soviet victory. As he had told the Chinese, and as he repeated after returning from the United Nations, time could not be rushed: "History is not a horse. It cannot be hurried on with a whip." For the benefit of unnamed critics within the Communist family, a Moscow *New Times* editorial explained: "Anyone who thinks that our labors were in vain fails to understand what is happening. We have sown good seeds here. . . . The seeds have been sown and they will bear fruit." [42] Ultimately, the Soviet press commented, the Western Powers will have to "bow to the will of history." [43] Khrushchev's own formulation—in his speech of October 2 before the General Assembly—was: "If not today, then surely tomorrow." That morrow dawned earlier than Moscow, or anyone else, had expected. On September 18, 1961, Dag Hammarskjold was killed in action.

After Dag

The death of the Secretary-General produced not only a sense of void and confusion in the United Nations, but also a grave crisis that, some observers felt, might have led to the very demise of the U.N. Dag Hammarskjold had come to symbolize an institution and an outlook viciously assailed by the U.S.S.R. His removal from the scene at a time when the U.N.'s Congo operation was teetering between success and failure and the Assembly faced its most difficult agenda came at the worst possible time for the UN. and its supporters. Less obviously, the timing was also inopportune from the standpoint of the U.S.S.R.

The problem of Hammarskjold's succession forced Moscow to take a public stand when it would have wished to postpone it. It left the Soviet Union the option of either holding out for the *troika*—with the near-certainty of suffering defeat—or else retreating from its solemnly proclaimed demands and settling for less than it hoped to achieve at some future time.

In harmony with his broader assumptions about the course of world affairs and his priorities in the fall of 1961, Khrushchev was eager to avoid a showdown at the U.N. Precipitating a split of the organization over the *troika* (or insisting on a Communist as Secretary-General) would have left the Soviet bloc isolated, with at most half a dozen "neutrals" following its lead, and thereafter with even less opportunity to influence all other states. Moscow's desire to push its own solution was thus circumscribed by the striving for political effectiveness among other member-states.

The Soviet delegation could be expected to use Hammarskjold's death to press for some variant of the *troika* but yet be prepared to accept a *modus vivendi* well short of it. The strength of the Soviet position derived from Moscow's willingness to wait: A weaker United Nations, with or without a Secretary-General, was likely to suit it better than most other member-states. By the same token, any substantial impairment of United Nations authority and considerable delays in naming a new Secretary-General were bound to antagonize the smaller and predominantly neutral powers. While Moscow benefited from the widespread unwillingness of others to push through the Assembly any arrangement unacceptable to the Soviet bloc, any negotiated settlement had to be acceptable to the other Great Powers as well.*

Moscow gave prompt and serious consideration to the succession problem. It indicated, before its tactics had perhaps even crystallized, that it would not go along with the effort to appoint

---

* The U.N. Charter makes no provision for a Deputy Secretary-General or for succession if the Secretary-General is incapacitated or dies in office. The thirteen under-secretaries are formally all of equal rank.

an Acting Secretary-General immediately; it would try to make at least some headway in the direction of the *troika*. Moreover, the two candidates favored by the neutral and Western powers—the new Assembly President, Mongi Slim of Tunisia, and the outgoing President, Frederick H. Boland of Ireland—were not acceptable to the U.S.S.R. And once an informal conference of non-Communist middle-sized and small states came into being, Moscow frequently found itself outmaneuvered: in a moment of crisis, many of the leading neutrals groped for an understanding with the West. They soon agreed that a single successor should be elected (thus locking the door to the *troika*) and that the regular procedure be followed in having the Security Council recommend the appointment to the General Assembly (thus assuring the U.S.S.R. of an opportunity to exercise its veto).

This understanding doomed the first Soviet move of September 18. Probably an improvisation, it was an important straw in the wind: it proposed rotating the Secretaryship among three under-secretaries representing the major blocs (Ralph J. Bunche, Georgi Arkadiev, and Chakravarthi Narasimhan). Jointly the three would form a "coordinating committee," which would constitute a step in the direction of the *troika*. The proposal could presumably be carried out immediately—a clear advantage over the full Soviet reorganization proposals, which required Charter amendment.

Once this plan proved to be unacceptable, the position to which the Soviet delegation next retreated answered the question whether, in the Soviet view, the tripartite formula was susceptible to negotiation and dilution. By September 27, Deputy Foreign Minister Valerian Zorin had come around to recommending that the office of the Secretary-General be left vacant but that four under-secretaries (one each from America, the U.S.S.R., Asia, and Africa) collectively assume the Secretary's functions and responsibilities, rotating the temporary chairmanship among themselves.[44] The somewhat unexpected Soviet endorsement of such a beheaded "four-horse *troika*" involved Moscow's acceptance of a geographical principle of selection tailor-made to maximize numerical support in the Assembly and in conflict with its previous insistence on the "reality" of a world divided into three political and ideological blocs. Coming as it did after a year of vociferous argument about the need for equal rights for the three blocs—nothing else would do—the new move exposed the manipulative and opportunistic nature of Soviet demands.

In the face of overwhelming sentiment in favor of a one-man administrator, as the Charter demanded, Moscow decided late in September to seek an accommodation on the best-possible terms. Foreign Minister Gromyko almost avoided the subject in his major Assembly address of September 26, but indicated the general tenor of Soviet thinking: "Let it be an interim solution for the start, but one which will not widen the gap which already exists between states. . . ." An interim solution required no acceptance by others of Soviet "principles." In turn, the Soviet delegates proved to be remarkably flexible in the complex back-stage moves and negotiations that ensued. In its statement of October 1, the Soviet mission to the U.N. suggested as an explicitly "conciliatory proposal on the provisional leadership of the U.N. Secretariat" the appointment (until April 10, 1963) of an acting executive who would officiate "in the spirit of concord" with three deputies —one from each of the three major blocs. Within the following two weeks, Zorin made it clear that the Soviet Union did not envisage the use of the veto by any of these assistants."

This further concession removed what had loomed as perhaps the largest remaining stumbling block, and the following weeks saw agreement over the number of deputies and their geographical distribution.* In the end, all parties yielded somewhat, but the

* The extent of Soviet concessions is suggested in this passage from a *New York Times* dispatch of October 14, 1961: "As proof of their conciliatory spirit, Mr. Zorin said that the Russians had given ground from their original demand for a three-man directorate, each member with veto power; that they had dropped their alternative demand for three deputies with the veto power and that they had made 'maximum concessions' on the procedure for electing the Acting Secretary-General. He said the candidate would not have to announce the names of his proposed assistants to the Security Council before its members voted on him, but would have to announce the geographical distribution." In the next two weeks, Moscow gave up even this last demand.

U.S.S.R. backed down most strikingly from its original demands—of course, the most sweeping ones to be made.

On November 3, 1961, the General Assembly, upon recommendation of the Security Council, unanimously named U Thant Acting Secretary-General for the remainder of Dag Hammarskjold's term. The appointment marked a triple Soviet failure Instead of a *troika*, a single individual was named; he was no required to make any prior commitments to the states sponsoring him; his authority was not circumscribed either by agreement o by the impinging prerogatives of political deputies.

Why had Moscow failed to push harder for its own proposals In the eyes of the Soviet leadership, developments at the United Nations had lost the priority of attention they had commanded the year before. In the fall of 1961, a combination of circum stances riveted Soviet attention to more immediately sensitive problems: the overt rift with Albania and its implications fo Soviet relations with China and the Communist movement as whole; the struggle over defense policy and consumer goods a home; the new de-Stalinization and revelations about the Stali era, with their implications for the future; the new struggle with the opposition ostensibly headed by Viacheslav Molotov. The U.N negotiations took place against the background of simultaneou Soviet-American feelers, culminating in the Rusk-Gromyko con versations aimed at "resolving," or at least easing, the Berli crisis; and the apparent Soviet desire to stabilize its internationa posture on the eve of the Twenty-second Congress of the Com munist Party of the Soviet Union, which opened in Moscow o October 17. In the face of urgent problems elsewhere, Moscov was eager not to become involved in an unpromising tug-of-wa at the U.N.

In the arguments within the Communist family between th advocates of a *détente* and those of a forward policy—betweer those who took their "peaceful coexistence" seriously and thos who saw it as a momentary cover for "direct action" abroad— Khrushchev and his *apparat* were eager to show that Soviet policy

ad not been (as critics were bound to allege) another failure
orn of weak-kneed concessions and "rotten compromise."

The election of a Burmese highlighted the change in the United
Nations: At long last, Moscow could prove its earlier contention
hat the United States "had lost control" of the U.N. As if to
demonstrate for the benefit of unnamed critics that the U.S.S.R.
vas conducting a vigorous policy at the U.N. (as Gromyko,
Khrushchev, and Adzhubei claimed at the Moscow Congress),
Zorin, on October 13, alleged that the United States, through the
person of Andrew W. Cordier, had seized control of the U.N.
ecretariat, and the U.S.S.R. was "of course anxious to liquidate
he situation as quickly as possible." *

Moreover, one may take it, Moscow was somewhat alarmed
y the attitude of some neutral and Western leaders. After all,
whatever the public assertions, Soviet suspicions about their
natural" allies in the underdeveloped countries were reflected
n the tripartite proposals themselves. The Congo operation con-
inued to indicate that the Afro-Asians were by no means "in
Khrushchev's pocket." Even prior to U Thant's election, the
Assembly voted 87:11 to appeal to the U.S.S.R. to call off its
mpending 50-megaton nuclear-bomb test. (On this as on subsequent occasions, the traditional Soviet bloc of nine votes was
oined by Cuba and newly admitted Mongolia.) The following
veek, it voted 72:21 to appeal to all nuclear powers to refrain
rom further weapons tests: The neutralist resolution, opposed by
he U.S.S.R. and the U.S. alike, had a clear majority of U.N.
members behind it. The United Nations had indeed changed!

The unaligned and smaller powers were likely to exploit their
ivotal role more powerfully than ever, and they were apt to
dentify their own security and future progress with the United
Nations far more than Moscow did. While recognition of the

---

* The Secretariat, over the signature of its under-secretaries, took the
nprecedented step of issuing a statement in reply, indicating that "there
as been no change whatsoever in the responsibilities of each of the under-
ecretaries," and that even their meetings had been held without a chairman.

need for some organizational changes in the U.N. had made re
markable headway in the year since Khrushchev's *troika* speech
neutralist sentiment ran overwhelmingly against the tripartite
proposals. Now the Soviet Union was eager to show that it wa
not the Communist bloc but the United States that was holding
up agreement. This did have a tactical advantage in that ever
those who rejected the Soviet terms were reluctant to identif
themselves with any plan opposed by the U.S.S.R. In this regard
Moscow was the silent beneficiary of what has been called the
psychology of aloofness of certain non-Communist states from the
great issues of our age.[45]

As for the United States, Moscow for the first time seemed t
be aware of—or feign concern with—the possibility of the U.S
turning its back on the U.N. At a signal from Washington, *Pravda*
alleged, the American press had begun to cry about a "crisis
at the U.N. Yet "there is no crisis—except that manufactured b
the defenders of 'dictatorial rule' exercised by the Secretary
General." [46] Moscow interpreted a wide range of American com
ments as showing a growth of misgivings about the future utilit
of the U.N. now that the United States could no longer expec
to have its way. Whether the desire to keep the U.S. from pullin
away from the United Nations helped swing Moscow towar
more conciliatory tactics remains a matter of speculation; Sovie
policy is explicable even in the absence of this element. At an
rate, this consideration presumably strengthened the hand o
those arguing within Communist circles for the plausibility o
"coexistence" and, in a curious projection of Soviet attitude
pointing a propaganda finger at the "undemocratic" United State
which will not cooperate when it does not win.

In agreeing to the election of U Thant, the Soviet Union ac
knowledged its failure to achieve its expressed aim—the tripartit
reorganization of the Secretariat. Yet it had accomplished sever:
things. The U.N.'s new official was bound to have less authorit
than his predecessor had built up over the course of years. Th
temporary tenure of U Thant added to the precariousness of hi

position in office. After the object lessons of Trygve Lie and Dag Hammarskjold, any Secretary-General was bound to give more weight to the attitudes of the Great Powers—especially the U.S.S.R.—or else invite dismissal. Under the new dispensation there was likely to be a strong temptation for the Secretariat to equate neutrality with passivity—all of which was perfectly all right with the U.S.S.R.

Moscow had assured itself of another year or two before the reorganization issue came up again, at a far more propitious time, it no doubt hoped, for promoting the *troika*.[47] The crisis created by Hammarskjold's death was seemingly resolved—until April 1963. The U.N. had won the immediate battle against collapse. But, to Moscow's ill-concealed satisfaction, it had lost considerable ground in the struggle to grow from a conference machinery into a constitutional authority. The future political physiognomy of the United Nations remained in doubt.

BERLIN AND THE UNITED NATIONS: A NOTE

The Soviet demands for making West Berlin a "free city" were, in November–December, 1958, accompanied by a proposal that the four occupying powers "and perhaps the United Nations" guarantee the status of Berlin. The offer "that the United Nations should take part in these guarantees" was reiterated in the joint communiqué issued on March 11, 1959, at the end of Khrushchev's talks with the East German leadership. In April, 1959, he was reported in agreement with Field Marshal Montgomery's proposal that a United Nations force of neutral troops might gradually replace the Allied troops stationed in Berlin. No less cautiously, Khrushchev remarked during his French trip (April 2, 1960) that "it could be very useful if the U.N. were involved to a certain extent" in safeguarding West Berlin's "free" status.

Finally, the Soviet proposals Premier Khrushchev handed President Kennedy in Vienna in June, 1961, were said to agree to the stationing of neutral troops under the United Nations as one possible variant guaranteeing the city's freedom (*The New York Times,* June 11, 1961). In his address to the U.N. Assembly on September 26, 1961, Foreign Minister Gromyko envisaged the "registration" of Berlin's status as a free city with the United Nations and other possible forms of "United Nations participation" in guaranteeing its status.

Soviet comments regarding the U.N.'s role in Berlin have always been evasive. The Soviet draft peace treaty with Germany (handed to the United States on January 10, 1959) made no reference to such a U.N. role. Moscow preferred a neutral U.N. force to continued U.S., U.K., and French presence, but undoubtedly was reluctant to give the U.N. more than nominal or token authority.

Secretary-General Hammarskjold himself at an early date indicated his reluctance to involve the U.N. in the Berlin crisis to any significant extent. While the United States gave serious thought to involving the U.N. in a Berlin settlement in the fall of 1961, West Germany and France firmly opposed such a move, and Britain demurred after Hammarskjold's death.

Characteristically, Moscow's desire to solve the issue "seriously" led it to keep the issue out of the U.N. Since September, 1961, however,

Khrushchev has demanded the admission of both West and East Germany to the United Nations as part of a German settlement "package," and on January 12, 1962, suggested making a free city of West Berlin into a sovereign state with membership in the U.N.—a proposal promptly rebuffed by the United States.

Chapter XII

The Soviet Outlook—Today
and Tomorrow

T<small>HE</small> United Nations has not fulfilled the high hopes that some of its sponsors had for it. A major share of responsibility for this failure has commonly been assigned to the Soviet Union, and not without reason. The Soviet view and Soviet conduct, however, have not been products of perversity or malice. They follow logically, first, from the world view held by the Communist leadership, which sees the United Nations as another arena in the struggle between the two "world systems" of our age, and, second, from the Soviet experience as a minority power seeking to frustrate the efforts of the hostile majority "in control" of the U.N.

ONE WORLD, TWO CAMPS, THREE BLOCS

The Soviet leadership sees world affairs as a secular conflict between irreconcilable opposites. "Forces"—and therefore attitudes—have an organic tendency to polarize around the two antagonistic camps. Deviations from this inherent law tend to be viewed as temporary aberrations that cannot alter or affect the basic dichotomy.

The presence of a superpower with a deeply engrained "two-amp" view in a "one-world" organization presents a challenging problem, for how can that agency function if one of its principal members fails to subscribe to its assumptions and rules? One must inquire, then, whether Soviet participation in, and praise for the principles of, the United Nations heralds the acceptance of a "one-world" view.

A new element in this picture has been the emergence of the "underdeveloped" nations, thanks to the collapse of the colonial empires. Does Soviet recognition of the "emerging states" as objects of particular attention and as presumptive allies—indeed, under the proposals for tripartite reorganization, their inflation into a coequal third bloc in the U.N.—mark a retreat from the Soviet commitment to the dichotomic perception?

The evidence points overwhelmingly to the continued acceptance of the two-camp view. Neither one nor three, but two, remains the magic number. Whatever its appeals to universal goals and values, Moscow does not see the world as one international community. And, however vigorous its assertions of solidarity with the Afro-Asian world, it does not in fact recognize the permanent fissure of the globe into three homogeneous and mutually antagonistic blocs. As the 1961 Program of the Communist Party of the Soviet Union declares, "The basic contradiction of the contemporary world [is] the contradiction between socialism and imperialism." The events of recent years have undoubtedly reinforced the Soviet belief in the correctness of its bifocal vision and in the inevitability of the shift in the balance of power in favor of the "socialist camp."

Premier Khrushchev's frequent and facile comments bear this out. They abound in such images as the balance, the see-saw, and communicating vessels in which the emptying of one (the capitalist) is tantamount to the filling of the other (the Communist). The United Nations itself, he reasserted upon his return home from New York in 1960, was the stage for "a struggle of the new and progressive against the old and the moribund." Identifying the Soviet Union, as usual, with the fight for "peace," he continued: "Lining up the forces for peace and war is a process that will quicken and develop and will augment the forces that stand for peace. The peoples of the neutral countries face a historic choice"—between the two camps.

It has become standard for Soviet writers on foreign affairs—and particularly on the U.N.—to juxtapose "the two lines" or "two opposite approaches" to world affairs, not three.[1] Bracketing the "objective" interests of the Communist and unaligned states, the Communist Party's official organ, *Kommunist*, commented on the 15th Assembly session:

> The historic struggle taking place on the world stage in our days finds expression within the walls of that Organization [the U.N.], where the world is represented in all its manifold and, of course, contradictory complexity. Here a polarization is taking place in the course of which the forces of peace, freedom, and social progress unite, while the advocates of aggression and colonial slavery doom themselves to isolation.[2]

Allowing for the contrived optimism of the prognosis, the approach is clear: It permits of no lasting neutrality. Leading Communists have from time to time spelled out the purely tactical and manipulative nature of their present support of the neutral states.° Indeed, in the Soviet definition neutrality no longer means what it did: An active struggle against "imperial-

---

° Paul de Groot wrote in *Kommunist* (No. 2 [1957], p. 63): "For a state over which America rules at present, neutrality guaranteed by both world camps would constitute a step forward toward national independence. For a socialist state, neutrality constitutes a step backward toward the subjugation to American imperialism and its sphere of influence." Similarly, Hungarian Foreign Minister Imre Horvath declared (June 2, 1957): "We approve of the neutrality of certain capitalist countries since it signifies that they do not join the imperialist military blocs. . . . [But] neutrality for a socialist country represents an underhanded attack on, and betrayal of, peace and socialism." For a systematic exposition of the Soviet view, see E. A. Korovin, "Neitralitet v proshlom i nastoiashchem," in his *Osnovnye problemy sovremennykh mezhdunarodnykh otnoshenii* (Moscow, 1959), and Boris Ganiushkin, *Sovremennyi neitralitet* (Moscow, 1958). See also George Ginsburgs, "Neutrality and Neutralism and the Tactics of Soviet Diplomacy," *American Slavic and East European Review*, December, 1960.

ism" is a "necessary condition" of Soviet recognition of a state's neutrality.[3]

The typical Soviet policy has been to keep the United Nations alive but weak. While it has sometimes advocated U.N. action in defiance of other nations' claims of domestic jurisdiction or of regional doctrines elsewhere in the world, Moscow's normal aim has been to safeguard its own freedom of action, to keep the United Nations out of the Communist bloc, and generally to minimize the organization's power. The Soviet Union and its allies have never brought a single dispute among themselves before the United Nations. When other states have raised issues relating to the "socialist camp," Moscow has labeled them illegitimate interference. Khrushchev, in April, 1958, reiterated Stalin's old warning to the "imperialists" "not to try to put their pig snouts into our socialist garden." Undiplomatic in form, the attitude itself follows inexorably from the hypothesis that the rest of the world—including the United Nations—is controlled by the enemy camp.[4]

The Soviet efforts to restrict the U.N.'s jurisdiction go back to the days prior to the adoption of the Charter. Ever since, the U.S.S.R. has favored a strict and literal construction of its terms and has invariably objected to attempts to broaden the prerogatives of the Assembly and the Secretariat. Subsumed under the obsessive emphasis on "sovereignty," the Soviet attitude springs from a determination not to be bound by the desires or decisions of others.

This has led Moscow to minimize the achievements of the United Nations. It has denied the U.N.'s role even where it is manifest. The Soviet press insists that the settlement of the Iran affair of 1946 was brought about not by the United Nations but by direct negotiation. The U.N. had nothing to do with the easing of international tensions after Stalin's death: The Geneva spirit of 1955 was a product of the Great Powers' own efforts. The Suez crisis of 1956, Khrushchev asserted, was settled not by the U.N., but by the Soviet Union's threat of intervention. More often than not, the United Nations has in the past acted either "under pressure from the U.S.A." (as in Korea) or as "nothing more than a passive registrar of world events."

The unique interpretation Moscow has given to the term *status quo* has been peculiarly advantageous to the Soviet approach. It gives the Soviet Union sanction to ignore the outside world when it comes to relations within its own bloc, and it permits the Soviet Union also to make the problems of other nations, in and out of the U.N., its own concern. For, as Khrushchev has repeatedly suggested, the essence of the *status quo* is revolution itself. Ultimately, this means acquiescence in the process of change whose culmination is the world-wide drift to Communism.

What to the outsider might appear to be a double standard turns out to be natural and consequent, once Soviet assumptions are spelled out. The seeming ambiguity or conceptual contradiction in such cases—for instance, the Soviet view of just and unjust wars—stems from the clash of two distinct categories of analysis—of "iron laws of history," as Moscow sees them, with man-made "international law in the epoch of coexistence." [5] In its internal analysis of the world scene, Moscow is bound to opt for the organic, fundamental laws that inform the historical process, rather than the "formal," "technical," and transient "bourgeois" rules.

It remains true that the Soviet approach is by no means free of unreconciled ambiguities and unresolved problems of analysis. As has been shown at various points, there have been conflicting priorities of revolution and diplomacy, of exclusiveness and universality, of sovereignty and "proletarian solidarity," of esoteric class analysis and tactics of compromise. Any of these may at times confront the Soviet leadership with genuine dilemmas. Thus, to accept the world as it is means to betray its long-range goals and visions; but to oppose it frankly and explicitly is to sacrifice all the advantages of propaganda, negotiations, and alliances—and, in this case, effective participation in international organizations.

While the Soviet view of the world and, more specifically, of the United Nations has remained fundamentally constant, Moscow has witnessed numerous disagreements over strategy and tactics to be pursued. In this context, Communist assessments of the United Nations have varied from total rejection as an "imperialist tool" to total espousal as an imminent Communist "front." While in the minds of some Communist leaders such expectations have vacillated over the years, others have adhered to the same position, more or less rigidly, regardless of new experiences and events.

As recently as October, 1961, at the Twenty-second Congress of the Soviet Communist Party, the major protagonists of the "moderate" line felt called upon to defend themselves against charges of "excessive faith in personal contacts and conversations" abroad; no doubt the United Nations was part of the target involved. Former Foreign Minister Viacheslav Molotov was identified as having been "opposed to contacts between our statesmen and Party leaders with foreign politicians, to visits abroad." The disarmament question was now added to the list of issues over which spokesmen for different Communist policies disagreed.

In the course of defending the Khrushchev record against charges of naïveté and failure at the United Nations, A. I. Adzhubei (in his speech of October 26, 1961) made a revealing comment about the Soviet performance at the 1960 Assembly session: Soviet behavior there, far from amounting to collaboration with the class enemy (as some comrades alleged), furthered the class struggle, for the Soviet delegation "organized obstructions when mendacious, provocative speeches were made from the U.N. rostrum," in order to "destroy the hypocritical quiet" and to show up "the attitude of the gentlemen who engage in the deceit of peoples." Proudly detailing the Khrushchev incidents, he proceeded to assert that Soviet fist-banging and shoe-waving were intended to "curb the pharisees and liars." These are no junkets, Adzhubei continued: "Comrades, behind personal contacts and visits, there is hard work, work until you are covered with sweat, often not leaving you time for sleep or rest, work that demands constant concentration and resourcefulness and the ability to use all the forces of argument. It requires if you wish, personal courage." After the break of relations with the Soviet Union, the Albanian Communist daily took issue with this argument from an unexpected angle:

> We have even reached the point [it wrote] where some stupidities committed by Khrushchev, which bring discredit to the Soviet Union—for instance, when he took off his shoes at the U.N. General Assembly—are slavishly elevated to a matter of "theory" and presented as "magnificent examples of a Marxist attitude." [6]

Undoubtedly we do not know the full range of disagreements relating to the U.N. Yet the experience of recent years is likely to have reduced the differences in the Soviet assessment of the United Nations: Neither total withdrawal from nor total reliance on the U.N. is likely to find many advocates among the leaders of the Soviet camp.

International organizations are after all expected to be but a passing stage. Both the strategy of the "zone of peace" and the pursuit of "peaceful coexistence" are deemed appropriate for the "given historical epoch"—the transitional era in which "capitalist" and "socialist" states exist side by side. Moscow has been frank in stating not only that the principle of "proletarian international-ism" among Communists is a law superior to "bourgeois" codes and mores, but also that it is intended "for a longer period of time" than "peaceful coexistence" is.[7] The cause of the Soviet camp is bound to win, Khrushchev asserts, because it has both "justice and force" on its side. Or, as he put it another time, "reason and right are not on their side but ours." [8] Unlike the more "pragmatic" responses of other states, in the Soviet case such perspective is by no means irrelevant to the conduct of actual policy.

U.N.—For What?

It is commonplace to argue that Soviet "conflict strategy" encompasses a practical, if somewhat condescending, willingness to use any individual or group, institution or symbol, to advance its aims. In Moscow's estimation, the United Nations is—or can be —one such tool. Until about 1954, it was considered an instrument of subordinate importance;* since then, its potential, in Soviet eyes, has substantially increased.

This statement is not in conflict with the underlying skepticism about what the United Nations can do and what the Soviet Union can expect to gain from it. Fundamentally, Moscow continues to hold, an international body of diverse and antagonistic sovereign states cannot solve the problems of our days.

The Soviet Union has participated in the United Nations for limited purposes and certainly with limited expectations. If, some observers have found, there is in the United States an acute contrast between hopes and results in the U.N.,[9] no such hiatus exists on the Soviet side—simply because Moscow had no such naïve expectations to begin with. It sees membership as a contract based on the mutuality of certain interests. The United Nations, it maintains, has no rights or powers of its own—only those derived from its member states. It is at all times an organ subordinate to these states, not the independent voice of a world conscience or of a common will.

* The standard Soviet textbook of international law declared: "The importance of international organizations must not be overestimated. Such organizations materially facilitate relations among states and to a certain extent promote technical and scientific development. . . . They certainly do not put an end to the inherent contradictions of the capitalist world." (Durdenevsky and Krylov, *Mezhdunarodnoe pravo*, p. 407.)

Many Western observers found it hard to predict in what direction the United Nations would evolve. On a number of points, the Charter is inevitably, and perhaps intentionally, vague. If, in a widely held view, the U.N. can be considered either a locus for the exercise of national policy or else a nucleus of international government, Moscow has had no such choice: The U.N. must serve only the former, never the latter goal. Soviet writings continue to assail all projects giving the United Nations greater power; and to "expose" all advocates of "the reactionary idea of 'world law.'" [10]

By the same token, the Soviet Union has not indulged in any optimism with regard to "functionalism" or "welfare internationalism" through the U.N. Neither the faith that international "togetherness" will overcome basic rifts, nor the belief that the U.N. could or should attempt to resolve the economic and social ills of the modern world has characterized the Soviet view. This is not at all surprising. Indeed, in its predominantly political approach to the international organization, the Soviet Union has differed fundamentally from the spokesmen of underdeveloped countries whom it has sought to court—countries for whom the health, education, and welfare activities often loom as among the most constructive tasks of the U.N.

"Internal" Soviet estimates of the United Nations' utility appear to have changed in the course of time. The initial Soviet commitment to participate in the League of Nations, and later in the United Nations, was due in large measure to a desire to buttress Russian security. Since 1950, this has been a receding consideration. Experience showed that both the League and the U.N. were at best dubious guarantors of peace. And with the growth of Soviet military and economic power, with crucial breakthroughs in weapons technology, and with a deep reluctance to trust the mechanics of a "no-power" club, the Soviet Union has not relied and need not rely on the United Nations for its defense. One of the most bothersome of Khrushchev's arguments since 1959 has been that of Soviet reliance on its own forces—without the U.N. and even against the U.N.* In case of crisis, Soviet resort to the U.N. is of course considered infinitely less promising than its own armed might, its alliance system, and other instruments it controls.[11]

The subordinate place of the United Nations in the Soviet scheme is also reflected in Moscow's disinclination to have the U.N. handle issues requiring careful dosage or urgent action. For such purposes, it prefers "summits" and bilateral negotiations.†

A similar power-conscious realism is revealed in the omission of the United Nations from the most authoritative and detailed Communist analyses of contemporary affairs. The official handbook of the Communist Party of the Soviet Union, used for political training throughout the U.S.S.R. and translated into several languages, in its 890 pages (including a lengthy section on world affairs, the Korean War, and the Suez crisis) does not contain a single reference to the United Nations! [12] Likewise, the Statement of Eighty-one Communist Parties meeting in Moscow in November–December, 1960, the most significant theoretical and strategic document produced by the Communist universe in recent years, fails to make a single reference to the United Nations, as does the new program of the CPSU, adopted in October, 1961.

---

* This has permitted Moscow to assume a pose of unselfishness: "In reaffirming its proposals for reorganization of the United Nations structure, the Soviet Government is primarily concerned for the interests of independent Asian, African, and Latin American countries. The Soviet Union is, of course, in a position to defend itself against any aggression, but what would be the fate of weak ex-colonial nations if the imperialists, having tried out their strength in the Congo, launch an all-out offensive against the Afro-Asian movement for national liberation?" (Editorial, *New Times*, No. 10 [1961], p. 2.)

† In New York, Khrushchev commented that "the question of Germany is outside the limits of the United Nations." (*Pravda*, October 11, 1960.) See above, p. 180. To Senator Hubert Humphrey, Khrushchev intimated that "the United States should be discussing questions of outer space directly with the Soviet Union instead of raising them in the U.N. 'So now,' Khrushchev said, 'the United States discusses outer space with Guatemala—but Guatemala does not seem to be too advanced in outer-space science.'" (Hubert H. Humphrey, "My Marathon Talk with Russia's Boss," *Life*, January 12, 1959.)

This does not mean that Moscow lacks theoretical criteria by which to judge the U.N.:

> Under conditions in which there are in the world states with differing social systems, international political organizations—constituting phenomena that belong to the superstructure—have the right to exist only so long as they correspond to the actual relationship of forces that constitute their base.

If the organization fails to change in accordance with these "basic" forces, it tends to become "essentially a separate bloc, hardly distinguishable from aggressive military alliances." [13] This is the rationale of the Soviet proposals of 1960–61: the demand that the organization be brought in line with the "realities" of international power.*

What then does Moscow expect to gain from its efforts in the United Nations? Membership, even at times of considerable adversity, has given the Soviet Union opportunities

for the settlement of relatively minor disputes;

for international contacts, both to exchange views and to initiate and pursue negotiations, often informally rather than at official sessions;

for gathering information, political intelligence, technical know-how, scientific data, and securing economic and other goods and services, as a matter of self-interest;

for gaining prestige and respectability as a major power in the family of nations; and

for engaging in propaganda, in the broadest sense of the term, and attempting to influence the views, attitudes, political alignments and actions of other states.

---

* It is worth noting that an analogous insistence on significant changes in the real world has, on a different plane, involved Khrushchev in debate with "dogmatic" Leninists who, directly or indirectly, have questioned his conclusions on the possibilities of "peaceful coexistence" and peaceful accession to power.

Soviet analysts have frequently stressed the value of the United Nations as a "broad forum"; as a gathering point for the different blocs, including the young nations of Africa and Asia; and as a vehicle for the dissemination of Soviet declarative proposals (such as the draft declarations on peaceful coexistence, stopping nuclear tests, and pledges not to employ nuclear weapons; the total disarmament schemes; and the anticolonialist declaration). The convenient, but not necessarily unique, opportunities that the U.N. has provided are shown by the Jessup-Malik talks over the Berlin blockade in 1949, and the Rusk-Gromyko talks over the new Berlin crisis in 1961. Upon returning from the U.N. in the fall of 1960, Khrushchev declared that his trip had been "useful in that we had many meetings and exchanged views with the statesmen of various countries on a whole range of important international issues." With all its vagueness, this comment no doubt corresponded to his view.

In the pursuit of these objectives, Soviet policy-makers have the choice among several models of behavior in international organizations:

1. *Nonparticipation.* This course commended itself until 1934 with regard to the League and has been consistently rejected for the U.N.

2. *Minimum participation.* Basically an isolationist strategy, it is restrictive in its interpretation of U.N. authority, stressing Soviet prerogatives of sovereignty and strict interpretation of agreements, and minimizing outside jurisdiction in Communist affairs. Adopted at a time when the Soviet bloc was in the position of a perennial minority, it has been the predominant policy ever since 1945, though in the 1950's, Moscow, sensing a distinct improvement in its "position of strength" and opportunities abroad, began to shed some of the features of this approach.

3. *Selective cooperation* against a specific foe. This strategy—seeing the U.N. as the equivalent of a military ally—is practiced when the Soviet Union needs international support in some form of collective action or assurance against a third power. In this

fashion it sought to strengthen its position vis-à-vis Germany and Japan in the 1930's. An analogous situation has not occurred since World War II. While no one will admit it, Communist China may theoretically present such a problem at some future date.

4. A broad, expansive strategy of *maximizing United Nations authority*. This is the normal Soviet policy for a Communist-controlled organization. No doubt, Moscow would welcome a situation in which its "camp"—together with assorted camp followers—would emerge in control of the U.N. But, after a brief interlude of extravagant hope, Khrushchev seems to have convinced himself that the day is not at hand. This policy, therefore, has seen, and in the foreseeable future will see, no systematic application.

Perplexingly, Soviet policy in 1960–62 has fitted none of the above prescriptions. The Soviet role is no longer minimal in many fields: It has increased in economic and social work; there has been greater Soviet use of the Assembly; in Soviet propaganda, the U.N. "principle"—but not its practice—has unmistakably become a positive symbol. Yet it is precisely the threats and demands voiced by the Soviet Union that underscore the continuing gap between the "United Nations mentality" and that of the U.S.S.R.

Beyond the immediate opportunities that Moscow sees available for itself, is there a longer-range objective of Soviet policy in the U.N.? At one time it was conceivable that Moscow would merely maintain nominal membership, seeking neither to win control nor to withdraw. No longer is this a reasonable prospect; given the growth of Soviet might, activity, and ambition, such a retreat to silent partnership is difficult to conceive. Nor is the Soviet bloc likely to pull out, in spite of all its threats. If it stuck it out during the isolation of the Korean War, it is sure to feel that the present advantages of membership are infinitely greater and the prospects more encouraging still. Its threats of withdrawal, moreover, would obviously lose their bargaining value—

without netting the Soviet Union any commensurate gain—were it indeed to leave the organization.

The question remains whether (in President Eisenhower's words) the Soviet leaders "in alternating moods look upon the United Nations as an instrument for use or abuse"; whether (as others have put it) Moscow seeks "the power to manipulate the United Nations for its own designs" or whether Khrushchev strives to render the organization impotent.[14] One may suggest that the two objectives—to neutralize and to control—can coexist in Soviet minds. They may be most usefully thought of as maximum and minimum aims. The simultaneous identification of such divergent goals has a long history in Bolshevik experience and has often been characteristic of Soviet foreign affairs.[15]

No doubt the most extreme and optimistic Soviet vision is the transformation of the United Nations into a Communist "front" organization, in the manner of world peace congresses, "solidarity" meetings, and labor federations that, behind a non-Soviet façade, Communists seek to control (but not overtly to direct, so as not to drive non-Communists out). But obviously Moscow cannot bank on the U.N.'s conforming to this scheme. In practice, the Soviet bloc has never been close to controlling a majority of Assembly votes. Moreover, the Western Big Three still possess their veto power. Thus, of necessity, the Soviet Union has had to turn to more immediate and more modest goals—especially since, by 1960, Khrushchev considered it a matter of considerable urgency to stop the organization from being "used" by the enemy camp.

Even if Moscow prefers to have two strings to its United Nations bow, choices must sometimes be made that preclude the return to an alternative policy. In general, Moscow has sought to avoid such irreversible commitments, and from the Soviet point of view a major shortcoming of the tripartite proposal is precisely the fact that its adoption would make it difficult to return at some future date to a veto-free pursuit of majority control in the General Assembly and the Secretariat. As it now stands, the Soviet plan would guarantee the veto to both the West and the collective voice of the unaligned. At present, Moscow would not seriously expect to "sell" its proposal without giving such "equality" to the American-led "imperialist camp."

Thus Moscow finds itself prepared, for the time being, to freeze the tripartite relationship and accept a more limited goal than its control of the U.N. The most immediate Soviet task is to make sure that the United Nations will not be used against it and its friends. To some extent, the Soviet demands and threats of 1960–61 have of themselves accomplished a part of this aim.

This does not exhaust what Moscow expects to achieve in or through the U.N. The Soviet bloc can hope to use it in a variety of ways—until such a time as, hopefully, the Charter may again be altered to bring it in conformity with what Moscow expects will then be the reality of even greater Soviet might.

CONTINUITY AND CHANGE

A substantially constant ideological framework has permitted significant variations in Soviet strategy and tactics at the United Nations. The contrast between Moscow's policy in Stalin's days and in the Khrushchev era measures both the extent and the limits of variation.

But what has determined shifts in Moscow's policy? The primary determinant is to be found outside the U.N. system: This has been the Soviet view of changes in the "real world" —above all, changes of power and of opportunity. It was precisely the contrast between the glorious sense of growing Soviet world power and the lack of commensurate success or influence in the United Nations that permitted Moscow to argue for "realistic" adjustments in the organization's system of staffing and representation.

Another determinant is the system of ideological preconceptions. True, certain fundamental axioms—conflict, dichotomy, optimism—have shown remarkable tenacity, and certain generalities in the Soviet world view—the call for "realism," the approach to "sovereignty," the verdict that the United Nations is "useful" but not "important"—have remained virtually unchanged. Yet the doctrinal revisions of the Khrushchev era have been important in rationalizing the Soviet policy of nonviolent competition and widening the framework of permissible techniques.

This is not to suggest that the doctrinal reformulations preceded the new perception of a changing world. It should be clear, moreover, that the specifics of Soviet policy, in or out of the United Nations, are not explicable in ideological terms alone. Like the demand for parity, the *troika* proposition exemplifies a Soviet effort to gain as much as the other powers might concede—a demand fully consistent with, but not predictable solely in terms of, its world view. Political realism, as Moscow sees it, is thus superimposed on ideological commitments. Only the combination of the two can explain the nature and the timing of the Soviet reorganization proposals.

Soviet policy has been capable of crude and unprincipled practicality when the rewards have seemed to warrant it. The traditional commitment to the tenet of *pacta sunt servanda* is not allowed to stand in the way of demands for greater rights due to greater power. The most "principled" insistence on the reality of three power blocs easily yields to a plethora of Soviet formulae for four, five, six, or seven under-secretaries when Hammarskjold's successors are being discussed. Moscow refuses to finance or back U.N. action in the Congo, but simultaneously attempts to dictate U.N. policy there. Soviet opposition to the existing order in the United Nations, Moscow admits at times, is due not to the belief that a *single* group of powers controls the U.N., but that the *wrong* group—"reactionaries" and "monopolists"—does.[16] Soviet insistence on unanimity as a *sine qua non* in the United Nations, which Moscow does not control, contrasts dramatically with its efforts to promote majority rule within the conclave of international Communism, where it does have most member-parties on its side, against Chinese Communist advocacy of unanimity. Even the sacred principle of sovereignty can be suspended when political utility demands it. "Principles," too, in other words, can be weapons in the struggle of systems, in and out of the U.N.

Among the strains of Soviet experience that contribute to the reassessment of strategy is the record of the United Nations itself. The U.N. action in the Congo is a case in point. While on the whole, events inside the U.N. have played a subordinate part in the crystallization of Soviet policies, the Soviet Union's own experience of being a "loser" for over a decade has no doubt reinforced Moscow's inclination to keep the United Nations' power down. The minority position of the Soviet bloc, during the early years, intensified its members' resentment and sense of isolation. Then their collective nonparticipation for a time set them apart even more. While a portion of this gap was bridged in the post-Stalin era, the suspicion that the United Nations was part of the hostile camp remained.

It was, of course, true that the majority of the United Nations —and of the Great Powers—was anti-Communist. With some exertion, the Western powers could usually command a majority of votes—something the U.S.S.R. could not do. At every step, from San Francisco to Korea and Suez, it must have seemed to Moscow that the United States had won out. Even as late as 1960–61, the U.N. was perhaps more indulgent toward the United States—over the U-2 flight and the attempted invasion of Cuba—than it might have been toward other nations. All this did not make the U.N. a "tool of the State Department," as Moscow alleged, but it provided an objective basis for the Soviet claims.

Finally, the Soviet world view contains a strong self-fulfilling element. George F. Kennan, among others, has suggested that Soviet expectation and behavior are bound to engender precisely the sort of response abroad and create just such a dichotomy as Moscow professes to see. In practice, too, many United Nations agencies became "Western" during the formative years, when the

U.S.S.R. refused to take an active part in their work. The realization that this was the case was probably among the reasons for the later change in Soviet tactics—from absence to participation in many, though not all, activities of the U.N.

Nothing would be further from the truth than to suggest that the Soviet Union has been the only culprit at the U.N. In fact, most powers have violated the spirit of the Charter, and many have ignored its letter time and again. Most members have failed to rely on the United Nations as a primary instrument of national policy—and with good reason. All nations have valued the U.N. for what they can get out of it. All states have loyalties transcending those to the U.N. All the Great Powers would refuse to surrender the veto. Others, too, have insisted on keeping the domestic-jurisdiction clause. Rather than entrusting their security to the United Nations, most states have bolstered their defenses or moved to regional-alliance systems. Other countries, too, have at times resisted U.N. regulation of their commerce and have preferred to put their own label on economic aid and exercise direct control over its distribution.

Moscow is right in arguing that if universality is an objective, the absence from the U.N. of Communist China and Germany is hard to defend. It is correct in stressing that "Great Power unanimity" *was* the original presupposition of the United Nations; if it implies the essentiality of agreement, it also spells the impotence of the U.N. when no such consensus exists. Many outside the Soviet bloc have also found the formula of "one state, one vote" in the Assembly highly unrealistic. Many new nations have felt their interests inadequately reflected on the United Nations staff and in the Security Council. Just as the Soviet Union came to look askance at a plain majority principle after its experience in the Assembly, so the United States and the United Kingdom appear to have lost some of their enthusiasm for that body since the accretion of Afro-Asian votes and the loosening of the Latin American bloc have made the Western powers a minority group, too. In its insistence on the imperative of change, the Soviet Union finds a considerable echo among other states, for there are many who—in H. G. Nicholas's words

> have joined the U.N. less to preserve, by mechanisms of law and order, an existing state of affairs, than to effect, by the pressure of their votes and their voices, a change not only in their own circumstances but often in their relation with the rest of the world.[17]

Even in its refusal to think and act in terms of a world community, the Soviet Union is by no means alone. Indeed, a series of studies on the U.N. prompted the conclusion that the idea of universal solidarity of man has not yet penetrated deeply. To use Maurice Bourquin's expression, people the world over "don't *feel* the unity of humankind." [18]

And yet, when all is said and done, the Soviet outlook on the United Nations remains unique in some essential ways. This unique feature is not so much Soviet defiance of the U.N., including its asserted willingness to use force to resist it, as illustrated by the Hungarian episode in 1956, when it ignored the body's verdict—at the same time that other violators of the Charter's spirit after all obeyed the U.N.'s call and stopped before Suez. Other states—notably France—have been known likewise to challenge and ignore the U.N.

The area of uniqueness lies above all in the Soviet view of the historical process and its translation into action. The profound conviction that, in the long run, neutrality and impartiality are impossible or nonexistent vitiates the fundamental assumption on which international organizations such as the United Nations are built. The Communist image of the United Nations as an arena of struggle is not a reluctant recognition of a tragic fact, but an exhilarating ride on the wave of the future.

The Soviet view, in sum, combines a revolutionary outlook with a conservative pursuit of its security and a pragmatic effort to make the most of the complex and shifting United Nations scene.

The hardheadedness of the Soviet approach contrasts strikingly with the fuzzy thinking about the U.N. that has often characterized others abroad. Yet—on this point the record should be convincing—Moscow has made its full share of errors and miscalculations. Soviet policy, Stalin told Anthony Eden in 1945, was "neither as simple as some thought nor as skillful as others believed." [19] Indeed, we have too often mistaken absence of information for absence of conflict or absence of doubt on the Soviet side. We have been too much inclined to endow the masters of the Kremlin with infallible cleverness—and they to an even greater extent have seen a pattern, a design, a purpose, a conspiracy in every move and gesture of the outside world: "There are no accidents."

Soviet analyses and expectations have, in the Khrushchev era, tended to be fairly realistic about power relations, capabilities and vulnerabilities of states. They have permitted Moscow to ignore the United Nations as a decisive obstacle on its path. Indeed, what *could* the U.N. do in the face of overt Soviet hostility? But a substantial lack of realism intervenes when Soviet analysis concerns a pluralistic world. As bipolarity is the natural shape to which, Moscow imagines, the universe tends, the standard Soviet image of the United Nations, too, has been one of two opposites. So long as the facts can be made to fit such formulas, Soviet analysis is simple and often shrewd, even if its view of capitalism and democracy remains hopelessly out of date. But they don't always fit.

It is precisely with regard to neutralism and nonalignment that the Soviet view is apt to go awry. Which way the uncommitted will go when forced by the logic of international strife and Soviet (and American) prodding remains in doubt. But it is clear that the assumption that the ultimate interest of the neutral bloc is on the Soviet side is unwarranted and naïve. Moscow has ignored the fact that the United Nations occupies a far more important place in the thinking and expectations of the developing nations, with regard to their own security and progress, than in the thinking and security of the U.S.S.R.; their view of the U.N.'s welfare and economic activities is far more positive; and their perspective on U.N. financing differs drastically from the Soviet. While on issues such as anticolonialism the Soviet bloc has naturally identified itself with the new nations, Moscow may in fact have begun to realize that the "third" bloc is not necessarily—and surely not yet—to be counted on the Communist side. And it is no doubt at least a subsidiary purpose of the Soviet plan to deprive the United Nations of its ability to compete with the Communists for leadership of the "national-liberation" movement. In the last analysis, the Soviet assumption that the unaligned world—any more than the Western grouping —constitutes a cohesive, homogeneous, lasting bloc is plainly wrong. Whether or not the Communist orbit does, only the future will tell.

THE LIMITS OF LOGIC

The Soviet stand, enunciated in the fall of 1960, and reiterated since, is logical within the framework of Soviet assumptions and objectives. It is, to be sure, more extreme than the view Moscow had previously propounded about the United Nations. Allowing for some improvisations in the actual proposals, it has the virtue that the assumptions behind the *troika* plan remove an area of suppressed ambiguity that, during all these years, has inhered in the Soviet compromise between inward Communist hostility toward and outward identification with the U.N. The view that there exists no just arbiter or administrator above the two major camps revives, almost verbatim, positions voiced in days of greater Soviet candor.

The Soviet formula made little constitutional sense: it would have frozen the balance of three blocs by institutionalizing a haphazard and transient political alignment from which the sovereign member-states might choose to withdraw at some future time. Many borderline states could not easily be put into any of the three categories. The assumption that each of the blocs had unity and permanence was obviously open to serious challenge.[20] Indeed, Soviet insistence on sovereign equality of states seemed to be violated by its plan to give equal weight to nine Communist states, some fifty neutrals, and the forty-odd Western powers and their allies.

Administratively, objections no less weighty were voiced by the United Nations staff itself. The *troika* would have stymied the Secretariat's work and made the use of the U.N. in another Korean or Congolese crisis impossible. But this was at least part of Moscow's purpose.

No elaborate evidence is required to show that Khrushchev has not been willing to tolerate an analogous *ménage à trois* either within the leadership in the Kremlin, or in Soviet industrial management, or in relations among Communist parties. Soviet insistence on tripartite equality and veto in the executive organs conflicts directly with the time-honored Bolshevik administrative principle of *edinonachalie*—unity of authority—which has been reaffirmed on innumerable occasions as "the basic method of operating the Soviet economy and the Soviet state." [21] Since the objective of *edinonachalie* is above all maximum efficiency, one may conclude that the Soviet purpose in opposing it in the United Nations is its reverse.

The political incongruity of the *troika* is well illustrated by Adlai Stevenson's remark that the application of the Soviet plan in the sixteenth century would have produced an organization "in which the administration of international affairs was entrusted to a triumvirate consisting of the Pope, the Sultan, and Martin Luther." [22]

If adopted, the proposals would reduce the United Nations to the highest common denominator of its members' views. Moscow has gone so far as to insist that "the main goal of this organization consists in finding solutions acceptable to *all* its members." [23] That this is no slip of the pen is shown by the recurrence of the theme on a number of occasions since Khrushchev's U.N. speech of September 19, 1959, in which he declared that "only such decisions should be taken in the United Nations that everyone would vote for." When asked, the following year, whether he would let a two-thirds majority of the member states decide whether or not Hammarskjold should stay, Khrushchev replied: "This is not a parliament. It is a forum in which questions should be resolved in such a way as not to endanger the interests of even a single state. . . ." [24]

There is ground to question whether Moscow means quite what it says. While the extension of the unanimity rule to all members of the United Nations is consonant with one strain of Soviet thinking, the *liberum veto* would permit a single member—say, the Union of South Africa—to prevent the adoption of a decision favored by all other states. This clearly would not be welcome to the U.S.S.R. It would be impossible, under the circumstances, to "isolate" any state or bloc of states; yet this is precisely what Soviet spokesmen have time and again called for at the U.N.

What Moscow means, one may surmise, is that its own concurrence—as the leading power of the world, or so it likes to think—should be required at all times and in all organs of the United Nations. Tsarapkin reportedly told Arthur H. Dean in June, 1961, "Never again will any international organization take a vital decision without our consent." But this it cannot say openly, any more than it can afford to ask for a selective extension of the veto to a few favored nations at a time when it courts precisely those countries that would not benefit from such a move.

That the operation of a United Nations in which all of its hundred-odd members would possess a *liberum veto* would be destructive not only of the United Nations but of Soviet interests as well is nowhere better put than in a Soviet critique of the League of Nations. As Grigori Morozov writes in his volume on the U.N., a recent and authoritative Soviet account,

> This impotence of the League flowed, in particular, from the fact that the Covenant required unanimity of all its members for the adoption of all political decisions taken by its Council and Assembly. This harmful pseudo democratism vitiated the role and

responsibility of the several states in the cause of supporting international peace and practically rendered impossible the effective operation of an organization for the maintenance of peace and the prevention of aggression.[25]

An extreme expression of the Soviet view is the contention that the "sovereign" member states need not be bound by what the United Nations says and does. This has been implicit in Khrushchev's references, since mid-1960, to the use of force. Speaking initially about the failure of the Security Council to support the Soviet demands stemming from the U-2 incident, he remarked (on June 3, 1960) that under such circumstances in the future "we have no other way out but to rely on our own strength." At the U.N. that fall, he went further: The Soviet Union would ignore United Nations decisions it deemed incompatible with its own interests. If it did not get its way, it would "uphold our interests outside this international body, outside the United Nations, by relying on our own strength."[26] The final step in this progression came in Khrushchev's speech welcoming President Kwame Nkrumah of Ghana to Moscow in July, 1961:

> Even if all the countries of the world adopted a decision which did not accord with the interests of the Soviet Union and threatened its security, the Soviet Union would not recognize such a decision and would uphold its rights, relying on force. And we have [plenty] to rely on.[27]

What constituted a threat to its security was, of course, at all times up to Moscow to decide. Such strident formulations reveal the extent of Soviet determination to maintain its full freedom of action. Once again, Soviet insistence on "unanimity" and "sovereignty" turns the clock back. The unanimity rule, Nicolas Politis said in 1928, amounts to an admission that "among nations no real organization is possible, for the rule of unanimity may lead to paralysis and anarchy."[28]

Moscow watched with unmitigated enmity the tragic—or pathetic—search for an international authority to deal effectively with forces greater than itself. The United Nations had not been expected to cope with disagreements among the Great Powers, and Moscow vigorously protested Western attempts to shape the U.N. into a serviceable tool in the conflicts between the "two camps." To its mind, what has taken place is an illegal "triple play" from Security Council to General Assembly to Secretariat, as the United States and its allies tried to use one organ after another for their ends. The Council, stymied by the veto, declined in importance and use, and was widely recognized to be unable to do its job.[29] The General Assembly, even under the Uniting-for-Peace Resolution, could not compel compliance with its recommendations; and there were political and constitutional limits to what it could do. Disappointment was widespread—in the Soviet judgment as well as in that of the West.[30] Both the inherent weakness of, and the increased membership in, the General Assembly finally encouraged an expansion of executive power in the U.N. Secretariat—a process likewise furthered by delegation of authority to the Secretary-General by the Security Council.

The United Nations Charter granted its Secretary-General explicitly far more authority than his inconspicuous and apolitical prototype in the League of Nations had possessed. If, in a recurrent pun, the problem of Trygve Lie and Dag Hammarskjold had been whether to be a Secretary or a General, one may claim that, by intent as well as by performance, the top executive of the U.N. has been a marshal rather than a clerk. His office has been not merely administrative but also political—legally, under Article 99; politically, "in response to developing needs."[31] This was one reason why Hammarskjold's death initially left such a glaring void.

Experience shows that there are inherent flaws in the way the Secretariat was conceived. Stalin could choose to ignore the Secretary-General, who, like the Pope, "has no divisions." For the Secretary-General to exercise all the authority of his high office in a crisis often means antagonizing one or more of the Great Powers. The Secretary-General's effectiveness presupposes heir continuous and unanimous trust. Both Lie and Hammarskjold antagonized the Soviet bloc. To have avoided doing o would have meant failing in the fulfillment of their duties.* To put it differently, the more effective the Secretary-General s in strengthening the U.N. itself, the more inevitable the opposition to him—especially on the part of the U.S.S.R.[32]

The necessity to perform political tasks does not make "disinterested" or "objective" service impossible. Dag Hammarskjold put the problem sharply into focus in his Oxford speech, on May 30, 1961: If the demand for neutrality implies that an international public servant cannot take a stand on a political issue, even at the request of the General Assembly or the Security Council, the demand is in conflict with the Charter itself. If, on the other hand, neutrality means that he must remain wholly uninfluenced by national or group interests or ideologies, the obligation to observe such neutrality is just as basic to the Charter as it was in the Covenant of the League.[33]

It has been a matter of honorable tradition and established policy, reiterated over generations, that an international staff, to be fair and effective, must not be imbued with the values and special interests of any one state.† Yet this is precisely what Moscow has challenged. As Walter Lippmann reported on the basis of his interview with Khrushchev,

---

* H. G. Nicholas (p. 155) puts the dilemma effectively: "If the action of one or more of the members violates the Charter, the Secretary-General's duty is clear, but when the time comes, as it must, for healing the breach unless there is to be world war *à outrance*), the Secretary-General's partiality, though it be the partiality of righteousness, is likely to be an offense in the nostrils of the returned prodigal."

† Article 100 of the Charter stipulates that:

1. In the performance of their duties the Secretary-General and the staff shall not seek or receive instructions from any government or from any other authority external to the Organization. They shall refrain from any action which might reflect on their position as international officials responsible only to the Organization.

2. Each member of the United Nations undertakes to respect the exclusively international character of the responsibilities of the Secretary-General and the staff, and not to seek to influence in the discharge of their responsibilities.

the Soviet government has now come to the conclusion that there can be no such thing as an impartial civil servant in this deeply divided world, and that the kind of political celibacy which the British theory of the civil service calls for is in international affairs a fiction.[34]

Beyond a doubt, the *troika* formula does radical violence to the entire U.N. approach, seeking to substitute for a distinguished civil service the crude arithmetic of political patronage.

It may well be that, from the Soviet viewpoint, the Secretary General had gone beyond the original purview of his task. Once more, Moscow stuck to the minimal construction of the U.N.'s role, while the Secretary-General found support for his initiatives in the broad view (expressed, for instance, in the Report of the Preparatory Commission for the United Nations that he, more than anyone else, "must embody the principles and ideals of the Charter."

Moscow objected not only to his arrogation of authority (at the behest of the "imperialists," it would maintain) but also to his philosophy under which the United Nations must be interposed between the major camps and fill the power vacuum wherever it can. In Moscow's reading, this is a pernicious doctrine incompatible with its view of the inevitable course of history. It is this attempt, more than anything else, that identified the Secretary-General, for the Communists, with reaction and that prompted the vigorous expression of Soviet determination not to tolerate efforts that would frustrate potential Communist gains in fluid areas around the globe.

WHERE DO WE GO FROM HERE?

The Soviet Union may at times silence the expression of its belief that ultimately "one or the other must prevail." It has never abandoned the "either-or" approach.

The choice of when to mute and when to trumpet the

extreme formulation of incompatibility is up to Moscow. Even if the outside world can help fortify or provoke a given Soviet response, it can never expect to control it. The Soviet Union may alter at will its readiness to compromise on the organization of the United Nations or its resolve to cooperate on a given task. It cannot be compelled or effectively induced to do so. With some oversimplification, one may conclude that the United Nations is only as much as its least cooperative members want it to be.

The question was raised earlier whether a state committed to objectives at variance with those of the United Nations can—and should—operate in an international body such as the U.N. Sheer logic might well lead one to answer in the negative. In the long run, the contending forces as now defined and inspired may well be unable to coexist. Theoretically, or ultimately, one may indeed maintain that "international organization is hardly compatible with rampant imperialism by one state which seeks hegemony over the world." [35] Yet in the short run—even on the brink of the thermonuclear precipice—restraint from recourse to extremes, retreat from the logical to the political, from incompatibility to coexistence, from the inexorable to the possible, refraining from the *ultima ratio*, remain the essence of power politics. So long as this is true, there is continuing and important room for the United Nations, and for the Soviet Union as part of it, in the duel of our age.

This would be true even if the Soviet long-range objective of controlling the U.N. had greater chances of success than now seems likely. Once its efforts succeeded, of course, the need for the U.N. would promptly disappear, for in the future commonwealth of Communist nations, the United Nations with its present complexion and philosophy can have no place.

The Soviet Union can be expected to pursue its own ends with all the vigor and determination that its "active, aggressive struggle" demands.[36] Soviet policy-makers no doubt realize that their reorganization proposals are not likely to be adopted in their present form. On at least one occasion—the crisis induced by Dag Hammarskjold's death—Moscow has demonstrated that its demands need not always amount to ultimatums. In March 1961, no one would have dared predict that within six months agreement on a successor to the Secretary-General was possible —even as an "interim" solution—without fundamentally modifying the structure and operation of the U.N. The deadlock likely to obtain when U Thant's term expires in April, 1963, may be expected to be fraught with even graver dangers, at a time when the Soviet position promises to be considerably less flexible—unless, once more, broader considerations of policy produce a propitious climate for Soviet moderation unforeseeable today. While various compromise formulas have been suggested in response to the *troika* plan, Moscow has actually allowed itself little room for negotiation or retreat without sacrificing the heart of its proposals—a veto over the activities of the Secretariat. It remains to be seen whether anything short of this will satisfy the U.S.S.R.; it is highly improbable that anything like it will be acceptable to the major non-Communist states.

To this extent, the future of the United Nations is in Soviet hands. Moscow can wreck it or build it up: In the U.N.'s present state, Moscow is unlikely to do either. It is, however, certain to keep the United Nations from taking that giant step that Dag Hammarskjold, in his final months, spoke of as the transition from "institutional systems of international coexistence" to "constitutional systems of international cooperation." That bridge between standing international conference and organized international community, which he saw embodied in the U.N. Charter,[37] is certain to remain unfinished so long as Moscow has the right and the might to interpose its veto.

The Soviet bloc cannot be expected to adopt the philosophy of the U.N. and pursue the objectives of the U.N. As Adlai Stevenson put it to the Senate Foreign Relations Committee on January 18, 1961:

The United Nations—as an idea and as an institution—is an extension of Western ideas; of Western belief in the worth and dignity of the individual; of Western ideology. It is based on a Western parliamentary tradition. Its roots are in the Western idea of representative government. In short, it is thoroughly antitotalitarian.

Indeed, the United Nations is founded on the belief in a measure of perfectibility, gradualism, and consensus. In many respects, its outlook in international affairs is analogous to that of liberal democracy at home. We have been reminded that

> international organization rests upon the belief that man is at liberty, not only to surrender to the operation of the iron laws of the system, or to attempt an apocalyptic leap from an era of determinism into an era of freedom, but to shape his collective destiny in the here and now.[38]

The non-Western nations may, and perhaps will, overwhelmingly come to share these assumptions. The Communist states, as we know them, cannot.

But too much must not be expected, or asked, of the United Nations. It was never intended to clash with a Great Power or to resolve conflicts among them. Philip C. Jessup has realistically justified the veto as the safety valve "that prevents the United Nations from undertaking commitments in the political field which it lacks the power to fulfill." Senator James W. Fulbright has more recently argued that "the history of the United Nations has been in large measure a history of retreat from false hopes and of adjustment to the reality of a divided world. The veto is in fact an accurate reflection of that reality."[39] The United Nations can alter neither the power relations among the states nor the motives of their rulers. This is not an argument against the United Nations: With all its inherent limitations, its uses and values, for all mankind, are many.

The West, and above all the United States, cannot of course

expect the U.N. to "do its job" for it. The tendency occasionally implicit in American action (and inaction) to "let Dag do it" was a characteristic effort to escape responsibility. The Secretary-General himself was aware of it at one time. As he wrote, in a private letter, late in 1956:

> It is one thing that, in the vacuum which suddenly developed in the Suez crisis, I had, for what it was worth, to throw in everything I had to try to tide us over. . . . But it is an entirely different thing, every time the big powers run into a deadlock, to place the problem in the Secretary-General's hands with the somewhat naïve expectation that he can continue to turn up with something. It is a matter of course that a continued use of the office of the Secretary-General in that way sooner or later leads to a point where he must break his neck. . . .[40]

It may well be that Hammarskjold's own conception of the Secretary's office and authority contributed to such extravagant expectations on the part of some member states. His isolation and possible abuse of the Secretary-General's authority are problems that, sooner or later, deserve the most serious consideration. But the immediate task is to keep the U.N. and its Secretariat in effective trim.[41]

If the United States—or any other power—cannot look on the U.N. as a substitute for a dynamic policy of its own, it must not turn its back on it either. No longer is it merely bigots, jingoists, and self-styled superpatriots who rant against the United Nations and American participation in it. Adlai Stevenson has aptly predicted that "the crisis of our loyalty to the United Nations is still ahead of us," as the passing of the majority to the new nations is bound to produce doubts and hesitation and, at times, bitterness as well. Henceforth, unlike in the days of the Korean conflict, the U.S. cannot expect to have the U.N. solidly on its side: The resulting proposals to forge a new and tighter concert of free nations or a cohesive international community endowed with force must be seen as complementary to the United Nations, not antagonistic to it, in conception or in future role.

The United Nations is not, and was never meant to be, an association of the like-minded. John Foster Dulles was once moved to write that the U.N. would be best served

> if its Assembly is representative of what the world actually is, and not merely representative of the parts which we like. Therefore, we ought to be willing that all nations should be members without attempting to appraise closely those which are "good" and those which are "bad." Already this distinction is obliterated by the present membership of the United Nations.[42]

It is essential then not to exaggerate the part the United Nations can perform in solving the awesome problems of our time. Moscow, on its part, does not expect any major impact on its world policy to come from or through the U.N. The roots of conflict lie outside the world organization and extend far beyond it. In this regard, "their" and "our" view is likely to coincide, for, in the words of George F. Kennan,

> it is not fair to the Organization today to ask it to resolve the predicaments of the past as well as of the present. No international organization can be stronger than the structure of relationships among the Great Powers that underlies it; and to look to such an organization to resolve deep-seated conflicts of interest among the Great Powers is to ignore its limitations and to jeopardize its usefulness in other fields.[43]

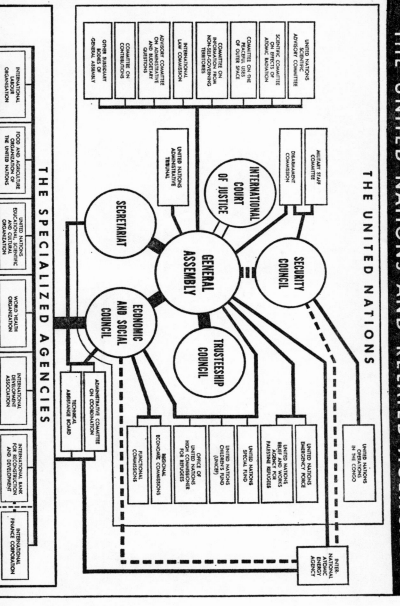

THE UNITED NATIONS AND RELATED AGENCIES

THE UNITED NATIONS

- UNITED NATIONS SCIENTIFIC ADVISORY COMMITTEE
- SCIENTIFIC COMMITTEE ON EFFECTS OF ATOMIC RADIATION
- COMMITTEE ON THE PEACEFUL USES OF OUTER SPACE
- COMMITTEE ON INFORMATION FROM NON-SELF-GOVERNING TERRITORIES
- INTERNATIONAL LAW COMMISSION
- ADVISORY COMMITTEE ON ADMINISTRATIVE AND BUDGETARY QUESTIONS
- COMMITTEE ON CONTRIBUTIONS
- OTHER SUBSIDIARY BODIES OF GENERAL ASSEMBLY

- UNITED NATIONS ADMINISTRATIVE TRIBUNAL
- DISARMAMENT COMMISSION
- MILITARY STAFF COMMITTEE

- INTERNATIONAL COURT OF JUSTICE
- SECRETARIAT
- GENERAL ASSEMBLY
- SECURITY COUNCIL
- ECONOMIC AND SOCIAL COUNCIL
- TRUSTEESHIP COUNCIL

- TECHNICAL ASSISTANCE BOARD
- ADMINISTRATIVE COMMITTEE ON COORDINATION
- FUNCTIONAL COMMISSIONS
- REGIONAL ECONOMIC COMMISSIONS
- OFFICE OF UNITED NATIONS HIGH COMMISSIONER FOR REFUGEES
- UNITED NATIONS CHILDREN'S FUND (UNICEF)
- UNITED NATIONS SPECIAL FUND
- UNITED NATIONS RELIEF AND WORKS AGENCY FOR PALESTINE REFUGEES
- UNITED NATIONS EMERGENCY FORCE
- UNITED NATIONS OPERATIONS IN THE CONGO
- INTERNATIONAL ATOMIC ENERGY AGENCY

THE SPECIALIZED AGENCIES

- INTERNATIONAL LABOUR ORGANISATION
- FOOD AND AGRICULTURE ORGANIZATION OF THE UNITED NATIONS
- UNITED NATIONS EDUCATIONAL, SCIENTIFIC AND CULTURAL ORGANIZATION
- WORLD HEALTH ORGANIZATION
- INTERNATIONAL DEVELOPMENT ASSOCIATION
- INTERNATIONAL BANK FOR RECONSTRUCTION AND DEVELOPMENT
- INTERNATIONAL FINANCE CORPORATION
- INTERNATIONAL

Notes

CHAPTER I

INTERNATIONAL LAW AND INTERNATIONAL ORGANIZATION: THE SOVIET VIEW

1. See Zbigniew Brzezinski, "Communist Ideology and International Affairs," *Journal of Conflict Resolution*, IV, No. 3 (September, 1960).
2. See Irene Blumenthal, "The Soviet Union and the United Nations" (MS), Chapter I.
3. Lazar Kaganovich, at the Institute of Soviet Construction and Law of the Communist Academy, 1929; cited in Ivo Lapenna, *Conceptions soviétiques de droit international public* (Paris, 1954), p. 36.
4. See *Sovetskoe gosudarstvo i pravo* (Moscow), particularly, 1951, No. 6; 1952, No. 7; 1954, No. 6; and Grigori Tunkin, "Coexistence and International Law," III (1958), *Recueil des Cours* (Academy of International Law, The Hague), 60, 72. On the Chinese Communist position, see *Sovetskii ezhegodnik mezhdunarodnogo prava*, 1958 (Moscow, 1959), pp. 544–48.
5. Nikita Khrushchev, Speech before the General Assembly, September 18, 1959.
6. See John N. Hazard, *Law and Social Change in the USSR* (London, 1953), p. 300; F. Kozhevnikov, *Sovetskoe gosudarstvo*

i mezhdunarodnoe pravo (Moscow, 1949), p. 24; V. F. Generalov, "Ob osnovnykh chertakh mezhdunarodno-pravovogo sotrudnichestva Sovetskogo Soiuza i stran narodnoi demokratii," *Sovetskoe gosudarstvo i pravo,* No. 7 (1950).

7. See John N. Hazard, "Le droit soviétique et le dépérissement de l'état," *Travaux et Conférences* (Université de Bruxelles, Faculté de Droit), VIII (1960), 99–100.

8. Jan Triska, "What Price Cooperation?" (Doctoral dissertation, Harvard University, 1956), pp. 163ff.

9. S. Sanakoyev, "The Basis of the Relations Between the Socialist Countries," *International Affairs* (Moscow), No. 7 (1958), pp. 23–24; and E. Korovin, "Proletarian Internationalism in World Relations," *ibid.,* No. 2 (1958), pp. 25–27. (*International Affairs* is the English-language edition of the authoritative Soviet monthly *Mezhdunarodnaia zhizn'.*) See also E. G. Panfilov, "Marksizm-Leninizm o demokraticheskom i spravedlivom mire," *Voprosy filosofi,* No. 4 (1958); L. Vasil'ev, "K voprosu o vneshnikh funktsiiakh sotsialisticheskogo gosudarstva," *Sovetskoe gosudarstvo i pravo,* No. 6 (1958); D. B. Levin, *Osnovnye problemy sovremennogo mezhdunarodnogo prava* (Moscow, 1958), pp. 28–39.

10. Tunkin, p. 26; and G. I. Tunkin, "Novyi tip mezhdunarodnykh otnoshenii i mezhdunarodnoe pravo," *Sovetskoe gosudarstvo i pravo,* No. 1 (1959), pp. 92–94. See also Curt Gasteyger, "Neue Entwicklungen im sowjetischen Völkerrecht," *Jahrbuch für Ostrecht* (Munich), II, No. 1 (May, 1961).

11. See Hazard, *Law and Social Change,* pp. 275–95. For a sophisticated commentary on the Soviet view, see Hans Kelsen, *The Communist Theory of Law* (New York, 1955), pp. 148–92.

12. Levin, p. 12.

13. See, for instance, Elliot R. Goodman, *The Soviet Design for a World State* (New York, 1960). See also pp. 48–49 of this study.

14. Blumenthal, Chapter I. On the "superstructural" and "class" character of international law, see Akademiia nauk, Institut prava, *Mezhdunarodnoe pravo* (Moscow, 1957), pp. 3, 6.

15. Vladislav Ribnikar, replying to Julian Huxley, at the first UNESCO General Conference; and *Uchitel'skaia gazeta* (Moscow), January 20, 1951; cited in John A. Armstrong, "The Soviet Attitude toward UNESCO," *International Organization,* May 1954, pp. 218–19, 232.

16. Inis L. Claude, Jr., *Swords into Plowshares* (New York, 1958), p. 139.

17. Oliver J. Lissitzyn, "Recent Soviet Literature on International Law," *American Slavic and East European Review,* December, 1952, pp. 262–63; and J. Frankel, "The Soviet Union and the

United Nations," *The Year Book of World Affairs 1954* (New York, 1954), pp. 70–73.

18. See, e.g., Eugene Korovin's article in *Bol'shaia sovetskaia entsiklopediia* (2d ed.; Moscow, 1954), XXVII, 23.

19. See, e.g., C. Dale Fuller, "Soviet Policy in the United Nations," *Annals of the American Academy of Political and Social Science*, Vol. 263 (May, 1949), p. 141.

20. Rupert Emerson and Inis L. Claude, Jr., "The Soviet Union and the United Nations," *International Organization*, February, 1952, pp. 1–26.

21. Fuller, pp. 143–44; Lissitzyn, p. 263; Lapenna, p. 297.

CHAPTER II

THE SOVIET UNION AND INTERNATIONAL ORGANIZATION: THE ANTECEDENTS

1. See C. Dale Fuller, "Lenin's Attitude Toward an International Organization for the Maintenance of Peace, 1914–1919" (Russian Institute Certificate Essay, Columbia University, 1948).

2. The First Congress of the Comintern in 1919 called the League a "holy alliance of the bourgeoisie for the suppression of the proletarian revolution." In his "Theses on the National and Colonial Question," submitted to the Second Comintern Congress the following year, Lenin wrote: "The so-called League of Nations is nothing but an insurance policy in which the victors mutually guarantee each other their prey."

3. "It has been proved, therefore, that the League of Nations actually does not exist, that the union of capitalist powers is simply a deception, and that it represents two vultures trying to tear the prey from each other." (Lenin in October, 1920, on Franco-British disagreements.) See Xenia Eudin and Harold H. Fisher (eds.), *Soviet Russia and the West, 1920–1927* (Stanford, 1957), pp. 121–22, 152.

4. Paul Miliukov, *La politique extérieure des Soviets* (Paris, 1934), goes so far as to entitle his chapter on the mid-twenties "L'anti-Ligue."

5. Alexander Barmine, *One Who Survived* (New York, 1945), p. 117.

6. Cited in Miliukov, p. 304.

7. See Kathryn W. Davis, *The Soviets at Geneva* (Geneva, 1934), p. 7.

8. Iu. Kliuchnikov and A. Sabanin, *Mezhdunarodnaia politika* . . . (Moscow, 1929), III, 238.

9. Henry L. Roberts, "Maxim Litvinov," in G. E. Craig and F. Gilbert (eds.), *The Diplomats: 1919–1939* (Princeton, N.J., 1953), pp. 346–49; and Louis Fischer, *Men and Politics* (New York, 1941), p. 147.

10. I. V. Stalin, *Sochineniia* (Moscow, 1951), XIII, 280.

11. Jane Degras (ed.), *Soviet Documents on Foreign Policy, 1917–1941* (London, 1953), III, 92–93.

12. Cited in Timothy A. Taracouzio, *War and Peace in Soviet Diplomacy* (New York, 1940), p. 195.

13. I. F. Ivashin, *Bor'ba SSSR za mir i bezopasnost' narodov* (Moscow, 1958), p. 7. (Italics added.) See also V. Zorin, "Leninskie printsipy vneshnei politiki SSSR," *Kommunist* (Moscow), No. 6 (1960), p. 143.

14. *Izvestiia,* June 26, 1959. See also O. Afanas'eva, *Kratkii ocherk istorii Ligi Natsii* (Moscow, 1945), pp. 11, 38.

15. G. I. Morozov, *Organizatsiia Ob'edinennykh Natsii* (Moscow, 1960), p. 11.

16. Now it was again called the "League of Warmongers." (P. Lisovsky, *Liga podzhigatelei voiny,* Moscow, 1940.)

17. Herbert Feis, *Churchill, Roosevelt, Stalin* (Princeton, N.J., 1957).

18. This theme is developed in Irene Blumenthal's "The Soviet Union and the United Nations," Chapter IV.

19. Soviet memorandum to the United States Department of State, "The International Security Organization," August 12, 1944. See Leland M. Goodrich, *The United Nations* (New York, 1959), p. 23; and Ruth B. Russell *et al., A History of the United Nations Charter* (Washington, D. C., 1958), pp. 393–422.

20. Edward Stettinius, *Roosevelt and the Russians* (Garden City, N.Y., 1949), p. 112.

21. N. Malinin, "Mezhdunarodnaia organizatsiia bezopasnosti," *Zvedza* (Moscow), No. 4 (1944); *The New York Times,* August 6 and 15, 1944; Frederick C. Barghoorn, *The Soviet Image of the United States* (New York, 1950), p. 98.

22. Robert Sherwood, *Roosevelt and Hopkins* (New York, 1948), pp. 854–57.

23. Winston Churchill, *Triumph and Tragedy* (Boston, 1953), pp. 356–57.

24. James F. Byrnes, *Speaking Frankly* (New York, 1947), p. 37.

25. Sherwood, pp. 875–76, 910–12. See also Herbert Feis, *Between War and Peace,* Princeton, N.J., 1960), pp. 86–123.

26. M. Nikolaev, "France and the San Francisco Conference," *War and the Working Class* (Moscow), March 15, 1945, p. 11.

CHAPTER III

THE SOVIET UNION IN THE UNITED NATIONS: THE FIRST DECADE

1. Stalin, interview with Associated Press correspondent Eddie Gilmore, March 10, 1946. See also Richard Van Wagenen, *The Iranian Case* (New York, 1952).
2. *New Times* (Moscow), No. 1 (1947), p. 1.
3. Sergei Samarsky, *Bor'ba Sovetskogo Soiuza v OON za mir i bezopasnost' narodov* (Moscow, 1956), p. 13.
4. The subsequent Soviet votes against the Indonesia settlement were apparently intended to embarrass the West by charging that United States and Netherlands interests continued to maintain a "stranglehold" on the Indonesian economy and, hence, politics. See also J. F. Collins, "United Nations and Indonesia," *International Conciliation*, No. 459 (1950).
5. See, e.g., Josef Korbel, "The Kashmir Dispute and the United Nations," *International Organization*, May, 1949.
6. See Oles Smolansky, "The Soviet Union and the Arab States, 1947–1957" (Doctoral Dissertation, Columbia University, 1959).
7. Triska, p. 291. See also Philip E. Mosely, "Soviet Policy in the United Nations," *Proceedings* of the Academy of Political Science, XXII (January, 1947), 28–37.
8. This point has been made, among others, by Hans J. Morgenthau, *Politics Among Nations* (New York, 1956), p. 450; and Lincoln P. Bloomfield, *Evolution or Revolution?* (Cambridge, Mass., 1957), p. 14.
9. United Nations Conference on International Organization, *Documents* . . . (London, 1945), I, 619; also VII, 263–64. See also Hans Kelsen, "Withdrawal from the United Nations," *Western Political Quarterly*, March, 1948.
10. While there is no specific information on the U.N. issue, the left-right feud over general Communist strategy in 1947–48 is well substantiated.
11. *Izvestiia*, January 29, 1949.
12. See also Harold K. Jacobson, "The Soviet Union, the U.N. and World Trade," *Western Political Quarterly*, September, 1958, p. 681.
13. Leopold Laufer, "Soviet and American Domestic Propaganda on the U.N. Unanimity Principle" (Russian Institute Certificate Essay, Columbia University, 1951), p. 89.

14. *Bol'shaia sovetskaia entsiklopediia* (2d ed.; Moscow, 1955), XXXI, 145.

15. E.g., Andrei Vyshinsky, speeches of November 8, 1951 (General Assembly) and January 12, 1952 (Political Committee), in his *Voprosy mezhdunarodnogo prava i mezhdunarodnoi politiki* (Moscow, 1952), III, 24, 320.

16. Emerson and Claude, pp. 14, 25–26.

17. Trygve Lie, pp. 229, 267.

18. For varying views of the Korean problem, see Allen Whiting, *China Crosses the Yalu* (New York, 1960); Leland Goodrich, *Korea* (New York, 1956); and Leon Gordenker, *The United Nations and the Peaceful Unification of Korea* (The Hague, 1959).

19. *The New York Times*, February 17, 1951.

20. See Chapter IX, pp. 115–17, and Alexander Dallin, "The Soviet Stake in Eastern Europe," *Annals of the American Academy of Political and Social Science*, Vol. 317 (May, 1958), 142–43.

21. *Bol'shaia* . . . XXXI, 144 and 146.

22. V. N. Durdenevsky and S. B. Krylov (eds.), *Organizatsiia Ob'edinennykh Natsii: Sbornik dokumentov* (Moscow, 1956), p. 3.

23. V. Kamenev and I. Korin, "The Results of the 10th Session of the General Assembly," *International Affairs*, No. 1 (1956), pp. 27–40.

24. M. Baturin, "The 11th Session of the U.N. General Assembly," *ibid.*, No. 1 (1957), p. 108.

25. See *International Affairs*, No. 6 (1956), pp. 157–60, and No. 10, p. 109; A. V. Topchiev, "Vsemirnaia Federatsiia Assotsiatsii Sodeistviia OON," *Mezhdunarodnyi politiko-ekonomicheskii ezhegodnik 1959* (Moscow, 1959), pp. 461–67. Topchiev, a prominent academician, has been chairman of the Soviet Association. It has been represented abroad by respected figures of academic rather than strictly political reputation.

26. E. A. Korovin, "Sovetskii Soiuz i sozdanie Organizatsii Ob'edinennykh Natsii," in *Voprosy vneshnei politiki SSSR i sovremennykh mezhdunarodnykh otnoshenii* (Moscow, 1958), pp. 61–68.

CHAPTER IV

CONSTITUTION AND POLITICS: SOME KEY PROBLEMS

1. General Assembly, *Official Records,* 4th session, pp. 232ff. (November 19, 1949); *Soviet Studies,* III (1951–52), 348–49; Blumenthal, Chapters II–III. See also Lidiia Modzhorian, *Sub"-ekty mezhdunarodnogo prava* (Moscow, 1958).
2. V. V. Evgen'ev, "Pravosub'ektnost', suverenitet i nevmeshatel'-stvo," *Sovetskoe gosudarstvo i pravo,* No. 2 (1955), p. 75. On the evolution of Soviet doctrine, see also Jean-Yves Calvez, *Droit international et souveraineté en URSS* (Paris, 1953), and Timothy A. Taracouzio, *The Soviet Union and International Law* (New York, 1935).
3. Leonard Schapiro, "Soviet Participation in International Institutions," *The Year Book of World Affairs, 1949,* p. 206. See also Bernard Demay, "L'URSS et l'Organisation Internationale" (Doctoral Thesis, Paris University, 1951), Chapter XVII.
4. See Jan F. Triska and Robert M. Slusser, "Treaties and Other Sources of Order in International Relations: The Soviet View," *American Journal of International Law,* 1958, pp. 699–726; and Lissitzyn, pp. 261–62.
5. According to Harold K. Jacobson, the Soviet Union tried to limit the work of the Subcommission on Devastated Areas to materials submitted by the government concerned and proposed a requirement that all sections of its report be approved by the government to which they referred.
6. A chapter in Samarsky's volume is entitled, "The Struggle of the Soviet Union in the United Nations in Defense of the Sovereignty and Independence of Peoples."
7. See the forthcoming volume, "The Soviet Union and the United Nations Economic and Social Work," by Harold K. Jacobson (based on his Doctoral Dissertation, Yale University, 1955).
8. Nikolai Poliansky, *Mezhdunarodnyi sud* (Moscow, 1951), p. 4. See also Hazard, pp. 297–99; Calvez, pp. 255–59; Levin, p. 88. The Soviet Union takes pride in having resisted attempts, at San Francisco, to give the International Court of Justice compulsory jurisdiction. (R. L. Bobrov and S. A. Malinin, *Organizatsiia Ob'edinennykh Natsii* [Leningrad, 1960], p. 9.)
9. S. B. Krylov, *Mezhdunarodnyi sud Organizatsii Ob'edinennykh Natsii* (Moscow, 1958), pp. 4, 163–64.

10. *Iuridicheskii slovar'* (2d ed.; Moscow, 1956), I, 573. This has not prevented Soviet approval of specific ICJ decisions. Thus the Soviet Union welcomed those parts of the decision in the Inter-handel case that affirmed "the priority, under specific circumstances, of domestic national jurisdiction over the international." (F. I. Kozhevnikov, "Nekotorye iuridicheskie voprosy v deiatel'-nosti Mezhdunarodnogo Sud za 1959g.," *Sovetskoe gosudarstvo i pravo*, No. 3 [1960].)

11. See Goodman, *Soviet Design.* This opposition has extended both to unfriendly states (such as the *cordon sanitaire* between the wars) and to other members of the "socialist camp" (such as the Yugoslav-Bulgarian federation schemes of 1947–48). "United Europe" plans are described as masking imperialist plans "of enslaving peoples and preparing aggressive war" (Vsevolod Kniazhinsky, *Proval planov "ob'edineniia Evropy"* [Moscow, 1958], p. 192).

12. Julius Stone, "Law, Force and Survival," *Foreign Affairs*, July, 1961, p. 552.

13. See, for instance, Fuller, p. 147; Levin, p. 167; Walter Meder, "Die Stellung der Sowjetunion zur UNO," *Jahrbuch für internationales und ausländisches öffentliches Recht* (Hamburg, 1949), p. 764. But see also Chapter IX of this study.

14. Bol'shaia sovetskaia entsiklopediia, *Ezhegodnik 1957* (Moscow, 1957), pp. 480ff.

15. O. Grinyov, "Who Wants an International Police Force?" *International Affairs*, No. 12 (1958), pp. 63–67.

16. See, e.g., a monograph devoted to the veto: Nikolai Ushakov, *Printsip edinoglasiia velikikh derzhav v Organizatsii Ob'edinennykh Natsii* (Moscow, 1956), p. 4.

17. Ivan Ivashin, *Ocherki istorii vneshnei politiki SSSR* (Moscow, 1958), p. 428.

18. Speech of October 10, 1950; Emerson and Claude, pp. 7, 9. An early analysis of the problem is Abramo Organski, "The Veto as Viewed by the United States and the Soviet Union" (Doctoral Dissertation, New York University, 1951).

19. *The New York Times*, November 25, 1948.

20. "He who raises his hand against the principle of unanimity . . . raises it against the very existence of the United Nations." (*New Times*, No. 42 [1948], p. 5.) "The crude guillotine of [majority] voting . . . would be a real threat to the principle of sovereignty." (I. D. Levin, "Problema suvereniteta v ustave OON," *Sovetskoe gosudarstvo i pravo*, No. 1 (1947), p. 18.) See also *International Affairs*, No. 7 (1959), p. 90; and *ibid.*, No. 8 (1960), p. 75.

21. E.g., Durdenevsky and Krylov, p. 3.

22. Triska, p. 402.
23. Ushakov, p. 60.
24. *International Affairs*, No. 9 (1959), p. 18.
25. *Mezhdunarodnyi politiko-ekonomicheskii ezhegodnik 1959* (Moscow, 1959), p. 441.
26. Bobrov and Malinin, p. 32.
27. *The New York Times*, October 14, 1960. See also G. Morozov, "Organizatsiia Ob'edinennykh Natsii i zadachi sokhraneniia mira," *Mirovaia ekonomika i mezhdunarodnye otnosheniia*, No. 10 (1960), p. 18.
28. Khrushchev, before the General Assembly, October 20, 1960.
29. For the Soviet position, see S. Borisov [pseud. of S. B. Krylov], "Protiv proektov peresmotra ustava OON," *Sovetskoe gosudarstvo i pravo*, No. 6 (1955); *International Affairs*, No. 1 (1956), pp. 38–39; *ibid.*, No. 7 (1957), p. 110. One of the purposes of the Durdenevsky-Krylov collection of documents (1956) was to show that there existed no need for Charter revision. For the various proposals submitted, see Francis O. Wilcox and Carl M. Marcy, *Proposals for Changes in the United Nations* (Washington, D.C., 1955). G. I. Morozov (*Organizatsiia Ob'edinennykh Natsii* [Moscow, 1960]) devotes his entire Chapter II to an "exposé" of alleged violations of, and plans to revise, the Charter.
30. V. Kopal and I. Mrázek, *Otázka revise Charty OSH* (Prague, 1957); reviewed in *International Affairs*, No. 1 (1958), pp. 114–15.
31. E.g., *International Affairs*, No. 7 (1957), pp. 109–10; Bol'shaia sovetskaia entsiklopediia, *Ezhegodnik 1957*, p. 481; *The New York Times*, November 3 and 11 and December 7, 1960.
32. *Izvestiia*, June 26, 1959; *International Affairs*, No. 1 (1957), p. 98; No. 11 (1957), p. 115; No. 8 (1960), p. 72; and No. 9 (1960), p. 61. See also Chapter IX of this study, pp. 122–24.
33. See Quincy Wright, *International Law and the United Nations* (New York, 1960), pp. 26–27.

CHAPTER V

SPECIALIZED AGENCIES

1. Cited in Arthur U. Pope, *Maxim Litvinov* (New York, 1943), p. 18.
2. Ruth Russell *et al.*, p. 422.
3. This is also the conclusion of Harold K. Jacobson in his valuable

unpublished study "The Soviet Union and the United Nations Economic and Social Work," in which he shows that the Soviet Union initially strove to demote the specialized agencies to a status similar to nongovernmental organizations, recognized by the U.N. but not a part of it. Bobrov and Malinin, p. 56, state in 1960 that the specialized agencies "continue actually to be outside the U.N." See also Raymond Dennett and Joseph E. Johnson (eds.), *Negotiating with the Russians* (Boston, 1951). I am obliged to Professor Jacobson for insights throughout the balance of this chapter.

4. Vyshinsky, pp. 90–91 (speech before the Political Committee, November 30, 1951). See also *New Times*, No. 13 (1950), p. 10. The U.S.S.R. expressed little interest in the numerous nongovernmental organizations with consultative status with the U.N. Communist states backed six groups for such status, and four were accepted: the Women's International Democratic Federation, World Federation of Democratic Youth, International Association of Democratic Lawyers, and International Organization of Journalists.

5. Trygve Lie, p. 304.

6. See John A. Armstrong, "The Soviet Attitude Toward UNESCO," *International Organization*, May, 1954, e.g., p. 222.

7. *Mezhdunarodnyi politiko-ekonomicheskii ezhegodnik 1958* (Moscow, 1958), p. 548. The United States does indeed have a major role in the activities of the International Monetary Fund, the World Bank, and the IFC.

8. "Readers' Questions Answered," *International Affairs*, No. 4 (1961), pp. 119–30.

9. Bobrov and Malinin, p. 64. See also V. Demidov, "The United Nations," *International Affairs*, No. 8 (1960), pp. 78–79.

10. See Harold K. Jacobson, "Labor, the UN and the Cold War," *International Organization*, February, 1957, pp. 66–67; and his "The USSR and ILO," *ibid.*, August, 1960; and E. John O'Rosky, "The Attitude of the Soviet Union during the United Nations Discussion of the WFTU, 1945–1946" (Russian Institute Certificate Essay, Columbia University, 1953). See also Alfred Fernbach, *Soviet Coexistence Strategy: A Case Study of Experience in the International Labor Organization* (Washington, D.C., 1960.)

11. *New Times*, No. 13 (1950), p. 10.

12. V. Zagladin, "Window on UNESCO," *New Times*, No. 23 (1960), and the reply by UNESCO Director-General Vittorino Veronese, *ibid.*, No. 35 (1960).

13. M. Negin, *Organizatsiia Ob'edinennykh Natsii . . . (Iunesko)* (Moscow, 1959), pp. 84, 99–104.

14. Soviet commentaries insist that the Charter provisions regarding standards of living, full employment, social progress, health, and human rights (Article 55) involve no infringement of sovereignty of member states. See, e.g., Akademiia nauk SSSR, Institut mirovoi ekonomiki i mezhdunarodnykh otnoshenii, *Mezhdunarodnye ekonomicheskie organizatsii* (Moscow, 1960), p. 35.

15. See David Wightman, "East-West Cooperation and the UN Economic Commission for Europe," *International Organization*, February, 1957.

16. See, e.g., Alvin Z. Rubinstein, "An Analysis of Soviet Policy in the Economic and Social Council . . . 1946–1951" (Doctoral Dissertation, University of Pennsylvania, 1954), pp. 245ff., which argues that Soviet refusal to support economic recovery schemes was due to an effort to keep Western influence out of Eastern Europe and the U.S.S.R., and to a belief in the imminence of a depression in the West, which would lead to an American economic withdrawal. On ECAFE, see Alvin Z. Rubinstein, "Soviet Policy in ECAFE," *International Organization*, November, 1958; and *International Affairs*, No. 5 (1960), pp. 64–67.

17. *Mezhdunarodnye ekonomicheskie organizatsii*, p. 27.

18. E. g., *International Affairs*, No. 10 (1956), p. 16. The prestige gains Moscow expected to derive are illustrated by the random report of 136 Indian engineers and 150 operatives of the Bhilai steel mill going to the Soviet Union for study under the U.N. technical assistance program (*Manchester Guardian*, February 15, 1958).

19. See Joseph S. Berliner, *Soviet Economic Aid* (New York, 1958); and Robert Loring Allen, "United Nations Technical Assistance: Soviet and East European Participation," *International Organization*, November, 1957, p. 630.

20. Bobrov and Malinin, p. 66.

CHAPTER VI

DISARMAMENT

1. Richard J. Barnet, *Who Wants Disarmament?* (Boston, 1960), p. 61.

2. *Sovetskoe gosudarstvo i revoliutsiia prava*, No. 2 (1930), p. 168.

3. *Ibid.*, No. 2 (1931), p. 172; cited in Lapenna, p. 290.

4. *Sovetskoe gosudarstvo i revoliutsiia prava*, No. 2 (1930), p. 163.

See also Kommunisticheskaia Akademiia, Institut mirovogo khoziaistva i mirovoi politiki, *"Razoruzhenie"—podgotovka voiny* (Moscow, 1932).

5. *The Sixth Congress of the Communist International* (Moscow, 1928), p. 37. See also Elliot R. Goodman, pp. 300–1.

6. For Soviet accounts of the disarmament efforts in this period, see Eugene Korovin, "The U.S.S.R. and Disarmament," *International Conciliation*, No. 292 (September, 1933); and V. M. Khaitsman, *SSSR i problema razoruzheniia* (Moscow, 1959). See also Maxim Litvinov, *Against Aggression* (New York, 1939).

7. For a perceptive analysis of the Soviet record with regard to atomic-energy negotiations, primarily in the Stalin era, see Joseph L. Nogee, *Soviet Policy Toward International Control of Atomic Energy* (Notre Dame, Ind., 1961). See also United States Senate, Subcommittee on Disarmament, *Control and Reduction of Armaments: Final Report* (Washington, D.C., 1958).

8. Philip Noël-Baker, *The Arms Race* (New York, 1960), pp. 8–9. On the initial Soviet reversal regarding the International Atomic Energy Agency, see John G. Stoessinger, "Atoms for Peace," in Commission to Study the Organization of Peace, *Organizing Peace in the Nuclear Age* (New York, 1959). By 1960, Moscow was arguing that United States insistence on free inspection by the IAEA was tantamount to " 'legal espionage' under the flag of an international organization." (F. Polomsky, "Espionage Under a New Guise," *International Affairs*, No. 8 [1960], p. 89.) When, on October 3, 1961, the annual conference of the IAEA elected Dr. Arne Eklund of Sweden as its new Director-General, the Soviet Union staged a new boycott. Once again, the frustration of its insistence on a non-Westerner, or on a collective *troika*, to direct the Agency, coincided with the new "toughness" in Soviet policy, to illustrate Soviet willingness to join and leave even such prestige bodies as the IAEA on a come-and-go basis. For the evolving Soviet view, see the articles of Vasili Yemelianov, then chairman of the Soviet delegation and a noted academician, in *Izvestiia*, August 6, and in *New Times*, No. 36 (September 6, 1961). See also George Ginsburgs, "Soviet Atomic Energy Agreements," *International Organization*, February, 1961.

9. League of Nations, Preparatory Commission for the Disarmament Conference, *Documents*, Series V (Geneva, 1928), p. 12.

10. Khrushchev, speech of October 20, 1960. It is quoted here and hereinafter from the translation in *Current Digest of the Soviet Press*, XII, No. 42, 3–14.

11. A. L. Horelick, "Deterrence and Surprise Attack in Soviet Strategic Thought," The RAND Corporation, 1960; cited by Donald S. Zagoria, in *Problems of Communism*, March–April, 1961, p. 3.

12. *International Affairs,* No. 4 (1960), p. 46.
13. While Khrushchev was eager to assure Adlai Stevenson and other Americans that he thought the United States could afford to disarm, Communist journals soon "clarified" that "nothing can stop the decline" of capitalism. (See, e. g., J. L. Schmidt, "Have Marxists Revised Their Views on Capitalism?" *World Marxist Review,* October, 1959.)
14. *Kommunist* (Moscow), No. 2 (1961), p. 122.
15. Cited in United States Senate, Subcommittee on Disarmament, "Disarmament Developments, Spring 1960," *Hearings,* June 10, 1960 (Washington, D.C., 1960), p. 16.
16. *Pravda,* June 13, 1960. See also *Kommunist,* No. 12 (1960), p. 12; and *Trud,* July 7, 1960. For other aspects of the Sino-Soviet controversy, see pp. 164–72 of this study.
17. N. S. Khrushchev, "For New Victories for the World Communist Movement," *World Marxist Review,* January 1961, pp. 16–17. For variant formulas, see his speech of October 20, 1960, and the draft Program of the CPSU, June, 1961.
18. *The New York Times,* June 22, 1961.
19. *Ibid.,* July 9, 1961.
20. This point is well argued by Malcolm Mackintosh and Harry T. Willets in Louis Henkin (ed.), *Arms Control: Issues for the Public* (American Assembly, 1961), pp. 141–73.
21. For a persuasive discussion of the relevant Soviet fears, see Barnet, pp. 88–90.
22. See, for instance, the issue of *Daedalus* on arms control (Fall, 1960); Thomas C. Schelling, *Strategy of Conflict* (Cambridge, Mass., 1960); and Jerome Wiesner, "Inspection for Disarmament," in Henkin, *op. cit.*
23. See, e. g., Henkin, pp. 153–54.
24. See Chapter XI, pp. 154–55.

CHAPTER VII

THE DOMESTIC IMAGE OF THE UNITED NATIONS

1. This point has been persuasively restated by Philip E. Mosely in his "Soviet Myths and Realities," *Foreign Affairs,* April 1961, p. 349.
2. Laufer, pp. 93–94.
3. In addition to the publication of some U.N. documents, the Soviet output included a volume of "Materials for the History of the United Nations," edited by S. B. Krylov (Moscow, 1949); no

further installments appeared. Other exceptions to the lack of attention were two studies of the Trusteeship System (by Boris Shtein, a veteran diplomat-scholar, and B. M. Shurshalov) and two on the International Court of Justice (by Krylov and Nikolai Poliansky).

For the most extensive Soviet listing of publications on international law and organization, see V. N. Durdenevsky (ed.), *Sovetskaia literatura po mezhdunarodnomu pravu; bibliografiia 1917–1957* (Moscow, 1959). A valuable English-language survey of Soviet publications on the United Nations is Alvin Z. Rubinstein, "Selected Bibliography of Soviet Works on the United Nations, 1946–1959," *American Political Science Review*, December, 1960, pp. 985–91.

To the above should be added five unpublished dissertations: U. Dzhekebaev, on the competence of the Security Council and General Assembly in the peaceful settlement of disputes (Academy of Sciences, Institute of Law, 1958); S. A. Ivanov, on the "principle of sovereign equality" and "its violation by American imperialists" (Academy of Sciences, Institute of Law, 1952); I. Kovach, on international arbitration and the World Court (Institute of International Relations, 1957); Kh. A. Sarkisov, on "Great Power unanimity" in the Security Council (Faculty of International Law of the Academy of Social Sciences, 1951); and A. T. Uustal, "The Struggle of the U.S.S.R. in the U.N. for Peace and Security of Peoples" (Tartu State University, 1949).

4. In 1955, G. P. Zadorozhnyi, *Organizatsiia Ob'edinennykh Natsii i mezhdunarodnaia bezopasnost'* (Moscow, 1955); in 1956, the pamphlets by Samarsky and Ushakov cited earlier; in 1957, A. P. Movchan, *OON i mirnoe sosushchestvovanie* (Moscow, 1957), and a brief account by a Ukrainian delegate to the General Assembly, Vera Bilai, *Na XI sessii Gen. Asamblei . . . notatki delegata* (Kiev, 1957); and in 1958, G. P. Zadorozhnyi, *OON i mirnoe sosushchestvovanie gosudarstv* (Moscow, 1958). Most of these were originally delivered as public lectures.

5. Anatoli Protopopov, *Sovetskii soiuz v Organizatsii Ob'edinennykh Natsii* (Moscow, 1957).

6. *International Affairs*, No. 12 (1956), p. 98.

7. *International Affairs*, No. 1 (1957), p. 160.

8. E. g., Bol'shaia sovetskaia entsiklopediia, *Ezhegodnik 1957* and annually thereafter; and *Mezhdunarodnyi politiko-ekonomicheskii ezhegodnik 1958* and annually thereafter. See also the yearbook of international law, *Sovetskii ezhegodnik mezhdunarodnogo prava*, published since 1958.

9. *Mezhdunarodnyi politiko-ekonomicheskii ezhegodnik 1959* (Moscow, 1959), pp. 571–80.

10. Akademiia nauk SSSR, Institut mirovoi ekonomiki i mezhdu-narodnykh otnoshenii, *Mezhdunarodnye ekonomicheskie organizatsii* (Moscow, 1960).

11. The series includes volumes by V. Vladimirov on ILO, M. Negin on UNESCO, B. Ganiushkin on WHO, I. Ornatsky *et al.* on FAO, and E. A. Shibaeva on international transportation and communications agencies. An earlier volume by V. Larin dealt with the IAEA (1957). M. N. Shmygov, at the Byelorussian State University in Minsk, has written on the Trusteeship Council; some popular pamphlets in Georgian were published in Tbilisi; but otherwise few provincial publications on the U.N. have appeared.

12. V. Demidov, "The United Nations," *International Affairs*, No. 8 (1960), pp. 72–80, ostensibly "published in reply to a request from readers."

13. R. L. Bobrov and S. A. Malinin, *Organizatsiia Ob'edinennykh Natsii* (Leningrad, 1959, 1960); and G. I. Morozov, *Organizatsiia Ob'edinennykh Natsii (k 15-letiiu Ustava OON)* (Moscow, 1960). Considering the large number of copies of other "scientific-popular" writings of comparable format, the editions of these two (4,500 and 10,000 copies respectively) are rather modest. There also appeared S. B. Krylov's revised *Istoriia sozdaniia Organizatsii Ob'edinennykh Natsii* (Moscow, 1960).

14. Ivan Ivashin, *Ocherki istorii vneshnei politiki SSSR* (Moscow, 1958), pp. 425, 482, 484.

15. "Soviet Red Cross Head on Children's Needs," *New Times*, No. 16 (1959), pp. 20–21. This was not always the case. During the nadir of Soviet-U.N. relations, in April, 1951, the Soviet delegate told the Social Committee of ECOSOC that UNICEF, as "a mere tool of the Anglo-Saxon bloc," was discriminating against children in Communist states and "incompatible with the purposes and principles of the United Nations Charter." (Doc. E/ AC. 7/SR 182.)

16. Irving R. Levine, *Main Street, U.S.S.R.* (Garden City, L. I., 1959), p. 157. For a discussion of the differences between domestic and foreign propaganda, see also Armstrong, pp. 231–32.

17. Communication from Professor Alvin Z. Rubinstein to the author, June, 1961. I must compliment him on finding the Center, since my own endeavors, in 1959, to locate it brought forth either blank stares or comments that the Soviet officials involved had never heard of it. None of the available Moscow city directories lists the Information Center.

18. See also p. 40 of this study.

19. E. g., CPSU, Central Committee, Section of Propaganda and Agitation, *Uchebnye plany i programmy na 1956–1957 god*

(Moscow, 1956). The U.N. holdings of the major Soviet libraries, such as the Lenin Library in Moscow, are highly selective, at least so far as volumes listed in the public card catalog are concerned.

20. See p. 191 of this study.

21. This point is suggested by Quincy Wright's criterion that "people tend to regard an agency which benefits them as important, valuable, and deserving their loyalty." (His *International Law and the United Nations* [New York, 1960], p. 10.)

CHAPTER VIII

AT THE UNITED NATIONS

1. Stephen M. Schwebel, *The Secretary-General of the United Nations* (Cambridge, Mass., 1952), p. 58.

2. Leon Gordenker, *The United Nations and the Peaceful Unification of Korea* (The Hague, 1959), pp. 244–45.

3. Sir Leslie Munro, *United Nations: Hope for a Divided World* (New York, 1960), p. 119.

4. He went on to complain that "during the last Assembly, there seemed to be a dearth of able free-world delegates who knew the practices and procedures of the Assembly and who were willing to assume leadership roles." (Francis O. Wilcox, "The United States and the United Nations," *Annals of the American Academy of Political and Social Science,* Vol. 336 [July, 1961], p. 120.)

5. E. g., Dennett and Johnson (eds.), *Negotiating with the Russians,* particularly pp. 231–35, 272–76, 290–96.

6. As a hostile delegate observed: "I can never make up my mind whether the Communist representatives really believe in the patent absurdities which they utter so blandly." (Munro, p. 123).

7. Robert E. Riggs, *Politics in the United Nations* (Urbana, Ill., 1958), p. 40. At times, Soviet behavior had its humorous overtones, as when the Soviet Delegation replied to the Secretary-General regarding forced labor in the following terms: "The Delegation of the Union of Soviet Socialist Republics to the United Nations presents its compliments to the United Nations Secretariat and herewith returns, unexamined, the documents attached to the Secretariat's letter of November 22, 1952, since these documents contain slanderous fabrications concerning the Soviet

Union." (Cited in Robert Asher *et al.*, *The United Nations and Promotion of the General Welfare* [Washington, D.C., 1957], p. 773n.)

8. *The New York Times*, August 4, 1960.

9. A. M. Rosenthal, in *The New York Times Magazine*, May 8, 1960.

10. See, e. g., Emerson and Claude, p. 23; *The New York Times*, June 26, 1959.

11. *The New York Times*, August 21 and October 23, 1959; *New Times*, No. 23 (1960), p. 25; and No. 43 (1960), p. 7.

12. I. Chernyshev, "The United Nations Today," *New Times*, No. 43 (1959), p. 8.

13. See Chapter X of this study.

14. This was also true of other U.N. agencies, such as UNESCO and the Economic Commission for Europe. The ILO, on the other hand, in March, 1961, turned down an analogous request to create a new assistant directorship for a Soviet citizen.

15. *The New York Times*, June 22 and October 1, 1961, and January 25, 1962.

16. *Ibid.*, October 26, 1960.

17. Calvin J. Nicholas, "Financing the United Nations: Problems and Prospects," Massachusetts Institute of Technology, United Nations Project (Cambridge, Mass., 1961), p. 15. For more recent data, see U.S. Congress, Joint Committee Print, *Information on the Operations and Financing of the United Nations* (February 6, 1962).

18. E.g., *The New York Times*, March 25, 1961.

19. See *International Conciliation*, No. 535 (September, 1961), pp. 197–205. Unfortunately, John G. Stoessinger's "Financing the United Nations," *ibid.*, No. 536, appeared too late for detailed consideration here.

20. The outstanding discussion of the problem is Vernon V. Aspaturian, *The Union Republics in Soviet Diplomacy* (Geneva, 1960).

21. See Sherwood, *Roosevelt and Hopkins*, pp. 875–77. When the Soviet demand for sixteen votes was trimmed at Yalta, Stalin originally held out for the Ukraine, Byelorussia, and Lithuania. The tentative inclusion of the latter shows that the argument on the Soviet side was based neither on "size and importance" nor on domestic political pressures, as has at times been alleged (Aspaturian, p. 105).

22. For students of international law, the question of Ukrainian and Byelorussian representation does raise interesting problems. See Romain Yakemtchouk, *L'Ukraine en droit international* (Louvain, 1954); Vsevolod Holub, *Ukraina v Ob'ednanykh Natsiiakh* (Munich, 1953); and Jurij Boris, "Den Ukrainska Sowjetrepubli-

ken och Förenta Nationerla," *Statsvetenskaplig Tidskrift* (Lund), No. 4 (1957).

23. Thomas Hovet, Jr., *Bloc Politics in the United Nations* (Cambridge, Mass., 1960).

24. H. G. Nicholas, p. 117. The monthly *East Europe* (New York), has a regular department entitled "Eastern Europe at the U.N."

25. See T. Zavalani, "The Importance of Being Albania," *Problems of Communism*, July–August, 1961, pp. 4–5; and William E. Griffith, "An International Communism?" *East Europe*, No. 7 (1961), p. 5. The Soviet Party's journal omitted the Albanians from its list of Communist delegations praised for successful performance at the United Nations (*Kommunist*, No. 14 [1960], p. 12).

26. For an interesting but perhaps overly schematic discussion, see George Modelski, *The Communist International System* (Princeton, N. J., 1960), p. 17. For the broader framework of relations among Communist states, see Zbigniew Brzezinski, *The Soviet Bloc* (rev. ed.; New York, 1961).

27. On the question of Chinese representation, see p. 57 of this study.

CHAPTER IX

BETWEEN SUCCESS AND FAILURE

1. *International Affairs*, No. 3 (1959), p. 85.

2. I. Lemin, lead article in *Mirovaia ekonomika i mezhdunarodnye otnosheniia*, April, 1961, p. 8. Numerous other statements to the same effect could be adduced.

3. For instance, the Declaration of Eighty-one Parties, in December, 1960; Khrushchev's speech of January 6, 1961; and the Program of the CPSU adopted in October, 1961.

4. *Kommunist*, No. 9 (1961), p. 101. For a detailed discussion, see Wladyslaw W. Kulski, *Peaceful Coexistence* (Chicago, 1959).

5. M. Baturin, "The 11th Session of the U.N. General Assembly," *International Affairs*, No. 1 (1957), p. 102; see also *ibid.*, No. 4, pp. 27, 35.

6. *Voprosy vneshnei politiki stran sotsialisticheskogo lageria* (Moscow, 1958), p. 68. In Khrushchev's later formulation, "the rise of growing numbers of nations through revolution provides most favorable conditions for an unprecedented extension of the

sphere of influence of Marxist-Leninist ideas." (Speech of January 6, 1961.)

7. D. Kraminov, "Ubeditel'nyi pereves sil mira," *Kommunist*, No. 18 (1960), p. 92. (Italics added.) See also *ibid.*, No. 17, p. 114.

8. When, in December, 1945, the U.S. asked to administer the formerly Japanese-mandated islands of the Pacific, Molotov advanced the view that all Great Powers were "directly concerned" in all trusteeship agreements. For a general analysis, see Joseph H. Sisco, "The Soviet Attitude Toward the Trusteeship System" (Ph.D. dissertation, University of Chicago, 1950).

9. See also James F. Byrnes, p. 96.

10. R. H. Chowdhuri, *International Mandates and Trusteeship Systems* (The Hague, 1955), pp. 57–58, 77, 87. Fuller (p. 150) has correctly remarked that the U.S.S.R. departed from the strict construction of the Charter, when it was desirable to obtain a voice over other states' trust territories.

11. Bobrov and Malinin, p. 41. See also P. Rzhanoy, "The Forthcoming Session of the Trusteeship Council," *International Affairs*, No. 6 (1958), p. 89; and Chowdhuri, pp. 101, 304.

12. English text in *New Times*, No. 41 (1960), p. 37.

13. B. M. Shurshalov, *Rezhim mezhdunarodnoi opeki* (Moscow, 1951), pp. 160–61. See also Levin, pp. 215–19.

14. Adlai E. Stevenson, *Friends and Enemies* (New York, 1959), pp. 4–5.

15. G. P. Zadorozhnyi, *OON i mirnoe sosushchestvovanie gosudarstv* (Moscow, 1958), p. 10.

16. That there was such an argument in Moscow is shown, for instance, by Robert C. Tucker, "Russia, the West, and World Order," *World Politics*, October, 1959, pp. 16–18. See also David J. Dallin, *Soviet Foreign Policy After Stalin* (Philadelphia, 1961), Part IV.

17. See, e.g., Kulski, pp. 235, 569–71; Walter Z. Laqueur, *The Soviet Union and the Middle East* (New York, 1959), pp. 254, 294–301, 336–37; Tucker, p. 18.

18. See Oles M. Smolansky, "Moscow and Cairo: Harmony and Conflict in Soviet-Arab Relations."

19. *Pravda*, January 28, 1959.

20. Interview of May 10, 1957, in N. S. Khrushchev, *Speeches and Interviews on World Problems, 1957* (Moscow, 1958), pp. 45, 49.

21. Interview of November 14, 1957, in *ibid.*, p. 274.

22. V. Zorin, statement on conclusion of 13th General Assembly session, December 12, 1958.

23. See, e.g., V. Alexandrov, "The 13th U.N. General Assembly," *International Affairs*, No. 12 (1958), p. 16.
24. *Izvestiia*, June 26, 1959.
25. *The New York Times*, September 22, 1959.
26. *Ibid.*, February 15, 1960.
27. For a case study of the Tibetan issue, see Sidney Bailey, *The General Assembly of the United Nations* (New York, 1961).
28. *The New York Times*, November 10, 1959. Hammarskjold did consult with the Soviet delegation before leaving, and private reports at the time had it that the latter would not object to a "normalization" of the Laotian situation—in line with the "spirit of Camp David"—but protested partly against the principle of expanding authority of the Secretary-General, partly to propitiate its Chinese Communist allies.
29. Y. Bochkaryov, "The Plot Against the People of Laos," *New Times*, No. 38 (1959), p. 11.
30. N. S. Khrushchev, "On Peaceful Coexistence," *Foreign Affairs*, October, 1959.
31. *International Affairs*, No. 2 (1960), p. 63.
32. I. Chernyshev, "The United Nations Today," *New Times*, No. 43 (1959), pp. 6–8. Italics added.
33. V. Cheprakov, "Shestidesiatye gody," *Kommunist*, No. 2 (1960), pp. 125, 136.
34. Pierre Villon, "War and the Working Class," *World Marxist Review*, May, 1960, p. 6.
35. Editorial, *Kommunist*, No. 14 (1960), p. 5.
36. A. Sovetov, "The Present Situation: Conclusions and Prospects," *International Affairs*, No. 7 (1960), p. 12.
37. *The New York Times*, July 14, 1960.
38. See p. 138n. of this study.

CHAPTER X

THE CONGO: THE LAST STRAW

1. See Chapter VI of this study. See also Daniel Cheever and H. Field Haviland, *Organizing for Peace* (Boston, 1954), pp. 482ff.
2. See Inis L. Claude, Jr., "The United Nations and the Use of Force," *International Conciliation*, No. 532 (March, 1961), pp. 346–55.
3. See Lincoln P. Bloomfield, *The United Nations and U.S. Foreign Policy* (Boston, 1960), pp. 48–49 and his Chapter V; Eichelberger, p. 37.

4. *Mezhdunarodnyi politiko-ekonomicheskii ezhegodnik 1959*, pp. 444, 450–51.

5. *Pravda*, October 2, 1949; Joseph Nogee, "The Diplomacy of Disarmament," *International Conciliation*, No. 526 (January, 1960), pp. 292–96; Thomas J. Hamilton, in *The New York Times*, October 4, 1959.

6. L. Fyodorov, "International Relations and the Battle of Ideologies," *International Affairs*, No. 3 (1960), p. 11. See also Morozov, p. 138.

7. S. Vladimirov, "Disarmament and the Plans for Establishing an International Police Force," *ibid.*, No. 4 (1960), p. 47.

8. *Ibid.*, No. 5 (1960), pp. 81–83.

9. *The New York Times*, June 4, 1960.

10. N. Talensky, "The Technical Problems of Disarmament," *International Affairs*, No. 3 (1961), p. 62.

11. E. Korovin, "Disarmament and Sovereignty," *ibid.*, No. 2 (1961), p. 57.

12. *New Times*, No. 17 (1960), p. 16; *The New York Times*, July 3, 1960.

13. *The New York Times*, July 14, 1960.

14. Editorial, *International Affairs*, No. 8 (1960), p. 65. The issue went to press on July 22.

15. Editorial, *New Times*, No. 9 (1961), p. 2.

16. *The New York Times*, July 16, 1960. See also *ibid.*, August 4, 1960.

17. *The New York Times*, September 11, 1960.

18. "Roundabout Methods," *New Times*, No. 35 (1960), p. 2. See also *The New York Times*, September 14, 1960.

19. *United Nations Review*, September, 1960, p. 54. An English translation of N. S. Khrushchev's speech before the General Assembly on September 23, 1960, appears as a supplement to *New Times*, No. 40 (1960).

20. See Hamilton F. Armstrong, "U.N. on Trial," *Foreign Affairs*, April, 1961, pp. 404–10.

21. E.g., "Hero of Africa," *New Times*, No. 5 (1961), p. 11; E. Primakov, "NATO Shadow over the Congo," *ibid.*, No. 6 (1961), p. 14.

22. The official text of the Khrushchev letter to Nehru, February 22, 1961, appears as a supplement to *New Times*, No. 10 (1961). Similar messages went to other neutral governments.

23. *Pravda*, February 15, 1961. The statement asked for the arrest of Tshombe and Mobutu, the repudiation of ONUC, and its withdrawal within thirty days.

24. The Soviet charges were repeated by Valerian Zorin and provoked a sharp reply by the Secretary-General (*The New York*

Times, February 16, 1961); they were again presented to the General Assembly by Foreign Minister Gromyko on March 21, 1961. In April, 1961, the State Publishing House released a 32-page pamphlet entitled "The Murderer on the East River" (M. G. Semenov, *Ubiitsa s Ist-River* [Moscow, 1961]). The same vicious attack on Hammarskjold, issued in 100,000 copies, appeared in various translations during the following months.

25. Claude, p. 379.

26. *Introduction to the Annual Report of the Secretary-General . . . 1959–1960* (GAOR, 15th Session, Supplement No. 1A, Document A/4390/Add. 1, pp. 2, 4). Claude (pp. 376, 378) points to UNEF as a precedent of U.N. action without participation of the Great Powers. The whole issue is analyzed by Theodore Draper, "Ordeal of the U.N.: Khrushchev, Hammarskjold and the Congo Crisis," Supplement to *The New Leader* (New York), November 7, 1960.

CHAPTER XI

THE SOVIET CHALLENGE

1. The sources used are primarily Khrushchev's speech of September 23, cited earlier, and his subsequent interventions before the General Assembly; and his revealing public report on the U.N. session on October 20, 1960 (here used in English translation, *Current Digest of the Soviet Press,* XII, No. 42, 3–14). The official Soviet account of his visit is available in English under the title, *Khrushchev in New York* (New York, 1960).

2. See p. 49 of this study.

3. See E. Korovin, "Ways of Reorganizing the U.N. Executive Organs," *International Affairs,* No. 12 (1960), p. 9.

4. Editorial, "The Principal Problems of the Time," *International Affairs,* No. 7 (1961), p. 7; *The New York Times,* November 22 and 27, 1960.

5. See, e.g., *The New York Times,* April 28, May, 5 and 10, 1959.

6. The sense of being outnumbered was reflected in Khrushchev's conversation with a group of nine governors of American states (which the author attended) in July, 1959. Seeking to monopolize the conversation, Khrushchev kept the governors from interrupting him, remarking, "Don't gang up on me, let me talk! What do you think this is, the United Nations?"

7. In his speech of October 20, Khrushchev inquired by what

right Britain and France could be considered Great Powers while India and Indonesia could not.

8. Editorial, "Triumf teorii i praktiki leninizma," *Kommunist*, No. 15 (1960), p. 7.

9. *The New York Times*, October 9, 1960.

10. Bobrov and Malinin, p. 10. For a discussion of sovereignty, see chapter IV of this study.

11. See pp. 138–39 of this study.

12. Leland M. Goodrich, *The United Nations* (New York, 1959), pp. 113–14; Blumenthal, Chapter VI; UNCIO, *Documents*, IV, 893; VII, 280–81; XI, 545–46. In 1961, Moscow was to argue that at San Francisco it had promoted the idea of "collective leadership" of the Secretariat. (*Mirovaia ekonomika i mezhdunarodnye otnosheniia*, No. 8 [1961], p. 39; and *International Affairs*, No. 8 [1961], p. 40.)

13. See Trygve Lie, pp. 20, 320–21, 369–70, 408.

14. *Pravda*, May 3, 1958.

15. Y. Bochkaryov, "The Plot Against the Peoples of Laos," *New Times*, No. 38 (1959), p. 11.

16. *International Affairs*, No. 10 (1958), p. 38.

17. *Kommunist*, No. 14 (1960), p. 11.

18. *Conference at The Hague . . . June 26–July 20, 1922: Minutes and Documents* (The Hague, 1922), p. 126.

19. *Pravda*, October 5, 1948. I am obliged for this reference to Joseph L. Nogee, *Soviet Policy . . .* , p. 243.

20. *The New York Times*, September 25, 1960.

21. *Ibid.*, October 4, 1960.

22. *New York Herald-Tribune*, April 17, 1961.

23. *The New York Times*, June 7, 1961. See also O. V. Bogdanov, "K voprosu o pravovom rezhime i strukture tsentral'nykh organov OON," *Sovetskoe gosudarstvo i pravo*, No. 5 (1961).

24. See Khrushchev's speeches of September 23 and October 11, 1960.

25. "The Soviet expert considers that the principle of geographical distribution should also be extended to all consultants and experts recruited by the United Nations secretariat. . . ." (Documents A/4776, June 14, 1961.) See also p. 103 of this study.

26. On the general problems of Sino-Soviet relations see Donald S. Zagoria, *The Sino-Soviet Conflict 1956–1961* (Princeton, N.J., 1962); Kurt London (ed.), *Unity and Contradiction* (New York, 1962); and G. F. Hudson, Richard Lowenthal, and Roderick MacFarquhar (eds.), *The Sino-Soviet Dispute* (New York, 1961).

27. Shih Tung-siang, "Refuting the Fallacy that the Nature of Imperialism Has Changed," *Hungchi* (Peking), June 15, 1960.

28. *Sovetskaia Rossiia* (Moscow), June 10, 1960.

29. *Izvestiia,* August 14, 1960.
30. See, e.g., Todor Zhivkov, "Peace: Key Problem of Today," *World Marxist Review,* August, 1960, p. 11.
31. On the Albanian stand, see p. 109 of this study.
32. *Pravda,* August 7, 1960. The basic exposition was given by N. Matkovsky in *Pravda,* June 12, 1960. See also *Izvestiia,* August 14, 1960.
33. K. Ivanov, "Present-Day Colonialism," *International Affairs,* No. 10 (1960), p. 22. Soviet writings abound in comments on the "complexity" of the world situation. "Marxists-Leninists take into account the full complexity of the situation." (*Kommunist,* No. 15 [1960], p. 10.) Attacking sectarian elements who favor a direct Communist bid for victory without first struggling for "democratic transformations," Moscow comments: "In real life everything is a lot more complicated." (*Ibid.,* No. 13 [1960], p. 22.) "It would be wrong to assume that the process of easing international tensions is a straight line, that there are no zigzags." (N. Inozemtsev, "U.S. Foreign Policy," *World Marxist Review,* July, 1960, p. 15.)
34. For instance, *Jen-min Jih-pao,* September 10, October 25, and November 21, 1959.
35. *Ibid.,* August 22, 1960.
36. *Ibid.,* October 12, 1960.
37. Edgar Snow, "A Report from Red China," *Look,* January 31, 1961, p. 98. Chou En-lai pointed to the U.N. as an example of different Soviet and Chinese outlooks and policies "owing to the different situation of the two countries" with regard to it.
38. *Jen-min Jih-pao,* October 19, 1960. The same line continued for months. See "In the Congo as in Korea the United Nations Forces are a Weapon of American Imperialism," *Jen-min Jih-pao,* February 16, 1961.
39. *Kommunist,* No. 14 (1960), p. 11 (sent to press October 1).
40. *The New York Times,* October 2, 1960. The next day he declared that a continuation of the Western powers' policy would "lead the United Nations to a collapse."
41. *The New York Times,* September 26, 1960. At the end of his stay in New York, he told the Assembly, after speaking of his strong nerves and military might: "I wish to declare to you, gentlemen, don't regard this as an ultimatum." (*Ibid.,* October 12, 1960.)
42. *New Times,* No. 42 (1960), pp. 1–2. Khrushchev cited "an old Russian proverb that a drop of water can move a stone" (*The New York Times,* September 30, 1960). General optimism was in evidence in Soviet assessments of the session; an anonymous commentary concluded that the influence of the Western

powers continued to decline. "This process, which will surely continue, is a guarantee of the *gradual* freeing of the U.N. from the imperialist grip. . . ." (*International Affairs*, No. 9 [1960], pp. 60–61. Italics added.)

43. *New Times*, No. 38 (1960), p. 2. In his speech of October 20, Khrushchev declared, "We believe that common sense will carry the day, that truth will prevail, and the good seeds yield abundant shoots. The time will come. . . ."

44. *The New York Times*, September 27 and 28, 1961. It appears established that, for whatever reasons, the system of alternating secretaries and three assistants was promoted by India's V. K. Krishna Menon—against the better judgment of his own President and Prime Minister. Whether the proposal was Soviet-inspired, remains to be ascertained (*Washington Post*, September 28 and November 5, 1961).

45. J. W. Fulbright, "For a Concert of Free Nations," *Foreign Affairs*, October, 1961, p. 2.

46. B. Strelnikov, in *Pravda*, September 24, 1961, and his "SShA i OON: Poteriannoe gospodstvo," *Za rubezhom*, No. 39 (September 30, 1961), in which he also accuses the friends of Hammarskjold of engaging in a "personality cult" of the late Secretary-General.

47. In his speech of October 17, 1961, to the Twenty-second Congress of the CPSU, Khrushchev gave somewhat perfunctory treatment to the need for "an essential improvement in the mechanism of the United Nations." He did, however, reiterate the demand for "the full equality of rights of the three groups of states in all United Nations bodies" and for representation of Communist China as well as West and East Germany in the U.N.

CHAPTER XII

THE SOVIET OUTLOOK—TODAY AND TOMORROW

1. For instance, Morozov, pp. 9ff.; *New Times*, No. 3 (1961), p. 3; D. Kraminov, "Ubeditel'nyi pereves sil mira," *Kommunist*, No. 18 (1960), p. 87.

2. Editorial, "Za mir, za razoruzhenie, za svobodu narodov," *Kommunist*, No. 14 (1960), p. 5.

3. N. Inozemtsev, "Razvitie mirovogo sotsializma i mezhdunarodnye otnosheniia," *Kommunist*, No. 9 (1961), p. 101.

4. The first time the U.N. plan was raised by President Roosevelt

(Bohlen Minutes of November 29, 1943, meeting at Tehran)
Stalin's immediate comment was "whether this body would have
the right to make decisions binding on the nations of the world."
(United States, Department of State, *Foreign Relations . . . The
Conferences at Cairo and Tehran 1943* [Washington, D.C.
1961], p. 570.) On the containment of conflicts within the Com
munist orbit, see George Modelski, *The Communist International
System* (Princeton, N.J., 1960), pp. 66–68.

5. I am obliged to Mr. Seweryn Bialer for a crystallization of thi
problem.

6. *Zeri i Popullit* (Tirana), January 9, 1962.

7. M. Airapetian and P. Kabanov, *Leninskie printsipy vneshne
politiki sovetskogo gosudarstva* (Moscow, 1957), p. 65. See als
Khrushchev's interview with the editor of the Tokyo *Asah
Shimbun* on June 18, 1957.

8. Khrushchev, speech in honor of Kwame Nkrumah, Moscow, Jul
11, 1961; and speech at the Twenty-second Congress of the
CPSU, Moscow, October 27, 1961.

9. See, e.g., Lincoln P. Bloomfield, *The United Nations and U.S
Foreign Policy* (Boston, 1960), p. 5.

10. The latter reference is to the Clark and Sohn proposals. (Moro
zov, p. 145.)

11. See William Welch, "Soviet Commitments to Collective Action,"
in Arnold Wolfers (ed.), *Alliance Policy in the Cold War* (Balti
more, 1959), pp. 294–300.

12. Otto Kuusinen *et al.*, *Fundamentals of Marxism-Leninism* (Mos
cow, 1960).

13. Editorial, "Reshit' problemu reorganizatsii OON," *Kommunist
No. 4 (1961), p. 14.

14. Hamilton F. Armstrong, "U.N. on Trial," *Foreign Affairs*, Apri
1961, p. 388.

15. See, for instance, George F. Kennan, *Russia and the West Unde
Lenin and Stalin* (Boston, 1961), and Henry L. Roberts, *Russic
and America* (New York, 1956).

16. "In the U.N. there continues to dominate a group of Western
powers, numerically small in terms of population and the most
reactionary in terms of its political goals." (Editorial, *Kom
munist*, No. 4 [1961], p. 13.) "This policy accords with the
interests of the colonial powers, the interests of monopoly capital
which now hold sway over the U.N. executive organs." (Khrush
chev, speech of July 11, 1961.)

17. Herbert G. Nicholas, *The United Nations as a Political Institu
tion* (New York, 1959), p. 145.

18. Maurice Bourquin, *L'état souverain et l'organisation interna
tionale* (New York, 1959), p. 17.

19. Anthony Eden, *Full Circle* (London, 1960), p. 7.
20. On this point, see also Michel Virally, "Vers une réforme du Secrétariat des Nations Unies?" *International Organization*, Spring, 1961, p. 246. Not long ago, a leading Soviet scholar wrote plainly: "It is entirely self-evident that the inclusion of this or that country within one of the types characteristic for the period of the disintegration of the colonial system is not immutable and given for all time." (A. A. Guber, cited in Kulski, p. 209.)
21. *Bol'shaia sovetskaia entsiklopediia* (2d ed.; Moscow, 1952), XV, 475–76.
22. Adlai Stevenson, address at the Princeton Club, Washington, D.C., May 17, 1961 (U.S. Mission to the U.N., Press Release 3724).
23. Editorial, *Kommunist*, No. 4 (1961), p. 15. Italics added.
24. *The New York Times*, October 8, 1960.
25. Morozov, p. 12.
26. *The New York Times*, October 4 and 8, 1960. He added that the socialist states would "not recognize [inimical] decisions and will rely on their own strength to defend the interests of their state"; and "if any one tries to interfere in our affairs, if you will excuse the rather indelicate phrase, we will just give him a punch in the nose."
27. Khrushchev, speech of July 11, 1961. In his interview with Cyrus L. Sulzberger, Khrushchev exclaimed: "If the United States opposes normalization of the situation in the United Nations, it will be rectified despite the United States, and the prestige of the United States will suffer." (*The New York Times*, September 8, 1961.) Since the U.S. has the veto over Charter amendments, it is hard to see what Khrushchev had in mind other than an attempt at intimidation.
28. Claude, *Swords into Plowshares*, pp. 128–29.
29. See Norman J. Padelford, "Politics and Change in the Security Council," *International Organization*, Summer, 1960.
30. See Vernon Aspaturian, "The Metamorphosis of the United Nations," *Yale Review*, Summer, 1957.
31. Dag Hammarskjold, "The Development of a Constitutional Framework for International Cooperation," April 29, 1960 (U.N. Press Release SG/910). See also Stephen M. Schwebel, *The Secretary-General of the United Nations* (Cambridge, Mass., 1952), and Nicholas, Chapter VII.
32. Geoffrey Goodwin, "The Expanding United Nations," *International Affairs* (London), April, 1961, p. 179.
33. U.N. Press Release SG/1035 (May 29, 1961).
34. *New York Herald-Tribune*, April 17, 1961.

35. Gerard J. Mangone, *A Short History of International Organization* (New York, 1954), p. 14.

36. V. Matveev and M. Mikhailov, "Bor'ba za mir, za svobodu narodov i Organizatsiia Ob'edinennykh Natsii," *Kommunist,* No. 15 (1960), p. 102.

37. Dag Hammarskjold, "Introduction to the Annual Report of the Secretary-General on the Work of the Organization," 16th Session, Document 1A (A/4800/add. 1); and "The Development of a Constitutional Framework for International Cooperation."

38. Claude, p. 15. Robert MacIver, in *The Nations and the United Nations* (New York, 1959), expounds a similar philosophy that sees as the true spirit of the United Nations the notion of peaceful and gradual change, increasing U.N. authority to help raise standards of living, and peaceful emancipation of colonies. See also Benjamin V. Cohen, *The United Nations* (Cambridge, Mass., 1961), p. 64.

39. J. W. Fulbright, "For a Concert of Free Nations," *Foreign Affairs,* October, 1961, p. 2.

40. Cited in *The Reporter* (New York), October 26, 1961, p. 22.

41. "For the moment, the vital task is to prevent the frustration of the Secretary-General in the conduct of his office, so as to keep the U.N. mechanism available for imaginative service to the world. In the long run, the task will be to devise an improved supervisory arrangement, so as to provide institutional assurance that the Secretary-General, when operating outside the limits of his autonomous realm as defined in the Charter, will be both sensitive to the legitimate policy guidance of and buttressed by the responsible support of an appropriately representative political organ." (Commission to Study the Organization of Peace, *Developing the United Nations . . . Thirteenth Report* [New York, 1961], p. 21.)

42. John Foster Dulles, *War or Peace* (New York, 1950), p. 190.

43. George F. Kennan, *Russia, the Atom and the West* (New York, 1958), p. 27.

Bibliographical Note

For a general familiarity with the United Nations, I have found the U.N.'s own publications, such as the *United Nations Yearbook* and the monthly *United Nations Review*, reliable, rich, and convenient guides. Leland C. Goodrich's *United Nations* (New York, 1959) is an expert's account. Among interpretations of the organization's performance and prospects, I was most stimulated by Inis L. Claude's *Swords into Plowshares* (rev. ed.; New York, 1959) and Herbert G. Nicholas's *The United Nations as a Political Institution* (New York, 1959).

Many of the relevant Soviet sources are discussed, in English, in Alvin Z. Rubinstein, "Selected Bibliography of Soviet Works on the United Nations, 1946–1959," *American Political Science Review*, December, 1960. Key materials available in English include N. S. Khrushchev's speeches and interviews (including his appearances at the United Nations); the periodicals *International Affairs* (Moscow), *New Times* (Moscow), *World Marxist Review* (English ed.; Toronto and London); and the *Current Digest of the Soviet Press* (New York). I fear I know of no guides to reading between the lines.

Abbreviations

ECA	Economic Commission for Africa
ECAFE	Economic Commission for Asia and the Far East
ECE	Economic Commission for Europe
ECOSOC	Economic and Social Council
EPTA	Expanded Program of Technical Assistance
FAO	Food and Agriculture Organization
GATT	General Agreement on Tariffs and Trade
IAEA	International Atomic Energy Agency
IBRD	International Bank for Reconstruction and Development
ICAO	International Civil Aviation Organization
IFC	International Finance Corporation
ILO	International Labour Organisation
IMCO	Inter-Government Maritime Consultative Organization
IMF	International Monetary Fund
ITO	International Trade Organization
ITU	International Telecommunication Union
NATO	North Atlantic Treaty Organization
ONUC	Organisation des Nations Unies au Congo
SSR	Soviet Socialist Republic (such as Ukrainian, Byelorussian)
UNEF	United Nations Emergency Force
UNESCO	United Nations Educational, Scientific and Cultural Organization
UNICEF	United Nations Children's Fund
UNSCOP	United Nations Special Committee on Palestine
UPU	Universal Postal Union
USSR	Union of Soviet Socialist Republics
WFTU	World Federation of Trade Unions
WHO	World Health Organization
WMO	World Meteorological Organization